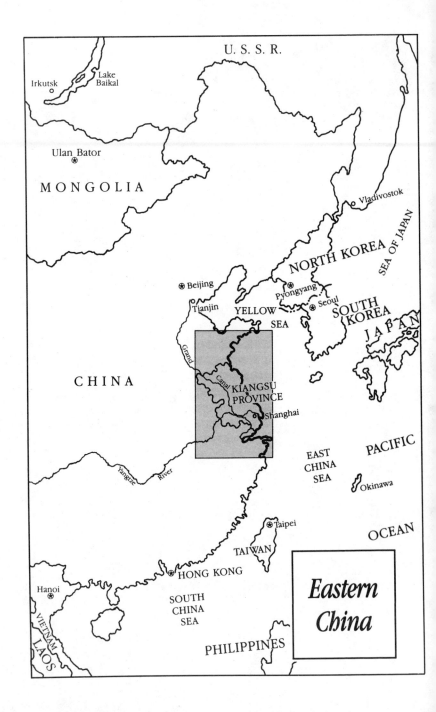

Eastern China

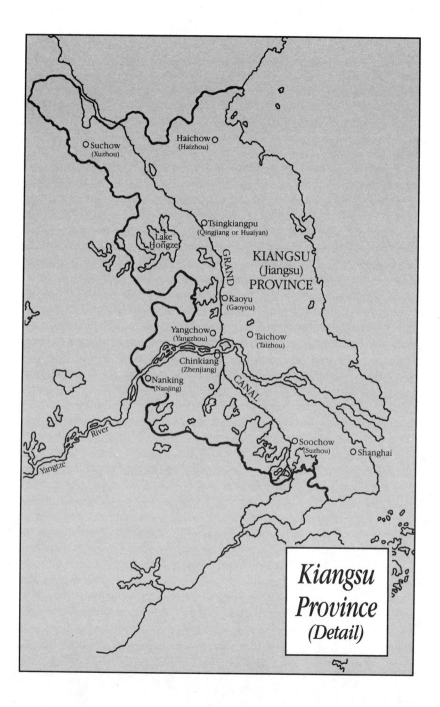

Suchow
(Xuzhou)

Haichow
(Haizhou)

Tsingkiangpu
(Qingjiang or Huaiyan)

Lake
Hongze

KIANGSU
(Jiangsu)
PROVINCE

Kaoyu
(Gaoyou)

GRAND

Yangchow
(Yangzhou)

Taichow
(Taizhou)

Chinkiang
(Zhenjiang)

Nanking
(Nanjing)

CANAL

River

Soochow
(Suzhou)

Shanghai

Yangtze

Kiangsu Province (Detail)

A FOREIGN DEVIL IN CHINA

By the same author:
The Apostle: A Life of Paul
The Master: A Life of Jesus
Billy Graham (1966, 1979, 1984)
Hudson Taylor and Maria
George Whitefield
Moody
The Siberian Seven
Wilberforce
Amazing Grace: John Newton's Story
Shaftesbury: The Poor Man's Earl
John Wesley
and other books

A FOREIGN DEVIL IN CHINA

The Story of Dr. L. Nelson Bell

John Pollock

World Wide Publications
A ministry of the Billy Graham Evangelistic Association
1303 Hennepin Ave., Minneapolis, Minnesota 55403

A Foreign Devil in China
©1971, 1988 by World Wide Publications

World Wide Publications is the publishing ministry of the
Billy Graham Evangelistic Association.

Library of Congress Catalog Card Number: 71-178825
ISBN: 0-89066-141-3
Printed in the United States of America

For His Grandchildren

Contents

Publisher's Note

In Dr. Bell's early days in China, people from other countries were usually referred to as "Foreign Devils" (and not without reason, considering the way China was often treated by other countries)—hence the title of this book.

But for tens of thousands of grateful patients, Dr. Bell was "Chong Ai Hua", or "The Bell Who Is Lover of the Chinese People." His genuine love for the Chinese people, his sacrificial service, and his respect for their culture caused him to be looked upon as a true friend and colleague.

It is significant that at the conclusion of World War II he was one of the first missionaries urged to return to China by the people who knew him best. Nothing would have gladdened him more than the new era of respect and friendship which has dawned in recent years between China and other countries, and the promise it holds of even greater fruit for the gospel of Jesus Christ in that ancient land.

Foreword

This biography of Dr. L. Nelson Bell was first published in 1971. It has been revised and edited by the author, John Pollock, with the help of my wife, Ruth, and other members of the family and staff. It has a number of new and exciting stories about Dr. Bell and adds the events of the latter part of his life when he was elected moderator of the Presbyterian Church in the United States.

When we went back to China in 1988 and visited the hospital where Dr. Bell labored for twenty-five years, we met a number of people who had not only been influenced by him but whose lives he had saved through his brilliant knowledge of medicine and whom he had influenced in a deeper spiritual commitment.

Dr. Nelson Bell was one of the major influences in my life and ministry. In fact, as I look back I am convinced that one of the reasons God, in His providence, allowed Ruth Bell to become my wife was so that Dr. Nelson Bell would become my father-in-law!

He had three successful careers: as a professional baseball player; as a medical missionary to China for twenty-five years; and as one of the most influential editors and writers in the evangelical world. I could add a fourth career—that of being my most faithful counselor and advisor right up to his death in 1973. Hardly a day has passed since then that I haven't found myself recalling his wisdom and how he would have met a particular situation or problem.

Nelson Bell, as much as any Christian I have ever known, had a singleminded commitment to Christ and a determination to be guided by His Word, the Bible. From the time he got up before daylight to spend an hour reading the Scriptures and praying, until he went to bed at night, he led a disciplined, dedicated life and spread happiness wherever he went. We who were privileged to know him marvelled at how totally and completely he lived to serve the Lord—and others! His compassion, his sensitivity, his delightful sense of humor, his love, his concern for God's truth—all came from his close walk with Christ and his uncompromising loyalty to the Scriptures. Following the example of our Lord centuries ago, Dr. Bell combined the healing of the body with the ageless message of the redeeming and life-transforming power of the gospel.

I am particularly delighted that this biography of Dr. Bell is being reissued in an expanded second edition. John Pollock has researched with meticulous care the life of this remarkable man and his equally remarkable wife and family. The reader lives with them through the dangers and joy of their years in China and afterward, and sees the roots of their strength and courage. Originally published before Dr. Bell's death, this second edition includes an account of his last years—which were among his busiest and most influential in spite of his declining health. This second edition also tells of the return visit of the Bell children in 1980 to the place in China where Dr. Bell served. No one would have rejoiced more than Dr. Bell at the way the seeds of the gospel planted by missionaries in previous generations are now bearing fruit in that land.

The story of Dr. Nelson Bell is one of the most exciting and thrilling narratives of our generation. But it is more than that. It is a vivid testimony to the transforming power of the gospel, and a powerful reminder that every Christian is to be faithful to Christ wherever He places us. Not many of us are called to undertake the kind of work to which Dr. Bell was called. But all of us are called to love Christ, to be faithful to Him and His Word, and to share the good news of the gospel with those around us. May this book be an inspiration and a challenge to every reader.

Billy Graham
Montreat, North Carolina

Preface

This book was one of the happiest experiences of my life. Billy Graham invited me to write it in 1969, which was four years before Nelson Bell died, and *A Foreign Devil in China* was published in 1971.

In the period between its going to press and Bell's death on August 2, 1973, his days were packed with further ministry, especially after he was elected moderator of his great denomination, the Presbyterian Church in the United States (Southern Presbyterian Church), at a time of crisis. I am delighted to have the opportunity of completing the story.

My own friendship with Nelson continued to deepen. Letters went frequently across the Atlantic between North Carolina and Devonshire, until the day when I received a cable from Ruth: "The Foreign Devil became an angel this morning."

It is especially fitting that the reissue of this book should follow Billy Graham's first preaching visit to China, an event which Nelson could only pray and long for as a distant hope. The great growth of the Christian church through the years of pressure owed much, under God, to the legacy of selfless service by men like Bell and his beloved Chinese associates. He died at a time when it might have seemed that their work had been washed away. He was sure in his heart that it had not been, and hopeful stories were already trickling out of China; but he walked "by faith, not by sight." Fifteen years later we walk with clear sight: we see the church in China, grown beyond measure because it was built upon the Rock.

We need to understand the background of this survival. Dr. Bell provides it. Soon after he and I began working together on this book he discovered that some eight or nine hundred letters, which he had written to his mother from China, typed closely on wafer-thin paper, were still in his possession, stuffed unsorted in boxes. The letters had a dual purpose: to give his parents the family news; and to provide information and description for his mother to read aloud to her prayer support group.

Nelson Bell was a natural, fluent writer, and he was writing for those who had never been to China. When the letters had been filed by years and photocopied, I found that I had a fascinating week-by-week account of a Christian family living with zest and fun in conditions of civil war, banditry, famine, epidemic, and bombardment. This was the childhood. background of Ruth Bell Graham and her sisters and brother, and they seemed to love every minute of it.

The letters proved to be the finest contemporary description of medical missionary work in China during the later 1920s and 1930s. Without realizing he was writing for posterity, Dr. Bell provided source material for an accurate understanding of motives, methods, problems, and the response of the Chinese. He shows what really happened—a foundation for the exciting events of the present time.

My new edition, therefore, ends not with Nelson Bell's death in 1973 and Virginia's the following year, but with the return visit of their daughters and son to Tsingkiangpu (now part of Huaiyin) in 1980, when China was still not fully open to Westerners, followed by the visit of Ruth and Billy Graham in 1988, where they saw moving testimony to the fruit of Dr. Bell's twenty-five years of healing and preaching.

A complete list of those who helped in the making of this biography can be found in the preface to the original edition. For help in providing the additional material, I am grateful to Dr. and Mrs. Billy Graham, Dr. B. Clayton Bell, Dr. John N. Akers, and Dr. Calvin Thielman; Dr. Akers has also given editorial supervision to this new edition. Russ Busby has helped with the photographic materials. I am grateful also to Mrs. Lucille Lytle and Mrs. Myriam van der Doef for organizing communication and typing. The original book was typed by Mrs. J. E. Williams of Bideford, North Devon. The additional material was typed by Yvonne Griffith, London, and Lucille Lytle, Montreat.

John Pollock
Rose Ash
Devonshire, England

Part One
FROM GENERATION
TO
GENERATION
1894-1920

Virginia Leftwich Bell

L. Nelson Bell

1
The Heritage

NELSON BELL'S early memories were of mountains and miners, an old-fashioned, roomy house, and a buggy-load of Bells behind old George the horse, singing their way down the forest road to the little church in the valley.

Lemuel Nelson Bell was born on July 30, 1894, the youngest in a close-knit, affectionate family. His heritage, through and through, was Scotch-Irish Virginian back to the fifth generation. The upper valley of Virginia was settled by his cousins. Their forebears had migrated from Scotland to Ireland in the days of Charles II for conscience' sake, and in the next generation to Pennsylvania where the Pennsylvania Dutch disliked them. The Presbyterians then pushed onward to Shenandoah to pioneer a new frontier for Virginia between the Blue Ridge and the Allegheny Mountains.

One of Nelson Bell's ancestors heard George Whitefield preach and sought ever afterward to bring men to faith. Whitefield wrote in 1740 that "the greatest probability of doing good in Virginia is among the Scotch-Irish, who have latterly settled in the mountainous parts of that province. They raise little or no tobacco, but things that are useful to the common life." Whitefield never crossed the Blue Ridge, yet his influence spread, and the ministers and elders of the upper valley and its mountains were warmly evangelical; they shed happiness and humor and allowed plenty of song in their services. Around 1800 two of the ministers of Augusta County were Nelson's great-great-grandfathers.

One, John McCue, preached at Tinkling Spring. He was

learned, humorous, slightly pugnacious, but widely loved, and had refused to pursue a legal career though Thomas Jefferson himself offered to train him. A missionary at heart, he had been the first Presbyterian minister to preach in Greenbriar County, in what is now West Virginia, before the call to Tinkling Spring. He lived to a ripe old age and died after a fall from his horse as he was riding to preach one Sunday morning of 1818.

The other minister was William Wilson, a man of such learning that once when recovering from illness—he too had fallen from his horse, striking his head—he could talk only in Latin or Greek. He preached—in English—at the Old Stone Church near Fort Defiance beyond Staunton, a few miles to the north.

Preacher McCue and Preacher Wilson each bred a physician among their numerous progenies. These were Nelson's great-grandparents, for the two doctors' offspring united when Thomas McCue married Elizabeth Wilson; their youngest child, Ruth Lee McCue (Lee for the hero of Virgina and the Confederacy, for she was born in 1862) was Nelson's mother. For some unknown reason she was nicknamed "Cora," and she grew up at Belvidere, the plantation house her father had built near the Old Stone Church.

Cora fell in love with a distant cousin, James Harvey Bell. He was descended from two of her ancestor Wilson's elders at the Old Stone Church: Alexander Nelson, a wealthy wheat planter, and Joseph Bell, a commissary in Washington's army whose younger son moved into the mountains after marrying Mary Ann Nelson in 1800. These farmed and lumbered more than eight hundred acres in Rockbridge County near the spectacular Goshen Pass; their valley of the Big Calfpasture River is still named Bell's Valley, now on State Highway 42. One of their many sons, Marshall Bell, married Charlotte Crawford, and had twelve children. James H. Bell was the second son.

James became head of the commissary of Longdale Mining Company which extracted iron ore some thirty miles from Bell's Valley, high up in the Alleghenies above the town of Clifton Forge on the James River. He married the twenty-year-old Ruth McCue in 1882. Their third child was Lemuel

Nelson Bell.

* * * * *

Nelson's birthplace, the superintendent's house, and all the miners' cabins have been swept away. The site of Longdale Mine is now a recreational area in George Washington Forest, but in the last years of the nineteenth century it was a setting for a happy childhood.

James Bell was forty at the time of Nelson's birth; he was of moderate height, rugged, ruddy-faced, and so strong that as a young man he once made several others pile on his back, then staggered to some platform scales and turned them at over seven hundred pounds. His McCue nieces thought him the "sweetest person imaginable." He had a fine singing voice and, Nelson recalled, "a very keen sense of humor. He was popular with people because he always saw the best side of them. He was a 'hail fellow well met,' popular with blacks and whites alike. He was courteous to all, and all seemed to like him."

James Bell was a happy Christian, and his son would say, "all the way through life his Christian commitment was known by everyone who had dealings with him."

His wife Ruth, who conducted a Sunday school for the miners' children, was thirty-two at Nelson's birth. Dark-haired, rather thickset, and always neatly dressed, she had good business sense and was determined and energetic, but too considerate to be hard. She held a deep belief in the power of prayer. Her children, neighbors, and the affairs of her church were the subjects of such detailed, persistent prayer that her concern sometimes seemed to border on worry. She was a natural homemaker, being both practical and highly affectionate.

Both the Bells had been raised in households manned by numerous servants, but at Longdale, as a neighbor said, the Bells' was "a home where economy is practiced." Money was not short nor comforts lacking, but spinster Cousin Maggie Crawford and a succession of tutors for the children were all the indoor help they needed to run their home themselves.

One of these young tutors, Ruth See, went to Brazil as a missionary, "and she had a profound effect on our family." Even more significant was a friendship with Frank Price, who as a seminary student in the late 1800s had held remarkable revival meetings among the miners while staying with the Bells. Two years before Nelson's birth Frank Price had sailed to China with the Southern Presbyterian Mission. The Bells had developed a strong missionary interest, and on Sunday afternoons when Mrs. Bell read aloud to the children, she often chose a missionary book.

Sunday was kept as the Lord's Day, and every day of the week began and ended with family prayer. "The position of the Bible as the Word of God was central in our training. Mother, who had more to do with the actual training of us children, raised us to look at the Bible as the final authority, the force determining the thing that was right or wrong. But there was no harshness in the religious life of my father and mother; they had such a warm, genuine Christian faith that we just sensed it. You couldn't miss it. Although often unexpressed verbally, it was very real, and this was evident because my parents were recognized as outstanding Christians in the community."

Nelson's early interest in the church and missions is seen in a letter he wrote (or more accurately, had his mother write for him) to *The Christian Observer*, a Southern Presbyterian weekly: "I am a little boy, four years and eight months old. I have recited the Child's Catechism to my teacher, Miss Ruth B. See, and my pastor, Rev. C. W. McDanald. I have commenced to learn the Shorter Catechism. I know the Twenty-third Psalm, most of the Nineteenth Psalm, part of the twelfth chapter of Romans, and almost all of the thirteenth chapter of First Corinthians, besides a number of other verses." Then he added, "I quote Scripture and exhort so much, and sing so loud, Mama says she is afraid I will be a shouting Methodist, instead of a Scotch-Irish Presbyterian, as she and Papa are. We have a Children's Missionary Society here, and we have undertaken the support of a child in Rev. P. F. Price's school, in Sinchang, China."

Nelson was six-and-a-half years younger than his brother McKim and nearly ten years junior to his sister Norma. Thus he was more like an only child, and despite a love for games and the outdoors, he might have grown introspective had they remained in the mountains. But in 1900 when Nelson was six, the Bells left Longdale, for the sake of the children's education, and bought a pleasant three-storied house, with a cupola and a good garden, on the western edge of Waynesboro, the small industrial town below Rockfish Gap in the Blue Ridge.

Waynesboro was only sixteen miles from Belvidere plantation with its apple orchards, grazing sheep, and view of the Blue Ridge Mountains, so Nelson saw much of his McCue relatives. His grandmother told him how Thomas McCue had freed his slaves (Joseph Bell had never owned any), after building his home with red-brown bricks made on the estate, and how all the slaves but one had stayed in his service, having known nothing from him but Christian compassion. Nelson saw the burn marks where federal soldiers had tried to set the place ablaze during Sheridan's scorched-earth treatment of the Valley. And he heard how his Aunt Betty, when a looting federal officer demanded her brooch, cried "Here you are!"—and drove the pin into his hand. "Madam," he replied, returning the brooch, "I admire your spunk!" "It's a wonder he didn't kill her," old Mrs. McCue would say.

Belvidere Plantation—birthplace of Nelson Bell's mother

*   *   *   *   *

At Waynesboro, James Bell opened a store with a partner—and hung a large bell over its entrance—but then changed to commercial travel. For thirty years he sold shirts, hunting clothes, coats, caps, and the like over four states, making a comfortable income. The Bells now kept a white servant, while Cousin Maggie was at hand when needed.

Nelson thrived in Waynesboro, as his quick step and cheerful grin made evident. By 1910, when he was sixteen and starting his senior year at Waynesboro High School, he had been named captain of the baseball team. He never played football because he had torn a cartilage in his knee at the age of six by falling on an iron toy—and was still troubled by the injury seven decades later. But, he said, "I spent a great deal of my spare time playing baseball." When not playing, he was practicing, "spending literally hours throwing the ball against a solid wall and catching it, and having it bounce on the ground." Already six feet tall, with strong arms and shoulders, he was a pitcher. His curved pitches fanned out many a batter, for he was experimenting already along a line that was to bring him fame in Virginia.

Playing and practicing could not exhaust his energy. With his great friend Ed Wayland, the school first baseman, Nelson would hike for hours in the mountains where the Skyline Drive and the Blue Ridge Parkway now run. He built his own boat, and the boys planned to sail down South River and the Shenandoah to the sea. "He was pretty strong-willed," Ed Wayland recalled, "and what he decided to do, he'd do. But we never succeeded in that."

Along with love of baseball and the mountains went a love of reading. Professor Kimler, the high school principal, a firm disciplinarian but a kindly man, did not consider that Nelson showed marked proficiency as a student "except as hard study gave it"; but Nelson studied hard. He worked fast and acquired a high standing—not brilliant, though always ahead of his age. The reading of biography, history, and a wide range of American and English literature strengthened his academic studies. He also developed a taste for detective fiction. His father had a pleasant conceit that they were descendants of the Joseph Bell who was the acknowledged model for Sherlock Holmes. The names were right, for James descended from several Joseph Bells. However Conan Doyle's model, the surgeon Joseph Bell of Edinburgh, died in 1911 having never lived outside Scotland. But it was an excuse to give his son a lasting love for detective stories.

Nelson's intellectual force and athletic ability were among the reasons why Kimler could write: "I have noticed him as a leader among students."

He was a determined person, "unusually persistent," as Ed Wayland commented a few years later. The school magazine joked that Bell "makes you think like he does, or say you do, anyway." He talked rapidly until you agreed with him, and the persuasiveness was all the more effective in that he never lost his temper. Nelson had inherited in full measure his father's sense of humor, love of fellowmen, and skill at telling a funny story.

In high school Nelson was known as a steady, unobtrusive Christian. The Bells took an active part at the First Presbyterian Church, and the ministers, Dr. Stribling and Dr. Walthall, who succeeded him in 1910, were almost like members of the family. The Bells never served "roast preacher" at Sunday dinner: indeed, "we were trained never to criticize the minister." Stribling, Nelson recalled, was "a warmhearted evangelical preacher, and Dr. Walthall also, though more of the Scottish type. Both were true preachers of the Word."

Evangelism was part of the church's program, and at the age of eleven-and-a-half, in January of 1906, Nelson went forward in an evangelistic service at his church. It was a deliberate, open commitment to the living Christ whose reality he had never doubted. Two weeks later, after instruction and the customary oral examination, Nelson was admitted to Communion, a full member of the church.

"From the time of my conversion to the time I entered college," Nelson wrote when he was twenty-two, "I was a regular church and Sunday school attendant and at times taught a class and was also identified with the boys' club of the church, but really did little active Christian work."

As was usual in the South, most of the high school students were from homes which attended the church of one denomination or another, but what was less usual, Professor Kimler, a layman, preached a short sermon every morning in the chapel. Some of the young people were indifferent and a few were in open or hidden rebellion. Therefore, the example of the school's baseball captain was important, though Nelson's commitment at this point went little further than strong convictions and determination to live cleanly, truthfully, and honorably.

Nelson Bell had no call to be a minister; on the contrary, he possessed a strong sense that he was meant to be a lifelong layman. He had often thought about the overseas mission fields which absorbed his mother's interest and prayers, but since Frank Price from China and all the other missionaries who visited the Bell home were clergymen, Nelson supposed that ordination was essential. Therefore, he could never be a missionary. The baseball captain would become a lawyer.

His parents agreed.

And so did the girl he was engaged to marry.

Nelson Bell, four years old

2
The Blonde With Gray Eyes

VIRGINIA MYERS LEFTWICH was a blonde with gray eyes. She was seven inches shorter and two years and three months older (born April 12, 1892) than Nelson Bell, attended the same high school, and lived some five blocks from his home.

They had been acquainted since the Bells first arrived in Waynesboro, but they didn't really pay any attention to each other until they got into high school. Virginia had a winsome personality and an exceptionally keen wit. She played the organ, sang, and was a good pianist, often accompanying her father's splendid baritone.

Douglas Lee (for the general) Leftwich was a traveling furniture salesman whose hobbies were fine cabinetmaking and, especially, music. He gave professional concerts and public readings all over the Southland. He was "a firm man, but he demonstrated his love."

Virginia's mother was a Wertenbaker, descended from the librarian of the University of Virginia in Jefferson's day. Virginia Leftwich had generals and colonels among her relatives, and the eminent Princeton historian, Professor Thomas Jefferson Wertenbaker, was her uncle. Her mother was a beautiful woman, and it has been said that she and Douglas had "a very happy life."

The eldest of a family of two girls and two boys, Virginia was slender, vivacious, and energetic. Nelson and Virginia played tennis, were members of the school dramatic club, the literary society, and the choir, and they sang solos and duets, for Nelson's voice had developed into a pleasant baritone. Virginia liked watching athletics too, which was fortunate: "The games I played in," said Nelson, "she was always right there."

The Leftwich family was Baptist. Waynesboro Baptists and Presbyterians were on excellent terms, with interchange of pulpits and a union service on summer Sunday nights. Virginia's home did not have such depth of spiritual life as Nelson's, but her parents attended church regularly. When Virginia was nine, she made public confession of her faith in Christ by baptism with total immersion. She later taught Sunday school and became president of the Young Women's Auxiliary. In high school her faith did not particularly stand out in the public eye. "I have always been rather diffident about taking active parts," she wrote in 1916, "and I cannot say that I have had much success in winning souls, but it isn't because of lack of desire."

With kindred interests, great sense of humor, and Christian dedication, Nelson and Virginia were a natural pair. Neither had eyes for any other. Nelson's early maturity—"I was always ahead for my years in everything I did"—offset the twenty-seven months between them, and when on August 13, 1910, they went for a walk in the fields and came back engaged, no one was surprised. Nelson was sixteen, Virginia eighteen.

Engagement meant that Virginia quietly abandoned a rather vague inclination toward foreign missionary service which had been in her mind since 1906. She would marry Nelson, and Nelson would be a lawyer.

*   *   *   *   *

Nelson's last year at Waynesboro High School (1910-11) passed in a blaze of glory. His academic work remained good, and he was popular. As a business manager he piloted the school paper, Kimler said, "through financial difficulties."

Under his captaincy the school carried off two baseball championships. "The heaviest and fastest team ever produced at the W.H.S. has been gotten together and completed by Captain Bell this year," the school annual declared. "Practice started early, and by the first of March the team was in excellent condition. The team, as the scores show, is not only fast in fielding but a team which hits the ball hard all the time, regardless of the opposing pitcher. The 'squeeze' play is worked with great success, being responsible for numbers of our runs. Bell is again in the box, and with Rusmiselle behind the bat, the two form an almost impregnable barrier to batters of other teams."

In the first six games of the season Bell's team had made ninety-three runs to their opponents' fourteen. As champions of Augusta County they then went on to win the state championship for 1911.

Virginia was always in the stands, and Nelson's classmates said his favorite phrase was, "Where's Virginia?" But their engagement was not entirely without tiffs. Once the two had a little disagreement, and Nelson, to express his feelings, started to climb up the narrow vertical ladder of the huge standpipe tank which held the town's water supply. One slip would be fatal. "Virginia was scared to death," related Ed Wayland, "watching him go up. She didn't want him to do it, but he went, and he got up on that tank. He had a good deal of courage!"

Another example of his strong streak of dare-devilry occurred on a chilly October night when Ed Wayland happened to be staying at the Bells. Nelson suddenly dared him to go down to the river, not far from the house, and swim. Ed accepted the dare; they stole out and swam dangerously in the ice-cold water in the dark.

* * * * *

There was only one university for Nelson Bell: Washington and Lee at Lexington, forty miles away near the head of the Valley. Relatives by the score had enrolled there since his preacher forebears, John McCue and William Wilson, had graduated when it was still named Liberty Hall. As Washington College, it acquired distinction under the presidency of General Robert E. Lee from 1865 until his death. Lexington revolved entirely around the university and the Virginia Military Institute, where George C. Marshall and

George S. Patton had trained a few years before Nelson's time. In 1911 when Bell stepped down at the depot of the Shenandoah Valley Railroad, the peaceful town possessed only two motor cars and stood in a lovely setting of hills, mountain skylines, and forests which looked glorious in their fall colors.

He was on familiar ground, for Longdale was not far away. A favorite cousin, Alexander Nelson, had been a professor of mathematics here, and his daughter still lived in Lexington. The Bells had arranged for Nelson to lodge with the Presbyterian minister, Dr. Alfred Graham. Most of the students roomed in private houses, and the Grahams kept six.

Ed Wayland matriculated in civil engineering and roomed at a home where he found the food insufficient. He moved across to the manse as Nelson's roommate and thought the world of the Grahams. "We had a wonderful time. They fed us to beat the band." Mrs. Graham—they were no relation to the Grahams of Charlotte, Billy Graham's family—was a mother to all her lodgers, and one of them, Jonah Larrack, who helped pay his board by grooming Old Rock their buggy horse, said they were "very, very understanding of us boys and our racket—we'd scrap upstairs sometimes."

Jonah Larrack recalled coming into Nelson's room one evening "when he was writing his sweetheart a letter on the big table. He had her photograph, and had three or four or maybe five mirrors reflecting the image of his sweetheart six or seven times. When I asked him 'Why all of that?' he said, 'It gives me inspiration!' We often teased him about his sweetheart."

The popular, athletic Larrack was impressed with Nelson: "Nelson was handsome, robust; he looked like a big athlete. A thorough Christian gentleman and student. I was not a very good student myself, but Nelson paid strict attention to his books. He was what we call a wheelhorse type of man: steady and tremendously sincere in his efforts—positive in all he did. He didn't waiver a bit. He knew what he was there for and did it. A good Christian boy; solid, sensible, substantial, dependable. He sometimes registered disapproval of some of the things the boys did, but he did it in a manly, helpful way." There was nothing of the prig in Nelson. As he said years later, "For me, being a Christian has always been a happy, glorious sort of thing." If Nelson was around, everyone else enjoyed life.

Washington and Lee had a strong law school, and Nelson set out to earn a good law degree and conquer his profession as his brother McKim, then just twenty-two, conquered his. McKim was a civil engineer who rose to be head of the company owning all the public utilities of southern Brazil, with headquarters in Rio de Janeiro. While he was never known as an active Christian, he was to help Nelson generously at one point.

Nelson Bell's ability was equal to McKim's, and being only seventeen in 1911, he had a good start. If not considered an outstanding scholar, he could reach any height in the legal world: "I regard Nelson as a young man of good natural ability and of extraordinary force of character," wrote President Denny of Washington and Lee in a confidential letter. "He has high ideals and a persistent energy in carrying out his plans."

*　*　*　*　*

The university had been founded by Presbyterians, and the Christian character of Lee, an Episcopalian, had strengthened the spiritual heritage, which remained predominantly Presbyterian and was enhanced by academic distinction. Nelson and his generation "had a feeling of rapport with our teachers, and I never heard one thing in the classroom that would in any way destroy the faith of a Christian believer."

Nelson and Ed Wayland centered their Christian activities on Dr. Graham's church with its Greek porch of large pillars, its squat colonial-style spire, and the stone facing which contrasted with the bright red of the university buildings higher up the hill. The church had been erected in 1843 on land once belonging to William McCue, the physician. Stonewall Jackson had been a deacon.

Nelson joined the choir and was soon in demand for solos. One of his fellow choir members was a classmate from Pennsylvania named Bill Hanzsche. Several years older, Bill was short in stature, but the tall Nelson looked up to him.

Bill Hanzsche was president of the Student Volunteers, who had signed the declaration: "We are willing and desirous, God permitting, to become foreign missionaries." Nelson was already in sympathy with his mother's concern for foreign missions. Moreover, Dr. Alfred Graham had a brother, Jimmy, who was an evangelist in North China at a rather unpronounceable place, as it seemed to Nelson, named Tsingkiangpu. Jimmy Graham was, by all accounts, a delightful fellow but, of course, a minister. Nelson's interest, therefore, was detached. For some years he had sought to live by the verse in Proverbs: "Trust in the Lord with all thine heart; and lean not unto thine own understanding. In all thy ways acknowledge him, and he shall direct thy paths." He often thought he should be a missionary, but was more than ever sure he should not be a minister, though he quite liked preaching. Being curiously ignorant of any other way, Nelson remained convinced that he could not be more than a lawyer who supported missions by purse and prayer, until one Sunday evening early in December 1911.

Bill Hanzsche and Nelson Bell were walking home to the manse after church.

"Nelson, did you ever think of becoming a medical missionary?" asked Bill.

That instant Nelson Bell knew.

He recalled: "That very instant I knew what God wanted me to do. This wasn't a thing of days after. It was just as clear as if I heard God speaking in audible tones, 'That's what I want you to do.' It was as sudden as a light striking through a cloudy sky."

Nelson immediately wrote to Virginia to say they would be medical missionaries. On Monday morning, not worrying about what she might reply, he switched from pre-law to pre-medical. The idea of being a doctor presented no difficulties. He knew about his physician ancestors, James Wilson and young William McCue, who had died of typhus. The medical profession was in Nelson's blood.

Virginia agreed with delight in her return letter. Her parents, however, were not too happy. "I've been praying for years for missions and missionaries," said Mrs. Leftwich when Nelson returned to Waynesboro for Christmas, "but I didn't expect that I'd have to give my own daughter." Nelson sensed no resentment, merely surprise; yet even as late as September 1915, when Virginia submitted her preliminary application, she answered the question, "Are your parents in sympathy with your missionary purpose?" with *"Partially."* By July 1916 she could change this to *"Reconciled."* And the reconciliation was complete. Their support thenceforth was total.

James and Cora Bell were thrilled at Nelson's decision. As for himself, from that day in December 1911 and that spot between church and manse in Lexington, he said, "I had one purpose: to become a medical missionary."

Waynesboro High School tennis club, 1910-1911. Virginia Leftwich and Nelson Bell, back row, second and third from right

Waynesboro High School baseball team, 1911. Nelson Bell, captain, first row, center; Ed Wayland on Bell's right

3
Baseball Pro

THE mayor of Maysville, the old tobacco market town in Kentucky, grew more and more excited during the Fourth-of-July baseball game against their greatest rivals in the league. The score was tied, and it was Maysville's seventh inning.

He saw an unknown tall fellow come out to bat and heard that it was a college boy from Waynesboro, Virginia, in town selling clothes. A friend had invited him to warm up with the home team, and the manager was trying him as a pinch hitter.

Nelson Bell took the bat and promptly hit a home run, driving in the runner ahead of him. The crowd roared as Maysville won the game. The mayor ran onto the field and flung his arm around Nelson: "You can have anything in town!"

Despite this winning hit, Nelson continued primarily as a pitcher. He was somewhat overshadowed at Washington and Lee by two of the greatest they ever had, Harry Moran, afterward of the Detroit Tigers, and Jap Efrid—but at least he was on the team. During summer vacations he welcomed an occasional game while traveling for the clothing firms his father knew; Nelson did five summers on the road, and this "business experience, starting very young, developing the ability to sell goods to those who sometimes didn't want them, was a help in learning how to contact people." It is a curious coincidence that both Nelson Bell and Billy Graham in their youth had stints as traveling salesmen.

By the fall of 1912 Nelson Bell had already finished with

Washington and Lee. Having gained the necessary credits in the pre-medical course, in September he registered at the Medical College of Virginia in Richmond. When this leading state institution learned of his intention to be a medical missionary, they canceled his tuition fees. "I never paid tuition the four years I was there. It was a voluntary action on their part; I never asked for it. I think they looked on it as a small contribution to the cause of medical missions."

At eighteen, Nelson looked older than his years with his height, broad shoulders, and big bones; he had a handsome, pleasant face and curly brown hair.

He worked unstintingly at the arduous courses and never failed an exam. "The hardest thing was inorganic chemistry. The professor was an old-fashioned, hard-boiled chemist who just gloried in flunking the students." The professor of anatomy, on the other hand, gloried in "flunking" the famous textbook, *Gray's Anatomy*—he had written his own. The professors of surgery, Murat Willis and Paul Howle, were interested in medical missions, and they encouraged Nelson's vocation and his aptitude and love for surgery.

He was initiated into the medical fraternity, Omega Upsilon Psi, and went to live in the fraternity house on Grace Street between the college and Jefferson's graceful capitol. The men were soon glad to leave the management to his inexhaustible energy. Vitality seemed to pour out of Nelson Bell of the class of 1916. In addition to athletics, academic and church work, he sang with the glee club, wrote for the college annual, and served in the Medical Corps. He paraded in Washington at the presidential inauguration of Woodrow Wilson in March 1913.

The other boys secretly admired Nelson's unwavering purpose to be a medical missionary and found him that rare breed, the man of intense conviction who was thoroughly popular, especially with his roommates. "One of his hardest tasks," chuckled one of them, Fred Van Pelt, "was to try to keep us straight on the right road, which was not easy. But he tried to keep us in line!"

One of the fraternity noted in Nelson's last year, "If other views conflict with his, he holds to his and believes them correct until it can be proved to the contrary." A little obstinate, a little excitable occasionally, yet Nelson was always in command of the situation.

And he could relieve any tension with his wit and humor. Without his merry heart the magnetic Nelson Bell might have been in danger of growing too good to be true.

One of his most remarkable achievements at Richmond was to start daily prayers in the fraternity house. After the dramatic call to be a missionary, he had joined the Student Volunteers and had attended a laymen's missionary conference, where his high school friend Ed Wayland also volunteered for the foreign field. From the Volunteers Nelson learned "The Morning Watch," introduced by John R. Mott after visiting Cambridge in England where Christian undergraduates signed a pledge: "I will endeavor, God helping me, to set aside at least twenty minutes, and if possible one hour, in the early morning for prayer and Bible study."

Nelson knew that his mother spent hours in Bible study, and he had often heard her, a poor sleeper, refer at breakfast to the previous night's intercession about a problem. He had absorbed much of her teaching, but he had not set aside a regular, disciplined time. The Volunteers' Morning Watch caught his imagination. From then on, year after year, he rose early to pore over the Bible and pray about his needs and those of his friends. He applied to Bible study the precision and clarity required in medical classes and practicals. He began, as he put it, to acquire "an absolute, complete confidence in the sovereignty of God, the fact that He is all-knowing, all-wise, all-powerful; and for that reason, when you pray and seek His guidance, He's got the answer. There's not a detail in our lives that God's not concerned with." He learned too that the psalmist's warning "is so true: 'If I regard iniquity in my heart, the Lord will not hear me.' You've got to get that cleared up."

The Morning Watch became an essential element in Nelson's life. He then discovered that although several of the boys were active Christians, none kept it. He felt a "deep sense of responsibility for these fraternity brothers." In his second year he began a brief devotional service for any who would come before they rushed out of the Grace Street house for breakfast at Mrs. Gentry's and other places over the way. He maintained it every day of every term for the rest of his time at Richmond.

Sundays were extremely full. Nelson attended Grace Street Presbyterian Church, a few steps from the fraternity house, and taught Sunday school before singing in the choir at morning service. In the afternoons he helped at the "Seventeenth Street Colored Mission" (which ministered to black families and individuals in the area) and in the evenings at the church young people's meeting, and in the evening service he again sang in the choir. The "Colored Mission" gave full scope to a sense of compassion which was strongly developed. Nelson did not yet have any marked reputation as a speaker or even as a personal evangelist; he was just an unwavering, cheerful Christian.

One evening he went from Richmond to Waynesboro. "I stopped by to see Virginia, my sweetheart, and then went home. After praying and reading my Bible, which I did every night, around eleven o'clock I had the most wonderful sense of God's presence in the room and in my heart: a sense of complete oneness with Him. God has been so real to me since a boy, and I have simply tried to know what His will was for my life and then to do it. And I think this was an experience of an in-filling of the Holy Spirit."

*   *   *   *   *

Virginia had remained in Waynesboro after high school, working two years as librarian of the Waynesboro Public Library. She and Nelson corresponded regularly, with or without the aid of mirrors to give inspiration, and during vacations used to drive by horse and buggy on Sunday afternoons to teach in a mountain mission school at Glenkirk, four romantic miles each way.

In 1914 Virginia studied at the Nurses Training School at St. Luke's Hospital in Richmond, followed by a course at the nearby General Assembly's Training School for Lay Workers. A fellow student was a daughter of the wealthy tobacco executive, John H. Reed. The Reeds' staunchly Christian home was an open house to young people and their son, afterwards one of Nelson's medical missionary colleagues, recalled his first sight of Virginia Leftwich when he was a small boy. "She wore a broad, white hat; it just vibrated with her vivacity. A handsome young man came to the door, and my sister found it was Nelson Bell come to see Miss Leftwich." Nelson became a hero to John Reed, Jr.: "Here comes a young doctor. Not a preacher, but a doctor who's going to be a missionary. So we began to look up to him as one of our ideal young men who was giving his life to the Lord's service."

John was excited, too, by Nelson's prowess on the ball field. Nelson played for the college team, and he pitched the first ball at the new Broadstreet Park, a dubious distinction because the batter hit it for a home run. Nelson was experimenting until he perfected a pitch which was most unusual at the time; it was known as a knuckle ball, though he used his fingertips. The ball did not twist in flight: the batter could actually see the seams. But just before it reached the plate, the ball would be jerked by the force of air compressed ahead of it, and neither Bell nor the batter could tell which way it would go.

In the summer of 1913 the manager of the Richmond club in the professional Virginia League was a catcher. He decided to try out this medical student who was only nineteen years old.

Nelson threw fast balls, curve balls, and straight balls, and the manager asked if he had any more. Nelson threw a knuckle ball. "It didn't twist at all. Just before it got to him, it jumped down and hit him hard on the shin! He didn't even have a chance to catch it. He could hardly wait to get to the club house to sign me up."

Nelson made one stipulation in his contract: he was not to be required to travel or play on Sunday. The club accepted this without demur, for Christy Mathewson of the New York Giants, one of the greatest pitchers of all time, had the same clause in his contract.

Throughout the summer vacation of 1913 Nelson traveled the Old Dominion as a professional baseball player, used in batting practice and relief. The Richmond club's leading pitcher was Burleigh Grimes, afterward with the Brooklyn

Dodgers. Nelson was on the field when Richmond beat the New York Giants in an exhibition game, 6-5 behind Grimes, to the fury of their manager, John McGraw.

The Richmond team was a mixture of characters. "There were some very fine men and some very rough ones: I have often thought that God's protecting hand and the prayers of my mother and father shielded me from a lot of meanness going on. It just went off me like water off a duck's back. I wasn't aware of it." The next year, 1914, Nelson played for Richmond through June and then was farmed to Clifton Forge in the old Mountain League. But in his second game near his mountain birthplace a line drive fractured the forefinger of his pitching hand and he could not pitch the rest of the season.

In 1915 when he was completing his junior year at medical college, the Richmond ball club was sold to the Baltimore Orioles at the forming of the ill-fated Federal League. Thus, unexpectedly, Nelson Bell had an opening which he had every reason to suppose could lead to the major leagues, but to report to Baltimore would involve abandoning his studies. He had thrown away the prospect of fame and fortune when he left law to train for medical missions. Now he had the chance to win fame and fortune in baseball.

"I had to say 'No' to myself and to that ambition."

It was a deliberate wrench to turn away from the big leagues, yet no real choice remained in Nelson's mind since that December day in Lexington four years before. Only his intense love for the game could stay.

As if to compensate for the decision, a "very coveted opportunity," in the words of the professor of surgery, came at medical college. Nelson was allowed to double the last part of his senior year as a student with the practical work of a resident intern at M.C.V.'s Memorial Hospital, the largest in the city. All senior students were sent out into the homes of the poor for obstetrics and treated the indigent patients in the hospitals under qualified supervision, but few were given the status and responsibility of an intern. "Owing to Dr. Bell's energy and ability," wrote Dr. Paul Howle, "the surgeons gave him exceptional opportunities in assisting in major operations....I counted myself fortunate in securing his services in working up all of my personal histories, which included the complete examination in each case....I regarded Dr. Bell as one of the ablest men of his class."

It is well that Nelson did not read what his professors and others said or his head might have been turned. "Dr. Bell is one of the best students graduated from the Medical College of Virginia during recent years," wrote the hospital superintendent, Frederic B. Morlock. "His service here at Memorial Hospital was worthy of praise of the highest type." Nelson's college roommate thought him "the finest, best, all-around *man* I ever met, and I have heard a great many reliable people say the same." Bell's popularity with students was proved by his election to the coveted fraternity of the Skull and Keys, "a right wild bunch," although the members knew he would not join the more uproarious of their proceedings.

He also was elected president of the Student Volunteers for the whole of Virginia. This took him frequently to Union Seminary.

"I see him crossing the campus," recalled a former seminary student, "tall, handsome, strong, bright, sunny, attractive, friendly. All of the seminary students liked him. He had a real influence on their missionary concern." One who was six years older recalled that "You were never conscious of his being younger. He had a gift of making people unconsciously look up to him." His former Waynesboro pastor did not exaggerate when he described Nelson as "One of the few young men who will receive the unqualified endorsement of all who know him....Physically he is almost a perfect specimen of manhood."

As a member of the Medical Corps of First Virginia Regiment, Bell marched in the inaugural parade for Woodrow Wilson, 1913.

Bell, intern at Memorial Hospital, Richmond, Virginia, 1915-1916

4
A Cable From China

ALL the Bell family's missionary contacts were with the Southern Presbyterian Mission, the overseas arm of the Presbyterian Church in the United States, which had been strongly missionary-minded since its separation from Northern Presbyterians at the start of the Civil War. It now had work in Africa, Brazil, Korea, Japan, and China.

During the first years of Woodrow Wilson's presidency there was a surge of interest in the Orient among American Christians. Korea had been the scene of the famous revival, in the fields of both Northern and Southern Presbyterians; Japan had caught the imagination of the West by its swift rise to a modern world power; and China had thrown off the Manchu emperors to begin its unsteady career as a republic—in which no citizen had a vote.

China had been open to the West since 1842, following the Opium War. Britain had forced her to cede Hong Kong, lease international settlements at five "treaty ports," and to abandon, at least openly, her profound conviction that the Celestial Empire alone possessed civilization and that all men on earth owed allegiance to the emperor in Peking.

Christian missionaries, like the men of commerce, had quickly taken up residence in the treaty ports, but no trader or missionary had legal right to venture into the interior, though a few Jesuits did so at risk of their lives. Even when a wider treaty granted access in 1860 after a second war, Protestant missionaries clung to the coast or the new up-river treaty ports. Then early in 1867, the year the first

Southern Presbyterian missionaries landed, a sickly little sandy-haired Yorkshireman, the young Hudson Taylor, led his recently founded China Inland Mission with incredible audacity into the unknown.

By the time Nelson Bell became a physician, almost half a century later, every province of the vast land had been entered by one or the other of a score of societies at the cost of many martyrdoms. The SPM had two spheres: the Mid-China Mission in the lower Yangtze valley, the hinterland of Shanghai, and the North Kiangsu Mission beyond the Yangtze (now called the Chang Jiang) River in the coastal plains of rice and wheat bisected by the Grand Canal. Both regions were densely populated. In these SPM areas, as elsewhere, Western missionaries and the native Christians were as a few grains of sand compared with China's millions who lacked knowledge of Christ.

Nelson Bell had been interested in China since Frank Price's visit on furlough to the Bell home. In the Lexington manse Nelson had heard frequent mention of Jimmy and Sophie Graham of Tsingkiangpu in North Kiangsu. Their two daughters also became Virginia Leftwich's close friends, so that Virginia and Nelson even knew by now how to pronounce Tsingkiangpu: *Ching-jahng-poo.*

In May 1916, shortly before Nelson qualified as a physician, a cable from Tsingkiangpu mission hospital caused Egbert Smith, the executive secretary of the Southern Presbyterian Foreign Mission Committee (as the board was then known), to make the long railroad trip from his office at Nashville to Richmond. A young and promising American doctor had died after a few months on the field. The forty-nine-year-old superintendent, Dr. James B. Woods, a veteran of twenty-two years' service, was overdue for his next furlough but could not leave until another associate arrived. Egbert Smith sought out Nelson Bell: "Can you go to China as soon as possible?"

"I'm perfectly willing," Nelson replied, knowing that he spoke also for Virginia.

Virginia was to join the Presbyterian church, with her Baptist pastor's approval, and they had planned to start their married life in the coal fields of West Virginia. Several professors had advised Nelson that a year spent as resident physician at some mines would be far more beneficial in preparing him to meet emergencies and rely on his own resources than a year spent as intern at some hospital, and he felt the same way. Egbert Smith now wanted him to cut this to a few weeks while the mission board organized the visas and papers.

At least one of Nelson's referees disagreed: "You are anxious to obtain thoroughly competent physicians and surgeons for the foreign field, and I do not feel that any man just out of medical college can fill these requirements. A man of Dr. Bell's qualifications and habits would undoubtedly be many times as valuable to you should he serve an internship in a general hospital for several years or an apprenticeship to some active man doing special work." The mission committee compromised. Sailing was postponed until fall to allow three months' experience at the mines.

When Nelson Bell received his medical degree on June 6, 1916, he was only twenty-one years old. To qualify so young was rare. It has since been argued that had Bell practiced in America for his first years, he might have become one of the world's greatest surgeons. But a world-famous surgeon must by definition be a specialist; a medical missionary must be ready to insert his scalpel anywhere.

*   *   *   *   *

Immediately after graduation Nelson brought his roommates home to Waynesboro to study for the Virginia and West Virginia State Boards. "But after one day," recorded Van Pelt, "we decided that if we did not know what we had learned, we just would not do any good trying to cram. So we had a good time and enjoyed Nelson's mother's wonderful food."

On June 30, 1916, Nelson and Virginia were married in the First Presbyterian Church, Waynesboro, nearly six years after their engagement. The best man was Ed Wayland, who had taken a small pastorate nearby at Stuart's Draft, and was hoping to join them in China. A few weeks later, on July 18, Nelson passed his state board examinations.

The Wedding Day—the bride wore navy

Going away—the new bride and groom

The just married, just qualified Dr. Nelson Bell and his bride set up house at the Summerlee coal mines of the New River Company in the mountains of West Virginia. His patients were rough miners, and he walked to all his calls. The Bells felt they were half in the mission field already, and Nelson busily made furniture in his spare time while Virginia not only cut dresses but rivaled Nelson as a handyman.

They also began a habit they continued: family prayers morning and evening. And during that summer in Summerlee Nelson wrote down some inner thoughts a few days after his twenty-second birthday. They do not foreshow his future literary skill but are a genuine indication of his mettle: "Altho I feel that I have made many mistakes and have not been as useful as I might, I have been trying earnestly for the past five years to do the Master's will and lead others to Christ....I can but feel a greater delight in doing His will and a greater desire to make my life one of service. Each year I realize my own weakness more and His love and mercy greater. It seems to me that my life has and is passing through a series of evolutions which I pray will some day lead me to the paths of the greatest possible service for my Master."

Meanwhile the SPM completed arrangements for the Bells' support. Their home church, First Presbyterian at Waynesboro, was missionary minded, yet unable to do more than pray for these latest recruits because of heavy commitments after rebuilding. The SPM committee invited the First Presbyterian Church of Houston, Texas, to adopt the Bells, who apart from one acquaintance had no connection with the church or city. This administrative decision was to have incalculable consequences.

All the medical and personal papers and references had now been received. The candidates' secretary, S. H. Chester, well-schooled in assessing the worth of favorable references, wrote of Nelson in a private letter to a committee member: "He is one of the brightest, and in every way the finest, young man we have ever had before us for appointment."

Years later one SPM executive secretary said: "The most unpredictable thing in the world is a missionary. You can tell about a horse, but the most elaborate system of checks and balances simply cannot guarantee what a missionary will be. Not until he is tried and tested on the field is his real character revealed."

5
Clear Water Depot

SLOWLY a long, crowded barge glided behind a steam launch up the ancient Grand Canal. Nelson peered out of his unglazed cabin window between a row of Chinese feet.

He wrapped his padded coat closer. There was plenty to watch when the cold or the stench of feet did not drive him back to the table where "Uncle" Jimmy Graham sat writing: market towns and walled cities, innumerable little farmhouses built of baked earth, and brick temples. Peculiar windmills brought water to the rice fields. Later the barge passed into the wheat country where fields were dry and brown. And everywhere he saw graves, like large molehills littering the land.

The Bells had landed at the International Settlement in Shanghai on December 4, 1916, after a stormy passage of nineteen days from Seattle. The next day Jimmy and Sophie Graham escorted them by the noon express 150 miles to Chinkiang on the Yangtze. Next morning they crossed the great river by ferry to board the launch which would carry them the remaining 125 miles up the Grand Canal. It promptly ran aground for four hours off the walled city of Yangchow.

In a riot half a century earlier, Hudson Taylor had nearly lost his life at Yangchow, once the city of Marco Polo. Anti-foreign feeling was now dormant, although never far from the surface, especially in country districts which seldom saw a "foreign devil." The Boxer Rebellion of 1900 had ended with the Western powers and Japan in closer control of China's policies and trade. Fear and suspicion of the white man still lay on the Chinese, while a Western newcomer could be surprised at some of their apparently primitive ways: when Nelson saw women nursing their young in public he was shocked. And soldiers at every stopping place, along with Uncle Jimmy's tales of bandits and violence, showed that China had not found internal peace by expelling the Manchu emperor. But Nelson at twenty-two relished excitement, and if Virginia—or "Ginny" as nearly everyone except Nelson called her—wondered what horrors might soon engulf them, she showed no disquiet.

That first journey took a mere sixty hours for the 275 miles from Shanghai, compared with much longer trips in years to come when the Grand Canal was too full, or too empty, or icebound, or a battle was in progress. They had only one night on board a barge, the two wives in a larger cabin and their husbands in an adjoining smaller one. The sleeping shelf was too short for Nelson, and a couple of hundred Chinese above chattered all night long.

Next day, the morning of December 8, they passed inside a great mud wall, twenty feet high, and saw the city of Tsingkiangpu. The canal was nearly a hundred yards wide at this point, spanned by two ancient bridges. On its southern bank, surrounded by the outer city, rose the strong gray stone walls of the original Tsing Kiang Pu, which means Clear Water Depot (or Stopping-place or Station). Over the gates leered decapitated heads of criminals.

Tsingkiangpu—the old city gate

Tsingkiangpu—the city wall

Houseboats, sampans, and small junks crowded the wharfs. The noise was indescribable as workers unloaded, merchants and boatmen bargained, and women argued in loud, cracked voices. Dr. Woods had sent sedan chairs for the men and their wives, while the luggage would come by wheelbarrow. The chairs swayed up narrow Ten Li Street. The bearers deftly threaded a way between mule-carts, donkeys, gambling wheels, shoppers who inspected piles of wares in the thoroughfare, and peasant women with tightly bound feet. Several times Nelson clapped his fingers to his nose at the stench of buckets of night soil carried by the workers. Uncle Jimmy pointed out an even narrower street which led to the church, and then, a *li* (third of a mile) further, they came to the hospital gate at the northeast corner of the outer city.

A board displayed five Chinese characters, one above the other.

"Ren si I Uen," Uncle Jimmy read them for Nelson. "'Benevolent Compassionate Healing Hall'; or you might translate it 'Love and Mercy Hospital.'"

*   *   *   *   *

The Bells instinctively felt at home in Tsingkiangpu. The mission had been opened as long ago as 1887 by Andrew

Sydenstricker, the father of Pearl S. Buck whose novel about China, *The Good Earth*, would be the best seller of 1931. Two China Inland missionaries, Miss Waterman and Miss Saltmarsh, already used the city as a center for country work, but the region of towns, walled cities, and villages had too dense a population to permit a breath of inter-mission rivalry: relations were excellent. Jimmy and Sophie Graham had joined Sydenstricker in 1889 as evangelists. Dr. Edgar Woods had started a medical mission the year before, which his youngest brother, James, joined the year Nelson Bell was born. The Sydenstrickers had afterward moved to the SPM Mid-China Mission, and the Edgar Woodses had been forced home because of illness. James and Bessie Woods had served at Tsingkiangpu ever since.

Nelson had vaguely expected the Chinese equivalent of a mountain mission in the backwoods but found a new (1914) gray brick structure under a red tin roof, comparatively well-equipped. It was efficient and clean, even if patients' relatives sprawled around the beds. It had two isolation wards, which stood a little apart, and an outpatient clinic. He was astounded at the numbers treated each day. The compound covered thirteen acres within a nine-foot gray brick wall. The only other buildings at present were the hospital chapel, a boys' school, a Chinese-style house for "the native physician," and the Woodses' home where the Bells would live until one of their own could be found. The Woodses' home was brick. To have built a frame house in modest American style would have been highly extravagant in a timberless plain.

Half a mile along the outer city earthwork, which served as a narrow road and overlooked the hospital, a second compound contained a famine orphanage, the Grahams' place, and another Western-style house for Addison Talbot. He was an absent-minded, lovable Kentuckian who was one of the best country evangelists in North China, and his wife Katherine, perhaps more than any white woman in Kiangsu province, was adored by the Chinese. She was always rescuing half-frozen or starved babies from the straw shacks used by beggars or abandoned on the canal bank or in the fields.

The Woodses' eldest daughter and two other single

women completed the missionary strength of Tsingkiangpu. "They are all such delightful people," Nelson wrote on Christmas Eve 1916. "This station has an unusual reputation for the quality and harmoniousness of its members, and we are indeed fortunate in being located here....These missionaries are without doubt the happiest lot of Christians I have ever seen."

Dr. Jimmy Graham was a gentle, amusing Virginian of fifty-three, young in heart. Nelson wrote after getting to know him well: "He is a good reader, plays a fine game of tennis, loves all kinds of fun, and is a thorough evangelist." Back in the 1880s Graham would return from the country covered with spit, and black and blue from stones and sticks. Once a dead puppy landed on his head. He worked three years without a convert, laughing off the insults, hatred, and blows. In later years when asked if he had ever become discouraged, he replied, "No. I knew the battle was the Lord's and He would win." Now he was pastor of a growing church, superintendent of the boys' school and the orphanage, and still traveled the country for weeks at a time.

His son, James Junior, said his Chinese was atrocious. Listeners had to use mental gymnastics to follow him. Sincerity, humor, and love offset this deficiency, but he regretted that pioneering had prevented study in his youth. "Aunt" Sophie Graham was the better speaker, yet even she put her meaning over partly by gesture: the Chinese would say they "loved to go and *see* Mrs. Graham preach." She was dynamic, with an instinctive grasp of Chinese gestures and facial expressions. The warm-hearted, lovable Uncle Jimmy and Aunt Sophie became almost like parents to the young Bells and later like grandparents to the Bell children.

Much would depend on Dr. Woods (whom Nelson never called "Uncle" James), especially as beneath the kindly courtesy of a Southern aristocrat he hid an extremely strong will.

Woods was a Virginian. No less than one hundred of his cousins were ministers, including thirty missionaries, and the noted Chinese scholar, Henry M. Woods, was his eldest brother. James Baker Woods was forty-nine, had reddish hair and an impressive mustache, and was shorter and more slender than Nelson Bell. Woods spoke as if he had

Dr. and Mrs. James B. Woods. Various members of the Woods family gave a cumulative total of over four hundred years of service to China.

carefully thought out each remark, while Nelson spoke rapidly, thinking as he talked.

Woods's wit was less keen than Graham's, but Nelson delighted to watch their "casual banter and kidding back and forth." The veterans were the closest of friends. Years before, they had stood side by side when murderous mobs, incited by the anti-foreign agitators, beat on the gate of the hospital, which was then at the heart of the city. As the SPM institutions developed, bringing a new era of trust and gratitude, Graham's admiration for the wisdom and spiritual discernment of his colleague, wrote Graham's son, "knew no bounds."

Woods had a deep conviction and was something of a scholar, fluent in Chinese and reading his New Testament in Greek and Latin classics in the original. He had a wide interest in current affairs and stored his mind with great literature.

It was obvious to Nelson, fresh from medical college, that Woods was an outstanding physician, leaning more to general medicine than surgery, but with useful surgical tricks not to be picked up in the sophisticated hospitals of America. He had graduated with high honors from the University of Virginia, followed by three years at the New York City Hospital. He had come up the hard way in China: in early days, when a pigtail and Chinese dress were necessary, he had even operated in a coal hole, using the patient's door as a table. In 1907 and 1912 he had been appointed director of famine relief for all North Kiangsu, with outstanding success, but at the cost of a severe attack of famine fever which left his hearing in one ear permanently impaired.

His reputation among the Chinese was enormous, not only among the poor. Years later, one of his sons was released by bandits immediately on his disclosing his parentage. "That old man saved my life," the bandit chief said. "I would not want to give you any difficulty at all. Your honorable father Ling Si Hsien San is a truly great man."

Woods's Chinese name was *Ling* (two trees, equals Woods) with the differentiation of Fourth Brother *(Si)*; thus Ling Si Hsien San means Mr. Four Two-Trees. But the Chinese showed their affection by calling him simply Mr. Four, and though there were many others so-called, if Mr. Four was spoken of over a wide area of North Kiangsu, the Chinese always recognized the reference as being to Dr. Woods of Tsingkiangpu. He was an autocrat of the old school. The Chinese told young Nelson: "Mr. Four can manage us much better than we can ourselves." This, Nelson explained in a letter to friends at home, meant "That he knows how to have his wishes carried out by the Chinese in little as well as big things—something very hard to do. And with all of his masterful dealings with them, he is famous for his *hsiao hua* or 'laughing words,' and that may be the secret of his wonderful success—they have to like him."

Nelson liked him too, although not with such deep affection as he felt for Uncle Jimmy; the older physician and the new were perhaps too contrasted in character, even though they shared a passion for detective stories.

Nelson quickly felt deep respect for his senior's experience, devotional life, and methodical ways, but realized some changes were indicated. For instance, Dr. Woods had a rooted objection to screened windows. He was not alone in his prejudice; many missionary hospitals remained without them for years to come. Even in Richmond, Virginia, in the 1920s a surgeon discovered on first using a fine new hospital building that the operating theater lacked screens. The architect explained that being on the third floor, it was above the fly line. The surgeon retorted that no one had explained this to the flies.

Dr. Woods declined Nelson's immediate suggestion of screens, so Nelson bided his time.

*   *   *   *   *

Once a day during the winter of 1916-17, when freezing northwest winds blew across the parched plain from the distant deserts of Central Asia, a suave Chinese gentleman named Kang, who had been a Confucian scholar and now was an elder in the church, taught the Bells the tones and characters of one of the world's most difficult languages.

A slight mistake of tone may produce a completely different meaning in Chinese so the Bells' good ear for music was useful. They needed all their youthful stamina and powers of concentration, but Nelson proved a natural linguist, driven onward by awareness that he must soon run the hospital. He was thrown into constant use of Chinese until he could speak the "low language" of the country people, the "earth words," almost like a native. No foreigner not born in China can hope to speak Mandarin like an educated Chinese, yet forty years later Bell was amused to be told after visiting General Chiang Kai-shek, who was born in a remote country district of the South: "Why, you speak better Chinese than the General!"

In the spring of 1917 Nelson knew enough Chinese to take the big clinic at the larger, rich city of Hwaian, ten miles south on the Grand Canal. Hwaian stood majestically with great battlements and gates and contained exquisite houses with rambling courtyards, their outer walls drab to deceive robbers and evil spirits. The prefect lived there in his *yamen*. And the poor huddled by the hundreds in filthy alleys where the stench and squalor could not deter the SPM women who taught there. The two stations worked closely together, and the Tsingkiangpu doctors looked after the health of their Hwaian colleagues.

Nelson went by sedan chair when the canal ran too low

for water traffic. The ten miles took three hours each way, much too long for Nelson.

Uncle Jimmy had brought back a motorcycle with sidecar shortly before the Bells arrived. No one had known how to ride it until Nelson learned and taught the others. They laughed at his enthusiasm, but when the Talbots borrowed the machine they did a two-day wheelbarrow journey in four hours with less bone-shaking. The machine happened now to be out of order, and as soon as opportunity offered, Nelson took it down to Shanghai for repair. On the outward journey the low water required six different boats and two tedious transfers by land. On the return, he left the canal eighty-five miles below Tsingkiangpu, and to the astonishment and alarm of country folk, he roared and bumped home along the Imperial Highway, narrow and rough, easily beating the record for a journey between Shanghai and Tsingkiangpu.

* * * * *

In April 1917 the Bells were joined by a couple of their own age.

The slender, dark-haired Kerr Taylor had been at Union

Rev. Kerr Taylor and his wife, Fannie Bland Graham Taylor

Seminary when Nelson was at medical college, and they had often talked missions. Kerr married Fannie Bland Graham (daughter of the Lexington manse and niece of Uncle Jimmy) and took a pastorate in a Kentucky town where the Bells' train to Seattle stopped for five minutes. As it drew out again, Nelson called: "We'll see you in China *soon.*"

"Seeing off a missionary couple has a good deal of influence on a man's life," Kerr Taylor commented. Five months later the Taylors were assigned to Tsingkiangpu to take over the boys' school; they arrived at the Talbots late at night. "Next morning Virginia and Nelson came up the half mile from the hospital and had breakfast with us. And I remember it just as vividly today after fifty-three years. Virginia and Nelson were brilliant and happy and dedicated and imaginative and very affectionate....Nelson said: 'I have already done three major operations this morning.'"

To Nelson and Virginia, the Kerr Taylors came as a breath of home and were thus doubly welcome, for there were moments of homesickness. Few friends bothered to write, though they had promised to pray. "I really wonder whether you wish to hear what we are doing," Nelson complained once.

His mother, however, wrote weekly and wished to hear all. Both the Bells and the Leftwiches—Virginia's mother died in 1918—were proud of their children on the field, but Mrs. James H. Bell's interest was intense. She fostered a small prayer circle every Tuesday afternoon, remembering local church needs, but mainly her son and all his colleagues in China. Nelson's detailed weekly letters, which survive almost complete from 1928, were written partly with this circle in mind. "STOP—Don't read aloud," he would insert before some highly confidential morsel...."READ ON." Dr. Wilbur Cousar, one of Mrs. Bell's pastors, wrote: "She seemed to take all those dear workers into her heart as though they were her children and became concerned for their safety and progress. She carried them in her prayers and talked about them as though they were friends of long standing." She pored over magazines and books about China and set herself to pray daily.

Mrs. Bell imagined as best she could not only the dangers

but the delights, such as the first vacation to Kuling in the mountains.

All Westerners in China, India, or other parts of the Orient made for the hills once a year; the heat was considered such a hazard to health that in India the entire government, from the viceroy downward, transferred to the Himalayas for the whole hot weather season. Summer in the plains of North China was especially humid and trying, even in a year like 1917 when the rains came just in time to avert famine. The Bells and Taylors went by launch down the canal to Chinkiang and thence by slow, foreign-owned river steamer some 350 miles up the Yangtze to Kiukiang. Then they walked, or were carried in chairs hanging between two poles carried on the shoulders of Chinese laborers, some ten miles up a steep mountainside.

Kuling perched dramatically above a gorge of the Yangtze which could be seen far below, the view being rather like that from Lookout Mountain near Chattanooga or Murren in Switzerland, magnified several times. This beautiful bowl in the hills, where the only Chinese were servants and shopkeepers, provided a safety valve in an age when mis-

On the way to Kuling, where the Bells spent vacation in their early years

sionaries had to serve long periods between furloughs, when letters from home took months, when no jet airliners offered a quick escape for the seriously sick or broken, and when the environment was often hostile or discouraging. Except in war years like 1917, the gathering was truly international and ecumenical. "We had a wonderful church in the middle of it," Kerr Taylor recalled, "where we all worshiped, a thousand at a time on Sunday. I'll never forget that worship, the singing and praying and preaching." Leaders from America or Europe addressed conventions. Missionaries discussed problems and shared encouragements regardless of differing outlook, area, or nationality.

The younger couples worked hard at language study: the Bells passed their examinations at the first attempt, while Kerr Taylor, already a theologian, developed his interest in literary Chinese. They also played games. Nelson and Kerr entered the men's doubles of the Central China Tennis Championship. Nelson had a powerful serve, played with finesse, and was quick at the net; Kerr was his equal. They won the championship that first year and were runners-up the next.

Back at Tsingkiangpu the Bells had a taste of the unsettled state of China in the years when the warlords ruled provinces on behalf of the government in Peking but were virtually independent autocrats clinging to power until toppled by another.

They borrowed the motorcycle and set off for Sutsien, some seventy miles north on the canal, the next Southern Presbyterian mission and hospital: there were no hospitals whatever in the thickly populated country in between. The great plain of China looked beautiful in autumn colors. But as the machine sputtered and whined through the dusty road toward one walled city, they noticed the bean fields deserted of the usual blue-clad figures in their straw hats. A city gate was generally so crowded that only deft maneuvering of the motorcycle prevented collisions, but this one stood empty except for guards. Inside the wall they found "a small cannon aimed at the entrance of the gate, and all along the street soldiers were stationed and a few on horseback were riding up and down. One of these had his carbine strapped on his back, and swung under his arm was a three-foot beheading sword wrapped in red cloth. That section had been terrorized by robbers, and they were prepared."

The Bells might have been kidnapped themselves, all the more easily in that today's soldier was often tomorrow's bandit—or even today's, when off duty. In the city streets no one knew who was a bandit come to town and who was an innocent countryman. The authorities found it easier to catch the innocent. When a high official was expected, they would execute sufficient numbers to "save face."

At Sutsien six bandits had been executed a few days before. "They cut off their arms, broke their legs, cut off their ears, punched out their eyes, skinned them, then cut off their heads, and finally cut out their hearts."

6
Love and Mercy Hospital

AT the end of October 1917 Dr. Woods left Tsingkiangpu on his overdue furlough, not to be back until 1919. Thus at the age of twenty-three, after being qualified a mere seventeen months, Nelson Bell became superintendent of the only hospital in an area where more than two million people lived.

Agnes Woods, the doctor's daughter, was Bell's head nurse until her marriage. She was in charge of some boys selected from the orphanage; there were no female nurses yet. Virginia was expecting her first baby, but she took the place of Mrs. Woods in running the hospital's housekeeping department and helping in the dispensary and at operations. Dr. Sun and Dr. Chao, the two Chinese physicians, were little more than faithful employees, scared of responsibility. One soon became sick and subsequently died. Nelson was head of both medical and surgical departments and was the administrator too: "I shall be buffer and shock absorber for the whole place," he wrote. But being administrator gave him opportunity to screen in the whole place before summer and thus control the flies and mosquitoes.

The next two years would make or break him. Nelson entered them with zest. He never knew what the next case would be: "I could go through the gamut of the entire medical dictionary." Gunshot or other wounds sometimes took as many as fifty of the 170 beds at once. Men and women were shot or knifed in family or neighborhood quarrels: one of Nelson's colleagues joked that the Republic should not have abolished the pigtail because in the old days anger was relieved by tugging your adversary's pigtail.

But bandit violence was no joke. Bandits blindfolded their kidnapped victims by splashing warm pitch on their eyes. Soon the distraught relatives received a small parcel. Inside was a finger or toe and a ransom demand. If they delayed, a larger packet would be delivered containing their beloved's left hand or right ear, cut, sawn, or even torn off. After ransom the victim would be taken to the hospital for repair. Often the bandits broke into farmhouses, stripped and tied up their owners, and burned their backs with lighted straw or red-hot pokers until they revealed the hiding place of their money.

Government soldiers would stretch out a suspect's arms and hold lighted candles to the flesh until he screamed information or confession. Other inhumanities—such as a father pouring quicklime in the eyes of a son who had disgraced him—could sicken even a doctor used to broken bodies. "I feel sometimes like I am looking down into the very mouth of hell itself," Dr. Woods had said. The tender mercies of the wicked were indeed cruel.

Sufferers often came to the hospital only as a last resort, held back by prejudice against the *yang kuei-tz*, "foreign devil." Though the phrase was seldom now used to a foreigner's face, except by children, the country people assumed that "outer barbarians" were ignorant and sinister and killed babies to make medicine from their eyes. Yet the Chinese folk-doctors offered no effective relief apart from a few herbal remedies or ancient drugs. Their favorite treatment was to stick needles in the patient (acupuncture). Nelson was once called to a child ill with meningitis: he found her in a stupor, sprouting fourteen large needles, several of which were on her face. Another child had been plastered with arsenic, as a cure for malaria, until the flesh and skin on parts of her body were entirely eaten away.

Tropical diseases were common, especially those which are aggravated by malnutrition, for drought or floods might ruin the crops, and even in a good year peasants and laborers subsisted on an inadequate diet. Kala-azar would in time make Tsingkiangpu famous, and elephantiasis gave Nelson some of his most interesting operations. Until shortly before this time no treatment for elephantiasis had succeeded, though Dr. Woods had developed a plastic technique for affected scrotums, and Nelson once removed one which weighed eighty-four pounds, the patient having arrived at the hospital pushing it on a wheelbarrow. Early in 1918 Nelson read of a new operative method devised by Kondoleon, a Greek surgeon. "The very next day a man came in the dispensary with the worst case I had ever seen," an ulcerous leg the size of a nail keg. Nelson tried the new operation. A month later the leg looked nearly normal, and after a second operation the delighted patient was soon spreading the news in his home district.

In October 1919 this operation was one of those described by Nelson in his first scientific article, published in the important journal, *Surgery, Gynecology, and Obstetrics*. The subject was elephantiasis, with pre- and post-operative pictures. It created a mild sensation among Nelson's friends in America because of his youth and the convincing proof of his surgical skill.

Cured and grateful patients could sometimes create embarrassment. An elderly mandarin—the title was still sometimes used unofficially—arrived from a city some sixty miles away. Nelson greeted him gravely in the Chinese way, not shaking hands but pressing the right fist into his own left palm and moving them up and down, but the mandarin did not return the greeting. He had cataracts in both eyes. Young Nelson had never actually removed a cataract but had watched his professors in America closely. He offered to operate. The mandarin agreed to pay the hospital's fee; no one was refused treatment if utterly destitute, but to give away what could be afforded would damage both individual and community. Whatever sum was asked, however small, was all that must be paid, however long the patient stayed. A mandarin could pay quite a sum and thus subsidize the poor.

The operation succeeded. Mr. Chiang, the mandarin, with the aid of glasses, now had excellent vision.

A few weeks later another cataract case reached the hospital from Chiang's city, and again Nelson operated successfully. Then came a woman with an entirely different eye disease. Nelson did his best. A few weeks later a man totally blind, led by his son, was puzzled and pained when Nelson said he could do nothing: "But Mr. Chiang said you make the blind to see!" In the course of a year the seeing but undiscerning old man dispatched no less than sixteen people to the hospital, most of them beyond help.

*   *   *   *   *

Li Song-Dsen was a little girl living in Hwaian. Half a century later in Taiwan, she had a vivid memory of the young doctor who had already achieved a storied reputation. "My mother adored the fine young doctor whom she regarded as a miracle man who could cure any disease anyone could have, and she would bring every one of her kin and acquaintance who had any ailment to the semi-weekly clinics at Hwaian. Since I was a sickly child, she would bring me frequently. I had attended church regularly and was accustomed to seeing the foreigners, so I was not afraid as the other children were when they came to the clinic for the first time and saw the big foreign doctor! But their fears were quickly dispelled, and all—adults and children—became his staunch admirers. They observed his loving interest in each case and careful inquiry into the history and symptoms of each, and he seemed to prescribe just the right medicine that would make them well.

"I was more susceptible to sickness than the rest. On one occasion Dr. Bell told my mother that I must come to the Love and Mercy Hospital for more extended treatment. So I went and stayed in the hospital for two weeks. I was not too sick or too young to notice, even at that age, how Dr. Bell moved around that great number of people who came in and out and showed the same care and tenderness to each one as he had shown at the little street clinics in our city. Here there were scores of people lying in all of the wards, and he and his assistants would go and visit each bed twice a day. We would also see them come in the morning and take some of the people from their beds and roll them into the operating room where Dr. Bell himself would have to perform serious life-or-death operations—but we rarely heard of any who had died. Then there were the early morning worship services where all who could leave their beds were urged to come and hear the message of the gospel. This was declared to be the heart of the whole institution and the reason for its existence. Dr. Bell would always attend these services, except when he was away, and very often gave the message himself."

Li Song-Dsen recalled "another feature which many doctors do not possess: Dr. Bell's blithe and happy spirit. The Book of Proverbs says, 'A merry heart doeth good like a medicine.' As Dr. Bell went through the wards on his rounds, he would have fun and laughter for everybody—a bit of personal banter here and a joke there. They would all roar at his jokes and loved to see him come and hated to see him go."

Nelson noticed that both Chinese and American jokes depend on plays on words and on exaggeration. "I could tell a joke that was typically American and they'd get the point right away." An SPM missionary from Japan was amazed at the jokes and grins that flashed back and forth between doctor and patient. "You could never get away with that in Japan," he said.

Without a sense of humor, a doctor in China at that time might well be driven to nervous breakdown by the delays, aggravations, broken promises, and a hundred and one pinpricks; or he might take refuge in a frigid relationship with the people. Nelson's humor not only bubbled over but frequently relieved tensions. He had never been a hot-tempered man, but occasionally in the early days he had to control himself by deliberate act of will.

Once his control broke. The gateman of the compound, who had the responsible job of barring undesirables and regulating the flow of potential admissions, made a serious error. Nelson bawled him out in a flow of choice Chinese which lost the man much "face." The older of the two national doctors promptly sought Nelson out. "Dr. Bell," he said gravely, "you are above that sort of thing. You shouldn't scold a man like that."

Nelson found the Chinese of his day "a delightful people. They had a keen sense of humor and a deep sense of gratitude; they were innately courteous and appreciative. In the China I knew, they were a most lovable people."

And they repaid the compliment. All foreigners were called by the nearest Chinese equivalent to their surname: Bell became *Chong* (a bell). They also received a *hzo* or nickname. The Chinese—very early—found one they considered appropriate for Nelson Bell. They called him *Chong Ai Hua*—"The Bell Who Is Lover of the Chinese People."

*   *   *   *   *

In letters to James Graham, Jr., then in the U.S. Marine Corps, Uncle Jimmy told of this "human dynamo who has hit our mission station." The younger Graham joined the SPM after World War I (and after World War II founded two Christian colleges in Taiwan) and he used to bring his family on visits to Tsingkiangpu. His father "would marvel at Nelson's exploits and chuckle for days over some of his quips and cracks.

"He would say with a perplexed shake of his head, 'That *Nelson*!! He's the greatest fellow I ever saw! What's that new expression I read, "Go-getter?" That's what Nelson is; he's a "Go-getter."' And my dad would tell of some amazing piece of surgery, entirely original and successful; yet it would never find its way into a medical journal because Nelson would not trumpet it or bother to write it up." Uncle Jimmy would describe Nelson's ingenious improvisations of equipment or tell how in administration the Chinese would bring up scores of reasons for caution or face-saving or tortuous action. "But Nelson won't fool around," Uncle Jimmy said. "He will cut the Gordian knot of delay, palaver, and appeasement and declare: 'This is the way we are going to do it.' And he even makes them like it because it turns out to be the best way."

Nelson could carry the heavy load of the hospital without lowering his medical standards or loss of health. He had youth, physical strength, and the skill of organizing time so that none was wasted. But he could relax too. The tennis court was Nelson's special delight, and one broiling July day while he and Uncle Jimmy were playing a hard singles, sweat pouring down their faces, a Chinese gentleman, hands carefully folded in the sleeves of his gown, watched utterly bemused.

"Honorable sirs," exclaimed the gentleman between two games, "could you not hire laborers to hit that ball for you?"

More important still was the happiness of home, for if two strong-willed characters do not always make a highly successful marriage, especially when alike in many ways, Nelson and Virginia did. On February 28, 1918, their first child was delivered by the proud father and named Rosa Wertenbaker after Virginia's mother. For the first-born to be a girl is reckoned a disaster by the Chinese, but the Bells were delighted. "Virginia has the great faculty of making a home and at the same time attending to her other duties," Nelson wrote when Rosa was a baby.

Most important of all was Nelson Bell's discipline of devotional life.

Rosa at ten months. Her mother—never one to waste anything—wore her wedding hat for the photograph.

Early every morning he had a cup of coffee and went to his desk for about an hour of Bible study and prayer. He set himself to master the content and meaning of the Bible, devising such study schemes as looking up every Old Testament reference which occurs in the New and typing it out. Then he turned to prayer, for friends, colleagues, and patients, praying especially for every patient listed for operation that day. Before breakfast he joined Virginia for a short reading in the Bible and prayer, and after breakfast the Chinese household gathered for prayer, according to custom long established by the Woodses. These prayers were simple, with Nelson helping each servant to repeat a memorized verse of Scripture. At 8:00 a.m. he was ready for hospital prayers in the chapel.

This cycle of reading and prayer did not strike Nelson as formidable but vital. It helped give him a strong sense of the Divine presence throughout the day and kept him alert to the Divine will. "I am often overwhelmed with the truth of the goodness of our Father," he wrote after a particularly difficult operation. "How much He will do through us if we will but let Him. The hard thing often is being willing to be led by Him."

It inevitably strengthened the urge to speak by word as well as by example: "I have seen men and women come into our hospital and leave there professing faith in Christ, and I have had the inexpressible joy of feeling that I had been the means God used to win that man or woman. Don't get the impression that all are gladly yearning for the message. This is not true; but many do hear, and the privilege of living and preaching the gospel to them is ours." Years later during the Japanese Occupation a Chinese man visited the hospital where, he told Bell, he had been a patient when a young man. "You or somebody gave me a tract and through that I accepted Jesus Christ. And now for a number of years I have been a preacher with the China Inland Mission."

From time to time there were more dramatic evidences, such as the Buddhist priest whose appendix was removed. He renounced his priesthood even before leaving the hospital. An old woman of seventy who needed surgery had the bed next to another woman who was recovering from the same serious operation. She heard about Jesus Christ and believed at once. Going into the operating room she told Dr. Bell, "I am not at all afraid. I have left my welfare to the heavenly Father." She made a swift recovery, saying, "It is God's goodness to me." After discharge she attended the women's church services regularly and one day came to a prayer meeting in the hospital chapel. She said, "I would like to thank Jesus for what He has done for me," and promptly climbed into the pulpit and said a prayer all by herself.

The Tsingkiangpu church was still mainly missionary controlled, although Southern Presbyterians genuinely desired indigenous churches and had succeeded dramatically in Korea, where the church was already self-propagating and almost self-supporting, if not yet self-governing. In China progress was slower. In 1917 Tsingkiangpu had less than a hundred full members of the church who lived in the city and perhaps another hundred throughout the region, for no one was admitted to church membership without careful examination. New believers not yet admitted, and non-believers, came to services, making a usual congregation of about 150, of whom many were connected with the hospital, schools, or orphanage. The church was cross-shaped, the sexes separated according to Oriental custom, with the men in the nave, the women and schoolgirls in the wings, and the preacher at the apex.

Dr. Graham generally was the preacher, wearing his hat as they all did, for to take off your hat in a public building or a neighbor's home was considered rude in China, while spitting on the floor was not; and when you prayed, you left your hat on but removed your glasses. Graham, however, frequently yielded the pulpit to a gracious old Chinese elder named Kao.

Elder Kao, like Elder Kang the language teacher, had been a Confucian scholar. As a young man he had known no other way than China's strange medley of religions, superstition, and ethics. Tsingkiangpu had numerous temples (and one mosque), and Kao, like his fellow-citizens, had uttered incantations before the Buddhas, great and small; if necessary he had entered one or the other dragon-guarded

Elder Kang, former Confucian scholar, and the Bells' language teacher

Taoist temples to inquire of the priest the auspicious days for this or that; he had lit joss sticks to placate the household spirits and had sent the kitchen god back to heaven each year by burning paper images. He had offered incense before the tablets commemorating his ancestors. Often he had visited one temple, the quietest, where the works of Confucius were honored. Kao mastered the great sage's sayings and passed the stiff examination in Confucian ethic which was China's immemorial road to education and morality.

None of this had satisfied. Kao was the first of his family to believe in Jesus Christ, and he became a mainstay of the pioneer church. By the time he died, his sons and daughters and immediate relatives, thirty altogether, were not only believers but strong, active Christians.

Kao's faith, character, and preaching were proof of the potential in the Tsingkiangpu region, as Nelson Bell looked to the future and dreamed his dreams. And an apt parable of Elder Kao's made Nelson more than ever glad he had come to China.

"A man fell into a dark, dirty, slimy pit," said Kao. "And he tried to climb out of the pit and he couldn't. Confucius came along. He saw the man in the pit and he said, 'Poor fellow, if he'd listened to me, he never would have got there,' and went on. Buddha came along. And he saw the man in the pit and he said, 'Poor fellow, if he'll come up here, I'll help him.' And he too went on. Then Jesus Christ came. And He said, 'Poor fellow!' and jumped down into the pit and lifted him out."

Nelson's trusty motorcycle, with Rosa

7
"Mr. Four" Returns

I N the winter of 1917-18 Nelson Bell yearned to do his share with the American army on the western front in France. It was easy to refuse to be surgeon on an ambulance team for Siberia, but many of his friends served in France and some had been killed. Nelson did not want to go as a doctor but as an aviator. He longed to learn to fly. If commercial flights had existed then, he would have rushed for seats, except that Virginia had a rooted objection to the very thought of flying.

Tsingkiangpu Hospital would collapse if he and Dr. Woods were both absent at once, yet "Sometimes I feel like I just must go. And then I remember I have this work to do, and the Lord has never shown me I could leave it. I think it has been one of the hardest things I have had to stand....Don't think I am dissatisfied with my work here. I was never happier in my life, but you know how the pull comes."

If he could not fly, he could roar. Friends at home clubbed together to give him a Harley-Davidson motorcycle with sidecar.

Nelson's prowess with the motorcycle became legendary at Tsingkiangpu, and he became a familiar sight sputtering across the canal bridge on a call to the inner city. Workers carrying their stinking baskets of night soil learned to jump nimbly out of the way. Farmers riding into market would hastily control astounded donkeys. Nelson tended to be a little frisky with that motorcycle. Once in a daredevil spirit he rode up the steep incline of the high outer mud wall of the city with Ed Currie, another missionary, in the sidecar.

Just before the top the engine stalled and the heavy machine turned turtle on Nelson, who by all the laws of gravity should have been crushed to death. He landed in a slight depression and emerged unscathed.

The Harley-Davidson was a big time-saver for distant calls from mandarins or officials which had to be accepted almost as commands. Previously Nelson would have gone by chair, "Just sit there and jog, jog, jog, jog," with a brick at his feet for warmth in winter and a book to read, and much time for prayer. He also could now ride his motorcycle to the twice-weekly clinic in Hwaian. Nelson loved these visits because in the fall of 1918 a young couple, James and Aurie Montgomery, had joined the SPM Mission there. Aurie Montgomery recalled how the Bells and the Kerr Taylors and the interchange of hospitality helped in their adjustment to the comparative loneliness of a small mission station after life in a state capital at home.

The motorcycle also played a part in the saga of Ed Wayland's arrival in China. Nelson's best man had married and was still a pastor near Waynesboro when "I got a call from Nelson; he wanted me to come over to China. He persuaded them over there to ask me." Ed had previously been hindered by responsibility for a widowed mother.

That bitterly cold winter the Grand Canal had frozen, and Nelson roared down the old Imperial Highway beside it until he reached open water eighty-three miles south of Tsingkiangpu, at Kaoyu. He met Ed and Rosalee Wayland at Shanghai on January 9, 1920. The Waylands were not sure they relished soup made from boiled canal water, "but we had to drink that stuff; they had nothing else," and Nelson assured them that all drinking water at Tsingkiangpu was carried up from the canal; sweet, soft, and purified when elaborately filtered and boiled. The cold was awful at night, and Ed spilled the pewter hot-water bottle in his bed. When he woke up next morning, the barge was frozen in, eleven miles south of the motorcycle.

Nelson left the Waylands on board, walked to Kaoyu, borrowed money from the restaurant keeper for his lunch, and rode back. He left the baggage in the care of the barge captain, installed Rosalee in the sidecar and Ed on the pillion seat, and set off at high speed. The narrow path was alarming enough to newcomers, not only because the frozen canal lay eight or ten feet below, but because of the numerous grave mounds, some of which had collapsed across the road. "Every now and then," recalled Ed, "the old thing would run up the side of a grave and go down." Ed grew alarmed and shouted to Nelson above the noise of the engine: "Isn't this sort of dangerous? We might run down into the canal."

"Oh," shouted Nelson, "if you do, you'll have the distinction of being the first one!"

Two hundred yards later the machine skidded on a grave mound and nearly turned turtle. Nelson's swerve to save it sent them down the bank straight at the canal. Ed jumped off, tugged hard at the machine, and stopped it just above the ice.

* * * * *

Dr. James Woods returned to Tsingkiangpu that winter to discover the entire hospital screened.

Nelson had been fully within his rights, but he had a hard time explaining. The Chinese murmured that of course there had been no flies in Mr. Four's time. Mr. Four Two-Trees discovered also that Nelson had allowed terminal cases to die in the hospital instead of sending them home. The Chinese had a strong tradition that a person must die in his own home, where the coffin stands before his eyes and he hears the chanting of the priests—if the family can afford them—and sees the funeral preparations which reassure him that his entry to the next world will be acceptable to gods and ancestors. When Woods came to China in 1894, he needed to walk warily, and he had respected custom. Nelson Bell felt that a quarter of a century later the dying no longer needed to be disrupted and hurt for convention's sake. Frequently he persuaded relatives to allow the patient to die peacefully and then be carried home for the funeral ceremonies.

These and other changes surprised Dr. Woods, but he proved extraordinarily understanding of his forceful young colleague. Tension could have permeated Love and Mercy

Hospital, yet argument never spilled over. "Chinese colleagues knew where we differed, but there was never a rift between us." Neither was quarrelsome, and neither carried professional differences into social life. Nelson could get on with anyone who did not resent frankness, and both men were forbearing.

Woods and Bell were undoubtedly aided in their personal relationships by the veneration accorded in China to age. Woods was twenty-seven years older and had been the doctor of Tsingkiangpu since before Bell's birth. No Chinese would dream of according the senior doctor less respect, whatever the qualities of the younger.

The bond of affection deepened between the two. James Graham, Jr. wrote: "It is to the eternal credit of Nelson Bell that coming into an institution as a product of a later stage in the advancement of medicine, with a brilliant mind, boundless energy, and an aggressive nature, he never to my knowledge or that of my father (who was very close to the situation) overstepped the lines of propriety and respect and loyalty to his senior. Dr. Woods's attitude also was faultless and showed no petty jealousy toward his brilliant young colleague."

The mission said that it was one of the miracles of Tsingkiangpu that James Woods and Nelson Bell got on so well together. But Nelson's admiration for his senior was proof against any differences on professional matters and never lessened throughout their long association. When, shortly after World War II ended, Woods died at the age of seventy-eight, Bell's published tribute came right from the heart. After detailing Woods's medical achievements, he wrote: "Although Dr. Woods was a great man in many ways, his true greatness was in his unswerving love for and devotion to his Lord. He loved to speak of Him, to tell of His goodness and of some new truth he had recently discovered in the Bible....

"One of Dr. Woods's most attractive characteristics was his love and affection for his friends. Coupled with this was a keen sense of humor and delightful gift for conversation. One never shared in a conversation with him that he did not learn something worthwhile from the Bible, or something about a flower, an insect, or some historical incident."

*   *   *   *   *

Dr. Woods's return gave Nelson opportunity for a new venture: to open dispensaries in the country "and use these as feeders to the hospital. I believe we can make them evangelistic agencies of the greatest usefulness at the same time." Addison Talbot had often looked out across the broad plains which stretched mile upon mile from the canal and said: "Oh, we do want help out there so badly. I am not touching more than one-ninth of my field, and the rest is going absolutely untouched." And wherever a foreign evangelist went, the people brought him their aches and diseases just because he was white. But going into their countryside meant taking one's life in one's hands. The only protection against bandits was their knowledge that no ransom would ever be paid for a missionary.

Nelson went off with Kerr Taylor riding pillion, the one to heal and the other to preach. "But always at a distance," recalled Kerr. "I couldn't hold the attention with a crowd watching what he was doing. He had his crowd of two or three hundred, and I had my crowd of two or three hundred as I preached. And he was preaching along with his healing. Nelson was a born preacher; he loved to tell the gospel, loved to share the religious experience. It was a joy to work with him. He never got tired. He had boundless energy."

The country dispensaries certainly proved to be feeders to the hospital. Wards for ten soon had to hold thirteen or fifteen, single-bed wards were crammed with two or three beds, and "rooms in and about the hospital never intended for patients have twenty-odd patients," Nelson wrote in May 1920. "We need a new building which will hold from seventy to a hundred more beds and at present have not the faintest idea where the money is to come from."

*   *   *   *   *

Virginia was now awaiting her second baby, and on June 10, 1920, Kerr Taylor heard that her labor had begun.

He hurried around to the Chinese-style house on the compound which had been the Bell home since the Woodses' return. It had two stories, but the boards upstairs had shrunk, so that anyone taking a bath had to be careful not to splash lest guests below receive a shower.

"I waited. And then I heard a baby's cry. And a few minutes later Nelson ran downstairs smiling and put his arm around me. 'It's all right,' he said. 'And it's another girl.'"

Like Rosa, she was named for a grandmother: Ruth McCue Bell. This name in particular symbolized Nelson's heritage. It was a heritage of unstinting loyalty to Christ from generation to generation, and he was determined that his own children should grow up, like his forebears, to rejoice in serving God and their fellowman.

Yet he and Virginia were determined also to give unstinting missionary service. Their priorities were sound. When a dear friend had a complete breakdown because her desire to be devoted in missionary service conflicted with the claims of motherhood, Nelson wrote: "I am so thankful Virginia takes the position she does. In my opinion the children and home come *first* with all mothers, yet some women on the field have neglected their children for the work, and I do not believe it is right."

Whether the Bells could reconcile their two determinations would be the test of the years to come.

The Bells' first residence in Tsingkiangpu, birthplace of Ruth Graham. On her first visit with her husband in 1988, Ruth Graham found the exterior much the same.

1918—The days of the warlords. Center, Generals Ma Yu-Ren and Pei Pao-Shan; front left, Rev. H. Kerr Taylor; rear, Bell on left and Rev. J. E. Wayland on right

Part Two
"LOVER OF THE CHINESE PEOPLE"
1921-1927

8
Enter a Texan

THE port of Haichow (now called Lianyungang) lies some one hundred miles north of Tsingkiangpu, with a pleasant view of low, rocky mountains and the broad Haichow River, twenty-five miles inland from the sea. For six months over the winter of 1920-21 Nelson ran the SPM hospital there while its regular doctor took his furlough. Work was hard and the winter severe, but two new missionaries, only a few years older than the Bells, made Haichow delightful: Gay and Edward Currie. Ed Currie was a former chaplain who had been known in the army as the "Wrestling Parson": he would take the men on, and any he pinned to the ground must come and hear him the following Sunday.

Since the canals and lakes and even the tidal river had iced over, Nelson invented a form of power skating for Ed Currie, who clung to the sidecar while Nelson whizzed down the smooth ice of a canal, stopped, turned around, and whizzed back. After several afternoons Nelson said: "Ed, I wonder what would happen if I tried to turn it real quick? If we could turn and continue forward down the ice?" He roared up to forty m.p.h. and made a sharp turn. Ed kept his balance, and they whizzed and turned until exhausted. Then Nelson tried another trick. Chinese boys would throw lumps of ice from the bank to slide into the middle. "Nelson being a great tease," recalled Ed Currie, "he would try to straddle these lumps, which I, following behind, couldn't see too well. He hoped I would hit them with my skates. That kind of thing was a lot of fun."

Irrepressible love—in Haichow

In the evenings when Nelson was back from his rounds and the Curries' baby and Ruth lay in their cots—"Little Ruth was so good and gave no trouble at all," the Curries recalled loyally—the two families played Rook or chess, or what they thought was chess. Gay had taught herself and then Ed, and Ed taught Nelson; but the senior evangelist, John Vinson, returned from furlough to discover that they set up their bishops and knights in the wrong places. Nelson became a keen chess player, making his moves rapidly. Even so, he won as often as he lost.

Nelson had already been back to Tsingkiangpu on an errand and so much enjoyed seeing Dr. Woods that he did not return to Haichow on schedule. Virginia sent him a wire. Nothing happened. She sent him two or three in vain. At that time a popular comic strip in the newspapers featured a man called Jiggs, his friend Dinty Moore, and Maggie, the nagging wife who ruled the roost with a rolling pin. Virginia sent a final, three-word wire: *"Rolling pin. Maggie."* A reply came from Tsingkiangpu: *"Jiggs left this morning. Dinty."*

In the spring the Bells left Haichow and returned to

Tsingkiangpu. Just after the wheat harvest the rains began, harder than the Bells had ever seen, and continued throughout July. Vast acres disappeared under water, the crops were ruined, and a partial famine became inevitable. Idle and impoverished peasants swelled the ranks of bandit hordes until on August 7, 1921, they captured a large market town twenty miles from Tsingkiangpu, killing two hundred citizens. The next day they looted a city thirty miles off, killed six hundred, and carried away the rich for ransom. Relatives in Tsingkiangpu began receiving severed ears and fingers. Merchants and officials were now terrified not only of the city being taken by storm but of the workers and the poor: during the Revolution of 1912 houses had been stripped bare and the oppressed and hungry became ravening, intoxicated beasts.

Virginia and Nelson and their two children were the only foreigners in the city. About ten o'clock on Wednesday evening, August 10, they were reading before going up to bed when two Chinese doctors, one church elder, and a teacher entered and took seats. Beneath their impeccable manners and their impassiveness Nelson could detect that something was up, and in a few minutes they asked him if he had heard any rumors. He told them, "No."

They said that the city was full of reports, apparently genuine, that the bandits were advancing. The doctor must take Virginia and the children to safety at once; there were few soldiers and the city would certainly fall. Nelson's own inquiries the next morning made him accept the advice, but since the Grand Canal flowed too high for traffic, the only escape was by motorcycle. Reluctantly he left the hospital after dark that evening, and with Virginia, three-year-old Rosa, and one-year-old Ruth rode down to the Yangtze.

Friends at Chinkiang took them in, while Nelson hurried upriver to Nanking, saw the American consul, and asked him to inform the military governor of Kiangsu of the position, which the local warlord had refused to report lest he be ousted by the arrival of fresh troops. Nelson returned to Tsingkiangpu alone, leaving a protesting Virginia who had already decided that in the future whatever dangers her husband might be in should be shared by all the Bells.

The bandit army had been stopped four miles from the city, more by flooded canals than government soldiers; before they could resume their advance, the troops, who had been set in motion by Nelson's intervention at Nanking, arrived from the north and south. Bandits never took on a superior force: they faded away. Virginia returned—in time for a typhoon which destroyed houses, put streets under water, and knocked down the hospital compound's wall in two places.

Nelson Bell's first term of service certainly had its excitements, but they were nothing compared to what would come.

*   *   *   *   *

The Bells were back in America in July 1922. On the way across the continent they stopped in Houston, Texas, to meet the First Presbyterian Church which had been contributing to their support.

Words which Nelson Bell wrote nearly a half century later help to explain what happened at Houston. For as in China, so in America: the first call each morning was the devotional hour, "a time when I surrender my mind, will, and body to the supernatural teaching of God my heavenly Father, Christ my Savior and Lord, and the Holy Spirit my Comforter and Guide. It is a time when I can *rest* on Him, *wait* on Him, *listen* to Him, and *talk* with Him."

That Sunday he preached morning and evening and told Houston that the Tsingkiangpu Hospital needed a considerable sum to build an additional building. During the following week he visited the offices of affluent businessmen who were members of First Presbyterian, and thus he entered the life of Benjamin Clayton.

Unlike Hudson Taylor, yet like D. L. Moody and William Booth, Nelson Bell was not reluctant to request funds openly. This was in conformity with SPM practice. But as another eminent member of the mission commented: "It would never have occurred to me to tackle one of the richest men in the state of Texas to get help for my work. If he had offered it, I would have gladly accepted it. But to go to him! Nelson lacks the kind of reticence, timidity, and hesitation that I would have. His cause is worthy, and he doesn't hesitate to go to the head of a great industrial concern." Bell could present his case without apology.

Benjamin Clayton, just turning forty, was with his brother William Clayton, head of the Anderson Clayton Company, the largest cotton exporter in the world.

As he listened to Bell, Clayton was especially impressed that Tsingkiangpu Hospital, while turning no one away, did not give free treatment to patients who could pay, which in Clayton's view would have been irresponsible. "Each patient," Nelson told him, "who applies for treatment goes through close scrutiny and questioning, often for several days, before we will admit him; in each case, when finally admitted, the patient has paid the limit we feel he can afford. In a way this sounds hard, but we know the people pay their witches and charlatans and pseudo-doctors. We know it is best for them, as well as absolutely essential for the continuance of this work, that they pay the hospital all they can."

Nelson Bell's integrity and evident efficiency convinced Clayton that any money he gave would not be wasted. Moreover, as he said, "Nelson Bell has an innate magnetism that has a spell on people." As a result of that weekend in 1922 the Houston church raised $20,000 for buildings to be called the Houston Unit. Clayton gave his share, but in the years to come he was to give a great deal more. In 1922 Benjamin Clayton began to play an important part in the lives of millions in North Kiangsu. Virginia later cherished an account book in which Dr. Bell kept meticulous records of the money from Mr. Clayton. Every penny was accounted for, in spite of the fact Mr. Clayton said he trusted Dr. Bell completely and would never ask for an accounting.

Bell had been awarded a grant in surgery by the Rockefeller Foundation. He first went back to the Medical College of Virginia, bought a cadaver, and with the help of his old professor of anatomy brought himself up-to-date by doing a complete dissection. At the Mayo Clinic he observed surgery as a visiting fellow, did urological work at the New York Postgraduate Hospital, X-ray studies at the Massachusetts General Hospital in Boston, and spent a short time at the

Medical School of Tulane University. He also attended a course at Moody Bible Institute.

Like all missionaries on furlough he undertook deputation speaking. When a wealthy man named Horace Hull heard him speak in Memphis, he promptly gave $1,000, which in the early 1920s was enough to put up a six-room tubercular ward. Hull became "a friend who meant much to me in later life," he wrote.

Naturally the four Bells spent time at Waynesboro, but even there no grass grew under Nelson's feet. The town telephone system had just been changed to automatic. He went to the company and begged enough telephones and equipment to install an exchange at Tsingkiangpu to link all the hospital departments, the gatehouses, and eventually every missionary home in the two compounds. It was another fourteen years before the Chinese telephone system could connect them with Shanghai.

Even at Waynesboro they itched to return. "It is a *happy life*. Mrs. Bell and I agree that the last six years have been the happiest of our lives; we are homesick for China right now."

He wrote this on January 27, 1923, to young American doctors who might join the staff at Tsingkiangpu. None came at that time, but this letter, after a detailed account of the medical and surgical opportunities, discloses what Nelson Bell considered essential as he embarked on his second term of service.

"The primary object of our work," he wrote, "is to win souls to Jesus Christ. I am more and more convinced that we must stress this. You do not necessarily have to preach, but I would say that you must have the love for souls and desire to win them to the Master if you are to be a successful missionary.

"And then one final word, and most important of all, we are but the instruments, and we have the Master's promise to be with us. Without prayer I would not dare go back, but with the knowledge of His presence and His promises I would not dare stay here. The most precious promise I have found in His Word you will find in Proverbs 3:6. 'In *all* thy ways acknowledge him, and he shall direct thy paths.' Think of it: *He will direct everything* if we will but let Him."

On September 4, 1923, the four Bells arrived back at Tsingkiangpu.

The wonderful welcome they received had its disadvantages: "The Chinese always show you their love and friendship by piling in on you as soon as you return, whereas you could enjoy them much more if they would give you a few days to get settled and composed." Especially when you have a new home. Just before they had returned to America, the Bells had designed and built a Western-style house, a gift to the mission from a Mr. Watts of Durham, North Carolina. The Taylors had used it until their own furlough, and now the Bells occupied it for the first time. It was the home of Ruth's childhood memories.

The Bells' permanent home in Tsingkiangpu, gift of friends in America. "Always open to our Chinese friends"—and countless foreign guests.

Nelson preaching to prisoners

9
Healing, Speeding, Expanding

IT was not without reason that the Chinese characters for hell and for prison were identical.

Soon after furlough Bell took over from Dr. Woods the Sunday morning medical visit to the city jail and the penitentiary. In his earlier days criminals were beheaded. Nelson had often seen decapitated heads sticking over the gates or floating down the Grand Canal. Later they were shot first but always in public, outside the city wall, to make a spectacle as in eighteenth-century England. The jail was living death. "The most filthy place you could possibly get into," a colleague recalled. "No cleanliness, no sewerage whatsoever. The sick were put in one room to stay there until they died. Almost every prisoner had scabies, most had worms, and all wore chains night and day."

The authorities gave Nelson the run of the prison. He and a boy nurse, carrying a large supply of medicine, wore white coats to protect their clothes. Nelson needed a strong stomach when he saw prisoners who had been punished by beating: the jailers "take a small bamboo strip that is slightly flexible and it can really beat the flesh to jelly. Just by thrashing, thrashing, thrashing so that the skin would not necessarily be cut, but more like a pulp. We would put a soothing ointment on these patients and give them something for pain, and that was all we could do."

Another patient might have been placed in the stocks and had a wedge driven in between the leg and the wood post, blow by blow, until he had confessed a crime, whether he had committed it or not, or endured until the bones of the leg were crushed. The Chinese seldom believed evidence unless extracted under torture, so that false accusations were a favorite form of vengeance. Nor were savage punishments and torture the sole prerogative of jailers and bandits. A young government soldier named Ma Er turned up at the hospital with a bloody bandage around his head and his two ears in a handkerchief. He had been absent without leave, and his officer had sliced off the ears and set him adrift, discharged in disgrace. Nelson sewed them back on again, but they did not heal. After that Ma Er always wore his hair long, topped with a large hat, to hide his disfigurement. He became a devoted servant of the hospital and eventually a Christian.

In the jail, with the beaten and tortured and the sick, were always a few toothaches for which Nelson carried forceps. Ed Currie, visiting Tsingkiangpu, remembered "a great big tall bandit who said he had a toothache in two teeth. Dr. Bell pulled out his forceps from his hip pocket and said, 'Which ones?' The bandit put his head right back and shut his eyes and said: 'This one here.' And before the man could say anything, Dr. Bell had a good hold on that tooth, started pulling, and pulled it out. But the bandit didn't let him pull the second. One was enough!"

After treatments Nelson gave out tracts and Scripture portions to any who could read, then stood on a box to preach. Once during treatments he overheard a prisoner whisper to another: "He doesn't want any money for the good he does us. He just wants us to believe on Jesus." The prisoners listened because they instinctively felt what Kerr Taylor said of Bell: "He has sympathy and understanding and kindness in that heart of his."

Early in 1926 Bell noticed "a marked awakening and interest in the gospel in the penitentiary. I date this from the time I urged them to pray for themselves....Their faces have changed, and they told me that they have God and peace in their hearts." Next Sunday he brought a visiting Chinese evangelist. Bell, busy with the week's mission, told the prisoners: "I'm sorry, but I've no time to treat your disease today; I just brought a friend I want to talk to you."

One prisoner replied for all: "We don't care about the

medicines. If you will just preach to us, that will be enough." Another added, "We get so anxious and hungry for more when you don't come." When Bell made his medical visit later that week, nine prisoners begged the Chinese pastor to begin a regular Bible class.

*   *   *   *   *

Jail visits and out-of-town calls were easier after 1924 because Nelson sold his motorcycle and bought a Baby Austin car, small enough to negotiate the city gates and just roomy enough to squeeze his legs under the steering wheel. Three years later Dr. Woods also bought one, so that thenceforth the hospital always possessed two cars.

Nelson's Baby Austin automobile

Nelson loved speed. He drove the Baby Austin as he had driven the motorcycle—as fast as it would go, which with luck was around thirty miles an hour, a fearful speed to every mule in the Tsingkiangpu countryside. He bought four cars altogether during his years in China, always at generous discount, and had only one slight accident. In 1932 a deaf young man ran across a wide, straight road; Nelson swerved, but the man bumped into the back of the car and broke a bone in his foot. Nelson gave him cash to get a ride to the hospital. The bystanders, who would have turned on any "foreign devil" if he was to blame, scolded the pedestrian: "There is a bus behind, and if you cannot hear, you had better be careful, for you won't get any money out of them if you get hit."

Nelson's virtually accident-free record (even in Shanghai, then the worst city in the world for driving) was nothing less than miraculous. A would-be suicide might throw himself in front of a car, a parent might chuck an unwanted girl-child under the wheels, and country folk knew the best way of killing their evil spirits was by dashing across the road in front of a car so that the pursuing demon would be run over by the vehicle.

"The first time I drove with Nelson," wrote a newly arrived young missionary, "he just honked the horn and kept going. What a pushing, shoving, and shouting as people jump out of the way—they just don't move until they have to. The car just barely misses this and that—and frequently touches this and that.

"The streets of Tsingkiangpu are so narrow that even with the little Austin one has to stop and back around to turn the corners. This would not be so bad if every corner did not have a vast array of pottery, iron, tin, reeds, bakery goods, fresh meat, or garlic hanging from the shack walls and dangling out in the middle of the street. Then, too, there usually are portable tea shops and gambling wheels which have to be removed when the car makes its appearance."

In the city Bell would drive in second gear, with finger on the horn to warn wandering babies, sleeping dogs, and pigs being driven to market. The slow speed allowed every yelling boy to climb on the spare tire and back bumper. If a donkey, loaded with rice, chose to poke its head into an eating shop, the whole street became a traffic jam and the horn merely encouraged the donkey to bray.

* * * * *

Meanwhile the new buildings of the hospital were going up: the Houston Unit.

Dr. Woods, as superintendent, had wanted to supervise the plans, but Nelson felt that the ideas were his, and he had raised the money. After some frank exchanges Woods gave way. He urged, however, that they employ local contractors who built the older buildings nine years earlier. Nelson argued that locals could not install elevators and the other modern equipment; he must have a leading firm from Shanghai. Once again he won his point. When Superintendent Woods opened all the business correspondence addressed personally to Nelson Bell, another argument arose. Again Woods retreated, and again these two strong-willed men remained the firmest of friends, never letting arguments grow into grudges. G. K. Chesterton once said, "People quarrel because they cannot argue." Woods and Bell knew how to argue.

The decision to employ a Shanghai firm was quickly vindicated: "Several things have shown so clearly the Lord's ruling in the matter," Nelson wrote. The best contractor in all North China had just completed a project in Kiangsu, and rather than have his men idle, he tendered a low bid.

The plans called for two buildings. Nelson intended to put up first the administration building, including operating suite, chapel, X-ray rooms, and business offices; then, when Houston paid the last of its $20,000 pledge and the contractor could return, they would erect the more expensive women's building. But administration buildings do not relieve congestion. Nelson almost hated going to the daily clinic "to have to face so many who wish and need admission whom we cannot admit now." On April 15, 1924, two men arrived from a town fifty miles away with ingrowing eyelids, causing intense pain which only surgery could relieve. Only one bed in the entire hospital was vacant, and that was in a small outbuilding. They begged to be allowed to share it. The next day brought another man from their town. When told there was no room, he dropped to his knees and asked with tears in his eyes to be allowed to sleep in the same bed with his friends. They made room by putting a bench beside the bed.

That same day five were sent away with promises of admission when beds were available, and room was found for four worse cases by discharging patients not really ready to leave.

Therefore, on June 28, 1924, one month and two days before Nelson Bell's thirtieth birthday, work began on the foundation of the women's building, which would relieve the congestion. And to the surprise of local inhabitants, it went up "like a mushroom." By mid-October the seventy Shanghai workmen had completed the gray brick walls and the roofing timbers, had laid the corrugated iron roof, and were ready for the airy windows, the Oregon pine floors, and the fittings.

Then fighting broke out again between warlords. Nelson and Virginia watched two thousand bandits march by the hospital compound on their way to join the Northern army while all Tsingkiangpu cowered. The bandits ignored the city and merely left a few wounded at the hospital, but the new war had an unexpected result: the contractor wanted to put up the administration building immediately on finishing the other because the fighting near Shanghai had stopped all his other projects.

Bell agreed and wrote at once to First Presbyterian in Houston urging them to fulfill their pledge to the last cent.

The administration building connected the old hospital and the new, designed like an H. The nine-room operating suite had walls of cement and marble chips rubbed smooth, easy to clean. And to the wonder of all, it had spigots and drainpipes, the first plumbing system in North Kiangsu. In spare hours, helped by hospital boys, Nelson did all the plumbing himself, having taught himself because he wanted to be sure of proper work. Even a Nelson Bell, however could not install modern sanitation in a Chinese hospital—"thunderboxes" (chamber pots) emptied by hand were universal. But his plumbing spurred Ed Wayland. Ed found the stench of the boys at school somewhat distracting and, therefore, gave them a shower room.

Ed Wayland, Nelson, and another missionary were looking over the administration block before its completion. The elevator was functioning so they decided to ride to ground level from the third story. But they soon realized the elevator was descending much faster than intended and would hit the bottom with a crash that could put them in their own ward for broken bones. Nelson shouted, "Jump in the air just before the impact...Jump!"

They jumped—and returned to earth unscathed.

On July 25, 1925, the Houston Unit was ready, only two months behind schedule. Nelson Bell had hustled the contractor and gotten away with it—perhaps because he never actually seemed to hustle.

"The buildings will last as long as mission work lasts," he told Houston. His prophecy was exactly correct, though not in the way he intended: The buildings were partially burned during the scorched-earth policy of the Kuomintang. Today, however, many have been renovated and are in use as a Chinese medicine clinic.

First Unit—Men's Hospital

Part of the Houston Unit—Women's Hospital

Unit connecting Men's and Women's Buildings, used for administration

10
Books Despite Bayonets

THE Houston Unit showed how the wealth of a strong, settled church in the West could help a young church in the East when the missionary challenged and inspired the one and provided technical leadership for the other—with prayer.

"Please remember us constantly in your prayers," Bell wrote to Houston, "that God will use us to *win souls.*" His mother, who not only put money in his account when she could, but regularly sent boxes of clothes and goodies to the family, once bemoaned that she could do nothing to help except pray. He replied: "That is worth more than all else combined, and your prayers are being constantly answered too. You have no idea what a comfort it is to know you are praying for us and the work."

Bell was alert to the danger that Western patronage or Western leadership might stifle Chinese sacrifice or initiative. When he arrived in 1916 he had had no theories, but experience had induced a strong desire to make the hospital independent of mission money in its year by year running, an aim achieved by the early 1930s when Tsingkiangpu became the only self-supporting SPM hospital in China.

Woods and Bell were equally determined to train Chinese doctors to be full partners. They now had Dr. Ch'ien, primarily a surgeon, whom Ruth Bell Graham recalled as "a very jolly, kindly person with a large round face, always smiling"; and Dr. Ts'ao, highly regarded in the city because of his local origin. His skill and good rapport with patients made him a tower of strength on the medical side. Bell wrote:

"There is hardly a day that I am not very thankful to the heavenly Father for giving us men like we have here. In many places where the Chinese doctors are professionally satisfactory they fuss and have factions among themselves, which hurts the work and is a constant source of trial to those in charge of the work. Here there is not the slightest breath of friction."

As for the hospital's relationship with the local church, each saw the other as partner in spreading the kingdom. Nelson was never so happy as when he could write, as on October 9, 1924: "Last Sunday was Communion Sunday, and among those admitted to the church was a man whose first knowledge of the gospel came while he was a patient here for severe eye infection. All that he knows, he got here. This fall I was called to his home to see his wife who was desperately ill. She was brought here, and he came with her for further eye treatment. She is about well now and very much interested in the gospel. These are people who probably would never have known Christ had it not been for the hospital, and it serves to illustrate what we are so earnestly striving to make of this institution: that it should be a place where God's love is manifested every day."

While the Bells had been in America, the local church had taken two leaps forward. The Chinese had put up a new building in a Chinese style, paid for entirely by themselves; and Dr. Jimmy Graham had resigned the pastorate so the Chinese could call their own pastor. They chose the eldest son of old Elder Kao, the converted Confucian scholar. Pastor Kao had been a boy in the mission school and later went to college and seminary. He was not strong physically, a little easily discouraged, and inclined to lean on missionary judgment, but his faith never wavered. Years later, after Japanese torture, his faith cost him his life.

Nelson Bell had no direct responsibility in the affairs of the Tsingkiangpu church, but he welcomed every move toward indigenous leadership. He was strong, too, for self-support and careful not to give large sums of money to the church, feeling certain that such gifts stifled growth. The Bells had nothing but their missionary stipends, but Nelson had tithed his income since college days, keeping an accurate record. He delighted to give money to Christian causes and decided that his way to help the Tsingkiangpu church financially was through Christian literature.

His literary interests had already made him local correspondent of the English-language *North China Daily News* (Shanghai), which thereby came to him free and fed his unwavering interest in current affairs. His own writing was maturing steadily; he had a growing conviction of the power of the printed word and knew money would be well-spent if put into literature. Several of his friends in America also sent gifts for this purpose.

The literary level in North Kiangsu during the mid-1920s was higher than in most parts of rural China, and many families knew enough characters to justify Bell's policy of saturating the region with bits of paper, each carrying a brief message and a drawing. When, for instance, a Chinese evangelist handed out a picture of a proud Chinese gentleman in fine silk robes, satin slippers, and silk hat, preening himself in a mirror which reflected not robes but rags and a face ravaged by sin, the peasants understood: God does not look on the outward man.

The SPM used a primer prepared by Dr. Frank Price: *Yu Chien Reh Sen (From Shallow to Deep).* It began with a few simple, large characters which almost anyone could read. By the last page an illiterate had acquired enough skill to read parts of the New Testament and at the same time had learned the rudiments of the faith. Nelson Bell took Price's book down to Shanghai to the Christian Book Room of Christopher and Helen Willis (in the future they would be the last Western missionaries in Communist China, for Helen Willis maintained the Book Room until expelled in 1959). To Bell's specification they prepared a special edition of *From Shallow to Deep* bound together with Mark's Gospel and about one hundred hymns, which they printed as cheaply as possible—and printing was cheap in China—and sold to him at cost. "We never sought to make a profit," they wrote, "and apart from the Chinese helpers, none of us took anything in the shape of wages....Dr. Bell never asked for discounts. His accounts were always paid promptly and paid in full."

Bell entitled this compilation: *Iong Sen de Hua (Words of Eternal Life)*. On admission every inpatient received a copy with his or her name inscribed, and the doctors would often see "people lying there reading these books. And if someone couldn't read, someone else in the ward would read aloud so the others could hear it." Most patients took their copies home, and Bell reorganized the hospital filing system so that a slip containing name and address reached the local Chinese evangelist. "Many, many people were converted after they went home because of their original contact in the hospital. And they became church members in the areas in which they lived." Then in 1926 Bell opened a Book Room for which the Willises supplied Gospels, tracts, and books for sale at nominal prices. In Bell's estimation, "The Book Room was one of the greatest single means of evangelization in our hospital. God used it directly and indirectly."

Another important means of evangelization was the evangelistic week which the Tsingkiangpu church held every January.

In 1926 the missioner was twenty-seven-year-old Leland Wang, afterward famous among the Chinese of Southeast Asia, who came from South China and had been converted to Christianity through the influence of his wife. After three years as a naval officer he had resigned his commission, at the age of twenty-five, "to serve the Lord as an evangelist."

"He is filled with the Holy Spirit," Nelson Bell wrote, "knows all of God's Word, has a sweet, humble personality, and preaches with wonderful simplicity and power. I have never seen a man in any country with the intimate and complete knowledge of the Bible that he has. The entire native church was deeply stirred, and if he helped others as much as he did me, his ministry here will be a great blessing to all. Many Chinese gave themselves to Jesus for the first time, among them a number we had been praying for especially, and there were a great many reconsecrations and a greatly renewed interest in Bible study and prayer. During the meetings there was a prayer service at the church each morning at seven. It was cold and hardly light but the last four or five mornings there were a hundred or more people there."

Leland Wang's influence on Nelson Bell was lasting, for it was Wang who gave him the idea of reading a chapter of Proverbs every day "because it is the book which allows us to relate our own lives to fellowmen." Some twenty years later Nelson Bell passed on the habit to Billy Graham.

*　*　*　*　*

Darby Fulton, an SPM missionary from Japan, was touring Korea and China before becoming associate secretary, and afterward for twenty-nine years executive secretary of the Foreign Mission Board. Fulton had heard of Nelson Bell "as a man of many parts, very attractive, good company, and someone I would like to meet, but that was about all. He had not yet made a name as a physician, simply because there hadn't been time."

Tsingkiangpu impressed Fulton with its size and scope and the happy, relaxed atmosphere in the midst of strenuous activity and unsettled conditions. In Japan the Fultons were the only Westerners in their city, living in a Japanese house on a busy street, with no aid from hospital, school, or orphanage, and reckoning fifty or sixty a good congregation. "At Tsingkiangpu I walked into the church and there were seven or eight hundred people. I was overwhelmed by this large company, and then I began to think, well, there are three hundred students at the boys' school, there are the

The Bells outside the Woodses' house, about 1917

Chinese doctors and nurses, and Christian teachers in the boys' school and the girls' home. And so you had a pretty good congregation to start with, and that normally tended to attract others. Young men and women in the city would come into the services because of all the young men and women who were going to be there. Whereas in my little work in Japan it was more like trying to pull yourself up by your own bootstraps."

Darby Fulton stayed in the Bell home, and his visit included the weekly social evening when all the American staff of both compounds, and often from neighboring Hwaian, met in one of their homes by rotation. "There was nothing they liked so much as to gather at the Bell home, whether it was for prayer or for pranks. The Bell home was a center of gaiety, fun, fellowship, hospitality, and faith....It was an altogether charming place where every minute was exciting. I don't believe there was a man on earth, regardless of his interests or his particular calling, who could have gone into the Nelson Bell home in Tsingkiangpu and felt bored. He might have hated everything the missionaries stood for, yet could have been charmed by the winsomeness and the contagious good cheer of that home."

Fulton soon detected where the roots lay. "You couldn't be in Nelson's home for half a day without being impressed by his own prayer life and the prayer atmosphere that pervaded the place."

Darby Fulton recognized "Nelson's tremendous love of people and his ability to minister to them. As he walked up and down the wards, the patients would call to him and he would smile and gesture. I didn't know what they were talking about, but it was perfectly evident that it was the language of admiration, love, gratitude, and respect."

When Nelson preached in chapel, Fulton saw how well it was understood "because people laughed or cried as they listened." Fulton learned that the other missionaries and the Chinese, despite their affection for Elder Kao, the hospital evangelist, and his son the pastor, rated Nelson Bell their number one preacher and evangelist. He prayed at bedsides as easily as he joked. He did not pray publicly in the operating theater like Sir Henry Holland of Quetta, because he found that patients under local anesthetic tended to suspect some crisis or difficulty. Before going into surgery, every patient was told that the doctor had prayed for him by name—alone in his study in the early hours, or at any time for an emergency case.

As Darby Fulton summed it up in a public speech in 1965: "Dr. Bell saw every patient as in need of bodily healing but also in need of the grace of God in Christ. He was happy when he could say, 'Take up thy bed and walk,' but he never felt his work was fully done until he could add, 'My son, thy sins are forgiven thee.'"

*   *   *   *   *

One afternoon from the top story of the hospital, Bell pointed out to Fulton the sunlight gleaming on distant bayonets in the grainfields on the other side of the Grand Canal. That night Nelson gave him extra blankets, saying: "If I call you in the night, don't stop to dress. Just pick up these blankets and come downstairs quickly."

"What's going on?"

"You remember those bayonets I pointed out across the canal? Cities and sections of the countryside change hands very quickly. Right now, General Ma with eight thousand soldiers has control of this city, but General Sun is advancing with ten thousand—those bayonets you saw. The rumor is he will attack tonight. But don't be alarmed; we're as safe here as anywhere."

Darby Fulton went to sleep with one ear open and woke in broad daylight to hear Nelson knocking to say breakfast was ready.

"Oh, yes," replied Bell, "it came off all right. General Sun is in possession of the city this morning."

"But I didn't hear a shot fired!"

"There wasn't a shot fired. General Sun sent secret agents to offer Ma's soldiers more money if they would change sides—six thousand of Ma's eight thousand did. General Ma and the other two thousand are several miles out in the country by this time!"

11
Home for Rosa and Ruth

RUTH said: "I can never recall going to sleep at night without hearing gunshots in the countryside around the house." If warlords or bandits were quiet, it was a neighbors' quarrel or robbery or even an accident. "I remember one tremendous fire in the city. We went up to the third-floor attic window where we could see it and hear the explosions. We thought the city was being invaded. The whole skyline was lit up. Later we learned that some barges containing five-gallon tins of oil had caught on fire and the oil tins were exploding.... I think the greatest tribute to Mother's courage is that we children never sensed fear and we ourselves never had any fear. Now this is bound to reflect your parents. If they had been nervous, we would have been nervous."

The formative years of Rosa and Ruth in the troubled China of the 1920s, before either had reached the age of ten, were years of security, affection, discipline, and fun.

"I remember our home," said Ruth, "as rather large, gray brick, with a red tin roof and a large porch around two sides of the house. As you came in the front door there was a vestibule, with a table and a mirror on the left and a wooden seat around two sides where visitors could sit and be greeted. To the left was Daddy's study with an old roll-top desk and bookshelves containing his medical books and quite a row of Edgar Wallace detective stories. In the corner was a big old safe. We kids used to crawl around the floor and sometimes we could find Chinese pennies that had been dropped when the money was deposited: we used to love to go hunting for pennies around the safe.

"To the right of the entrance hall was the living room, and it was blue—blue cushions, curtains, and flowered wallpaper. Mother had some furniture that her father had made, but most of it had been made by the local carpenter. A window seat overlooked the front porch, and two windows were at the far side with an upright piano between. In the center of the room was a table, and there were Chinese rugs on the floor, blue—with floral designs around the edge, and a little fireplace in the corner of the room around which we sat on winter evenings. I always remember home as being the most homelike, most comfortable place in the world."

The living room fireplace burned coal from Shantung, and the dining room had a coal stove with a tin pipe to heat the room above. Each bedroom had a little tin stove fed by soybean stalks or odds and ends of paper; in winter the children had their weekly bath in a tin tub in front of the little burner upstairs: "The half of you that was away from the trash burner would freeze and the other half would be red-hot!"

"We shared the same bath water. I always thought it was quite the normal thing, and I remember how horrified our own children were when they found out!"

The Bells usually ate American-style food. Although they enjoyed Chinese dishes frequently, the home was frankly American for the children's sake. One of the Chinese doctors said to Bell: "We don't mind you having houses much larger than ours; we like you to have them. All we want is that the door is also open to us." And it was.

By the standards of a later age complete equality was prevented by an invisible barrier, barely recognized by either side and not remotely resembling the arrogance of contemporary Western merchants or officials which helped sow the seeds of China's later fury during the Cultural Revolution at "imperialism." The Bell children were totally unaware of it. "I don't think it ever entered our heads that we were a superior race," said Ruth. "The non-Christian Chinese may have looked on the missionaries differently, referring to us as 'foreign devils,' especially in the earlier days, but between the Christians of both races there just seemed to be mutual respect and admiration. I don't think either felt superior to the other—just different." And Rosa added: "Never once were we made to feel that the Chinese pastor was inferior in any shape or form to the missionary pastors." The girls rather wished that Chinese children had been allowed to play more with them, but because of the kidnapping danger their parents could not risk them out of the compound unaccompanied, and to invite one or two members of the hospital staff to send their children to play would cause jealousy.

The Bells had servants. The Chinese would have thought it exceedingly odd if an American doctor had tried to do without servants when every Chinese professional man had them. And doing without would have complicated their work to the point of uselessness. They were in China to minister to the sick and needy, not to shop, cook, clean, and garden.

Wang NaiNai, with Rosa and Ruth

For Rosa and Ruth the most important servant was Wang NaiNai (pronounced Nanny; it means "granny"), their *amah*, who was with the Bell children until they grew up. Pearl Buck's autobiography reveals how lasting the influence of a Chinese nurse can be on a bilingual missionary child, for her Buddhist *amah* in the 1890s imbued her with feelings

The hospital gate. Although later torn down, the stone inscription over it reading "Love and Mercy Hospital" was preserved and shown to the Grahams during their 1988 visit.

for a civilization which owed nothing to Christ. Ruth's Wang NaiNai "made a deep impression on me. She was one of the kindest people I've ever known. Everybody loved her."

Wang NaiNai had been a procuress. She and her husband had run a traffic in small girls, buying some from debt-ridden parents and kidnapping others, selling them down to Shanghai for the teahouses as "little flowers" for the lusts of male customers. One day she was intrigued by the singing from a little gospel hall in Tsingkiangpu. She entered, heard a large, yellow-haired, blue-eyed "foreign devil" woman named Sophie Graham talk about Christ, and responded at once. She was a simple-hearted country woman who was converted through and through. When the church admitted her, soon after she joined the Bells' service, Nelson commented: "I never saw one I thought more worthy of admittance." She was still illiterate, and she saved stubs of candles and "late at night we'd find her lying on the floor in front of the fireplace with these candles, learning how to read." (The Bells were then in the Chinese house and had no electricity.) They bought her a little oil lamp, and in time she could read even the Old Testament. Like Mary Magdalene, she never forgot. Ruth, when small, knew nothing of her background but remembered her sitting on a little stool, with her battered Bible and hymn book, singing the Chinese translation of Cowper's "There Is a Fountain Filled With Blood," especially the lines:

> The dying thief rejoiced to see
> That fountain in his day;
> And there may I, though vile as he,
> Wash all my sins away.

Wang NaiNai had one weakness: she gave Rosa decided hints that Ruth was her parents' favorite, though they had no favorite. Rosa was already burdened with one dreadful handicap: every Chinese in the place, Christian or not, could not avoid disclosing their conviction that as first-born she had disgraced her father by arriving with the wrong sex. Nelson and Virginia apparently did not realize her feeling. "It took me ten years to get over it, until one night when I was crying about it, the Lord just seemed to say to me: 'Now Rosa, if I wanted you to be a boy, I would have made you a boy.' So from that time on I was glad to be a girl."

* * * * *

Each day in the Bell household began with family prayers. Like any children, Rosa and Ruth occasionally found these irksome or wanted to stay in bed longer. Whoever was not down by the end of the first verse of the hymn had no sugar on her porridge. Later the rule changed: if you missed family prayers, you stayed for servants' prayers after breakfast. But both girls noted, with the unfailing perception of childhood, that their father positively enjoyed these daily prayers; they came to realize the importance of his own devotional hour and their mother's devotional time after finishing her household duties.

Rosa spoke for both girls when she said: "I cannot thank God enough for the early training I had in Bible study, that I had parents who believed the Word and who believed in drilling it into their children. We did have to learn a lot of Bible verses, but Mother tried to make it just as interesting and as much fun as possible. They did not make it a punishment—ever. We never had to learn Bible verses because we had been naughty."

If they were naughty, they were spanked or switched, whichever was appropriate. "Punishments were generously dished out, but we knew they loved us." They—and the two younger children later—were disciplined without being repressed. With two adored parents who always "seemed very young," who never punished in anger or selfishness, the children did not feel nagged or scolded. Rosa and Ruth regard the strictness as one reason why they recollect childhood with such happiness.

Defiance or disobedience met inevitable doom. Elbows on the lunch table were swept off in a trice. Virginia was chief disciplinarian, but, Ruth joked, "It seems to me they ganged up on us."

"We could not divide and conquer them," added Rosa. "If we asked Daddy for permission to do something and he said 'No,' we might go to Mother and say, 'Mother, may we do thus and so?' And instead of saying 'Yes,' she would say, 'What did your father say?' 'He said no.' 'Then why did you come and ask me?' Then we'd do Daddy the same way. We'd ask Mother, 'May we do thus and so?' And if she'd say, 'Absolutely not,' we'd go and say, 'Daddy, may we do thus and so?' 'What does your mother say?' 'Well, she said we couldn't.' 'Then why did you ask me?'

"But if it was something that we really and truly wanted to do very badly, and Mother had said no and we couldn't approach her any further on the subject, we'd say, 'Daddy, this is something that is very important and won't you reconsider?' He would give it his attention. And if he felt that it was all right, he would check with Mother first. They would hash it out together without us eavesdropping. If there was a good, substantial reason why we couldn't be indulged, the answer would continue to be no. But if it was reasonable that we should have our way, they would say, 'We have discussed it and have decided you may do it.'"

* * * * *

Nelson once wrote: "We live surrounded by serious contagious diseases and are simply in God's hands. Unless it is His will that we should be taken ill, nothing can harm us." Virginia could say the same, but she had a daily fight against dirt and germs, especially the prevalent trachoma. Any lapse might lead to illness.

Twice in the old Chinese house Virginia omitted washing Ruth's hands before putting her to bed. Both children woke screaming with a rat running over them. Their mother rushed in, saw blood on Ruth's hand, and was terrified until she washed it and found that only a corner of a finger had been bitten, though that was horror enough.

This battle against germs, amid the tensions of civil disturbance and the pressure of her hospital work which, since she was a vital, highly organized person, she could take in her stride while bringing up the children, imposed a heavy strain on Virginia. Yet severe migraine headaches were the sole nervous reaction. She never complained. You

could only tell she had one by looking at her eyes. She
found, however, that the headaches could make her a little
short or spicy. And Nelson would be extra considerate and
relieve any tension with his marvelous humor: "He could
make a joke out of any situation and have everybody laughing. They were a wonderful balance for each other," their
children recalled.

While Nelson worked at the hospital, Virginia spent the
morning teaching the two girls.

The Southern Presbyterians preferred to teach their children on the stations rather than send them away to a school
in another part of China; "raising new missionaries" was
part of the vocation, a policy which paid off, as many of
the children returned to the field as missionaries or in other
forms of service. Virginia proved a born primary teacher,
obtained the best books from America, and taught all her
children up to the sixth grade; after that they had a tutor
until high school. And since all the missionary homes had
accumulated good libraries for every age group, the children
became great readers.

Virginia taught them music and handwork: embroidery,
knitting, crocheting, sewing. Rosa learned to play the piano,
while Ruth enjoyed painting and was interested in art. Their
mother was an accomplished needlewoman and dressmaker
who passed the skills to her daughters along with a delight
in being well-dressed. As Ruth has often told interviewers,
"My mother didn't see why we should look like the scrapings
from the missionary barrel." The "barrel" which the postman
brought from time to time included wonderful collections
of cast-offs from generous home supporters; once there was
a suit from Sak's Fifth Avenue. Nelson's sister, Norma Norris,
sent over the clothes her girls had outgrown, and materials
and dresses were bought or made by Mrs. James H. Bell in
Waynesboro. She could only guess the sizes, but Virginia
plied her needle after poring over *Harper's Bazaar* or *Good
Housekeeping*, while the local tailor, with true Oriental skill,
could copy exactly, though fortunately not, like one Shanghai
tailor, reproducing the darns and patches!

When lessons were over, their father came home to lunch,

having performed more operations in a morning than a surgeon in America would do in a day. Some were intensely interesting, and he would start describing them in all their gory detail.

"Nelson! *Not* at the table!" Virginia would command.

"Oh, Mother, let him," the children would cry; they loved every minute. Rosa watched her first operation at the age of six when Wang NaiNai's daughter (who afterward married a doctor) had her tonsils out, "And everytime she spat, I spat."

One lunchtime Nelson brought back a tray of glass eyes which had just arrived. For fun he inserted one over his own eye, giving a most gruesome effect. The houseboy, upon entering, nearly dropped the dishes.

After lunch both parents went to the hospital. Mrs. Bell had charge of the women's clinic and could be counted on to be out of the way for two hours. The two children then proceeded to scrap. These two little girls who afterward became such devoted sisters "hated each other. We fought all the time. When Mother was out of the way, we really tore into it. We fought verbally and with our hands and feet, and the servants used to line up and bet on who was going to win."

The children may have supposed their parents were in blissful ignorance, but when Rosa was twenty and Ruth eighteen and both in college in America, Nelson Bell remarked to his mother in a letter from China: "Their devotion to each other has been a comfort to us—they used to scrap like cats and dogs. Each is constantly writing something nice about the other."

Fighting was not the only way to get even. Once their mother lay upstairs with a migraine headache while the girls were quarreling downstairs. "I'm going to tell Mother," pouted Ruth, flouncing out of the room. She came back a little later: "Mother wants to see you."

Rosa went upstairs and started to justify herself.

"What *are* you talking about?" asked Virginia.

"Didn't Ruth come and tell you?"

"No."

"Ruth told me you wanted to see me."

"You tell Ruth to come here!"

The girls could lose their tempers with each other privately, but none of their missionary "aunts" and "uncles" knew them as anything but agreeable, relaxed, and well-mannered. They were not encouraged to be ostentatiously pious, nor held up to the Chinese as picture-book paragons: they were simply to be themselves, with plenty of play. Both were devout, Ruth being more open, while Rosa's feelings were buried deeper.

When Rosa was three years old, her young father heard her crying after she had been put to bed. "He went upstairs to see what was the matter, and as he leaned over my crib, I threw my arms around his neck and said, 'Daddy, I'm such a sinner.' Instead of saying, 'Well, you're a sweet little thing and we'll talk about this when you're twelve years old,' he just explained the plan of salvation to me right then and there. Then he said, 'Well, that's why Jesus died, honey, and if you would just ask Jesus to come into your heart and forgive you, He will.' And I did. And He did." Rosa's open dedication to Christ came when she was older.

Ruth, too, "cannot remember when I didn't love the Lord. My earliest recollections are of deepest gratitude to God for having loved me so much that He was willing to send His Son to die in my place. And there was such a contrast in China between good and evil, Christianity and heathenism. In America the lines have become so blurred; sin is glamorized and glorified until it is hard to detect. But in China sin was ugly and revolting, and there was such a contrast between the Christian Chinese I knew and the pagan Chinese—in their kindness, in their joy, and in their love."

No parent needed to labor the point. Evidence of the contrast between pagan callousness and Christian compassion was overwhelming, whether seen with a child's own eyes or casually related by grown-ups. Once someone fell off the launch on the Grand Canal, and Nelson dived in to attempt rescue. The other passengers remarked, "Never mind. It's only a little girl." Nelson never found her in the muddy water.

*   *   *   *   *

In late afternoon Virginia relaxed by gardening. She had a green thumb, and after a few years her garden or yard was full of shrubs, flowers, and fruit: cherries and strawberries in May; apricots and peaches in June; plums, grapes, and mulberries later. The porch had plants which were brought into the living room when the chilly weather began.

Nelson played his tennis, and Rosa remembered "as a very small child how my father and his friends would take time from their playing tennis on a summer afternoon and allow us to chase them. It was great sport, chasing after those men, and it was just a part of our living, not something that we considered extra special....This was one of the things that I appreciated so much about my childhood; none of us children in the family or in the mission station were ever made to feel that we were in the way, or that the parents could do a lot more work for God if they didn't have us to cope with. We always were included. Of course, there weren't too many children."

The younger Talbot boys were Rosa's and Ruth's ages, and later there were the Graham and Woods grandchildren from time to time. Every child out of the nursery was included with the "uncles" and "aunts" in the weekly social gathering, which included charades, Rook, or other games, and in Thanksgiving dinners, Fourth of July, and other festivities. Halloween, Christmas, Valentine's Day, birthdays, every celebration normal to American children received full treatment, for Virginia was a born hostess, and both parents took endless trouble to reproduce the excitements which would have been enjoyed at home, whether delicious suppers or fancy dress parties.

And every evening the Bell family changed their workaday clothes, ate dinner, and then gathered around the fireplace in the living room with its blue motif and fine old French etchings which Virginia had inherited. After dark the risk of kidnapping, gunfire, and banditry kept all citizens off the streets. Although a rare emergency might arrive at the gate escorted by a policeman or soldier, and Nelson occasionally drove to the city or to Hwaian on an urgent call, normally, except for the usual round of the wards after supper, he was free.

Every evening was fun for all the family. They played party games, word games, and popular pastimes now forgotten, such as caroms, Crokinole, and Flinch. But their greatest relaxation was reading aloud. Nelson and Virginia had discovered this special pleasure as early as the winter of 1918, starting with Dickens and Scott. For Rosa and Ruth they began with favorites such as *Little Lord Fauntleroy;* as they grew, the girls enjoyed *David Copperfield, A Tale of Two Cities, Ivanhoe,* Kingsley's *Hypatia,* and many other classics. Sometimes it would be just "a frivolous tale." Virginia read aloud to the children at other times of the day when they were small; in the evenings Nelson read the larger share while his wife and daughters sewed or knitted. He did not try detective stories, rightly concluding that fast plots and complicated clues are essentially a private delight.

Sunday was different, Ruth said, "but never dull or boring. Mother and Daddy were particular about the Lord's day being the Lord's day. We were not allowed to read secular books or magazines on Sunday, or listen to or sing secular music. We were not allowed to play secular games. Now if that had been all there was to Sunday, it would have been a dreary and horrible day which we would have dreaded with all our hearts from one week to the next. But they never, in all the years that we were growing up, said 'You cannot do this' without giving a happy substitute. The things we were not allowed to do on Sunday were replaced by things that we did only on Sunday. A variety of excellent Christian books and periodicals were saved up and used for Sunday."

On Sunday evenings they played Bible games. They had a variety of them, and Nelson was difficult to beat because he knew the Bible like the back of his hand. These exciting Bible games were probably the chief reason why the Bell children gained exceptional command of biblical detail.

12
A Grave in Tsingkiangpu

THE year that Ruth turned four, the Bells made the laborious journey to the holiday cottage at Kuling which Nelson had bought on a mortgage. Ruth has a terrifying memory of being carried in a chair, slung between two poles resting on the shoulders of Chinese carriers, up the mountain path which twisted so sharply that she was literally hanging over the vast abyss of the gorge while the carriers back and front negotiated the corners.

That year two new missionaries at Hwaian, Ray and Mary Womeldorf, were the Bells' guests in the Kuling cottage. Ray had lost a leg in France. He was a cheerful man and a terrible tease, and when he and his wife first met Nelson and Virginia, they were "overcome to find such youthful and charming folks as active missionaries." Womeldorf had supposed that all missionaries were old, solemn, and austere. The Bells' youth and vigor and their enthusiasm about the whole mission program, and the programs of other missions, impressed him from the first.

Along with conferences and meetings, Kuling sport was at full strength. Nelson again entered the Mid-China Tennis Championship, with Ed Wayland as partner. At baseball, with Nelson as pitcher, the Southern Presbyterians won the local equivalent of the World Series. Indeed, other missions would quip that athletic prowess was an essential qualification for an SPM recruit.

The SPM missionaries were renowned also for their singing. The North Kiangsu quartet became quite famous in missionary circles. Nelson with his guitar, Kerr Taylor with his mandolin, James Montgomery of Hwaian, and E. H. Hamilton ("Ham") of Suchowfu (joined sometimes by Ed Currie of Haichow and Lock White also of Suchowfu) would dress up as minstrels and sing the old plantation songs with local parodies. The British and other nationalities loved to hear "Are You From Dixie?" sung with the appropriate make-up and Southern dialect:

> Are you from Dixie—I say from Dixie,
> Where the fields of cotton beckon to?
> I'm glad to see you, tell me how be you
> And the friends I'm longing to see?
> If you're from Alabama, Tennessee, or Caroline—
> Just any place below the Mason-Dixon Line—
> Then you're from Dixie, Hurray for Dixie!
> 'Cause I'm from Dixie too.

This was followed by the North Kiangsu parody:

> Are you from Kiangsu? Old North Kiangsu?
> Where the six or eight stations beckon to me?
> Are you from Kiangsu? Old North Kiangsu?
> That's where you ought to be!
> Are you from Suchowfu or Chinkiang, Tsingkiang
>   or Hwaian?
> Tell me you live above the yellow Yangtze Ki-ang!
> Are you from Kiangsu? Old North Kiangsu?
> Well, we're from Kiangsu too.

In the tradition of minstrels, the two "end men" would exchange jokes, the most popular being the skit on the initials of missions.

Nelson would say: "What are all these initials we see around here? What does SPM mean?"

Ham would reply: "Don't you know what that means? That means So Proud of Myself." CIM (China Inland Mission), according to the minstrels, stood for "Come in Man," and FOR (the pacifist Fellowship of Reconciliation) became "Fight or Run."

But the following year, 1925, the Bells did not go to Kuling—nor ever again, and Nelson eventually sold his cottage.

One reason was that all the Bells could stand the heat of the plains. Then, too, the medical work slumped if one American doctor was on furlough and the other in Kuling. And the journey of nearly a week each way was a considerable strain to parents with two small children, excited at first but progressively more tired. First the rickshaws to the jetty, then the houseboat or launch down the Grand Canal. These were all infested with bugs, and Ruth must have been particularly tasty: as she recalled wryly, "If there was one bedbug on the boat, it would find its way to me!"

"Poor Ruth got her share of the bites as usual," runs a letter from Nelson to his mother. The family carried its own bedrolls and camp cots, and the legs of the cots would each be placed in a small can of kerosene, but the bugs would crawl across the ceiling and drop; at journey's end Virginia had to inspect every bedroll inch by inch, since one undetected bug in your home could bring hours of extra work.

After the Yangtze ferry, "Taking the steamer in Chinkiang is a perfect nightmare," Nelson told his mother, "with the steamers arriving from midnight to dawn, all the time waiting in a junk anchored in the river."

Virginia had to watch the children every minute lest they touch dirty woodwork and then rub their eyes with germs. She had to cook the food over a camp burner and boil all their water. "And all day long," remembered Ruth, "there would be people squatting on the little narrow decks peering through the windows at these strange foreigners on board, carrying on a running commentary: 'My, how big their feet are! My, what big noses they have!' Not knowing that we could understand Chinese."

It was far more restful at home. Moreover, 1925 brought an excellent reason against Kuling, for early the previous December the Bell family had been increased by the birth of Nelson Junior, whereby the servants considered that Rosa and Ruth had had their noses truly put out of joint now that Dr. Chong Ai Hua at last had a man-child. Little Nelson was a sturdy infant "and so full of life that he was a favorite with the foreigners and Chinese alike."

It was the summer that the Houston Unit opened, so

the staff invited their colleagues of North Kiangsu to hold the annual Mission Meeting at Tsingkiangpu; they gathered early in October when Nelson Junior was ten months old.

The Bells had a houseful of guests and were their usual efficient selves, so cheerful that it was hard to credit a rumor that their baby had fallen ill with amoebic dysentery. But Little Nelson's condition became critical.

Estelle Hamilton remembered "seeing Nelson and Virginia coming down the staircase, right downstairs to the living room, and going to the piano. They began to sing 'Where the Gates Swing Outward Never.' They sang it in a triumphant way. I was so impressed by their faith in God and their cheerful aspect, even though their child was dangerously ill."

The week of meetings ended, and the station almost emptied as several of the Tsingkiangpu people happened to disperse temporarily. Nelson and Virginia nursed their baby until by Friday, October 23, 1925, the eighteenth day of the illness, "It looked as though he was gradually overcoming the trouble," Nelson wrote five days later. "But his heart could not stand the strain of a very high and continued fever, and it gave way under it. Virginia and I realized he was going, and we were alone with him when the end came. It was so sweet and peaceful, no struggle, and no evidence of pain, just quietly leaving us and going back to Him."

They laid out the little body themselves, and then Virginia went straight up to the Talbots' house where Rosa and Ruth were at lessons: she did not wish them to hear the final news from the Chinese. "Mother and Daddy were very composed," they recalled, "though we knew their hearts were nearly broken. Yet there was no sense of hopelessness or grief beyond repair." Nelson saw the children's grief and found it a true opportunity "to bring," as he put it, "the great hope that is ours close and plain to them. If it were not for that hope, we would not be here in China."

The hospital carpenter made a casket, and they lined it with white silk from the Chinese silk-seller. Late that afternoon many Chinese and the Americans went to the little station cemetery outside the north wall. They sang "Praise God From Whom All Blessings Flow." Rosa and Ruth never forgot the sight of the Chinese weeping. "But though it was sad, there was a sense of assurance that Little Nelson was safe with Jesus; we would see him again someday."

As they left the cemetery, a sunset filled the western sky. Virginia said to Nelson, "I have a song in my heart, but it is hard to keep the tears from my eyes."

The next morning Nelson spent his usual devotional hour alone at his roll-top desk. Thoughts which a few days later he put in writing were in his mind: "His going has left an ache in our hearts, and our arms feel empty, but, oh, the joy of knowing he is safe. It has but drawn us closer to Him and given us a new tie and joy to look forward to in Heaven. We would not have him back, for we know it was His will that he should go. There is no repining, wishing we had used other medicines. We feel that everything that could possibly have been done was done."

Nelson turned to his Bible and found himself reading in Genesis—how Jacob, at the brook Jabbok, wrestled with a Stranger, found it was God, and received a blessing which made a new man of him, but at a price: God "touched him in the hollow of his thigh." When Jacob left the place of blessing, he limped.[1]

Nelson was comforted. "Jacob limped next morning as he went forward, but that limp was because God's hand had touched him. We may have a terrible sorrow which gives us an emotional limp, but it is where God, in His love and mercy, has touched us, bringing us a blessing, with a consciousness of God's presence. God has left in our hearts the mark of his loving touch."

The peace, the new sensitivity to God's presence which Little Nelson's death had brought to Nelson and Virginia, was soon put to a tough test.

---

[1]"Therefore the children of Israel eat not of the sinew which shrank, which is upon the hollow of the thigh..." Years before Dr. Woods had told Nelson a little known fact: in ancient China the name for the Jews had been *T'iao Ching Huei* (the religion that takes out sinew).

Nelson Bell, Jr.

Bath time for young Nelson—Rosa and Ruth watching

The grave in Tsingkiangpu

13
The Great
Evacuation, 1927

NELSON BELL told a tale about a professor at a certain mission medical school who was friendly with the local warlord.

"One day he broached to him the need in his department for more subjects for dissection, and the general offered to send over the bodies of executed criminals which were constantly available. The offer was gladly accepted, but when the bodies began to arrive, only too often they were useless because of mutilation. The professor then had his Chinese secretary write a polite letter of appreciation to the general, at the same time asking if he, in the interests of science, could not have his executioners exercise more restraint. The reply was that of a true friend—'Honored Sir: Your most honorable communication has been received, and your little brother understands and deeply apologizes. In order that things may be entirely in keeping with your needs in the future, I will send the condemned men to you, and you can just kill them any way that suits you best.'"

Warlord maneuverings continued to have an element of grim farce, with troops switching sides for higher pay and battles made more of noise than violence. The real sufferers were the peasants, forced to pay taxes two or three times a year as a district changed hands, and constantly preyed upon by soldiers or bandits and seized for forced labor. But by 1925 a new factor had entered Chinese politics which was eventually to change the situation. Communists began to play a hidden, but important part in South China, putting teeth into the Kuomintang or Nationalist party, hoping to use it as a means to a Soviet-style revolution, though Mao Tse-tung was unable to gain full control. The eventual Nationalist leader, after Sun Yat-sen's death, was Chiang Kai-shek, who hoped to use the Communists to help him unite China. He was not a Communist—nor yet a Christian—but an ally of Soviet Russia. In May 1925 the Nationalists and Communists revolted against the Peking regime, the nominal rulers of the chaos that was China, and in July formed a Nationalist government in Canton.

The new revolutionary movement was anti-foreign and anti-Christian because it regarded Christians as "running dogs of the Imperialists," agents of the foreign powers who exploited China's wealth, had imposed unequal treaties, and had ignored her right to German concessions which instead were foolishly handed to Japan.

High school students were fanned into agitation against England and Japan. For all the basic justice of China's claims, history proves Nelson Bell right in his deduction (in a letter of July 6, 1925) that the underlying stimulus came from foreign Communist leaders. "The majority of the students do not know this, and they are being filled with false and misleading propaganda which is more and more centering itself against England. These students are the tools of masterminds. Playing upon an appeal to patriotism, they are being led into most dangerous things." And some leaders of the recently formed Federal Council of Churches added to the confusion by exerting "a strong pull to turn the native church into a political organization."

While Nationalists and their Communist allies consolidated their hold in South China, the north remained under warlords who combined with each other and fought each other to strengthen their hold before the revolution swept up from the south.

Tsingkiangpu, one of the most strategic points on the Grand Canal, found itself in the middle of a seven days' battle fought with all the fury of a civil war.

Sixty thousand men were involved. A combination of northern generals under Chang Tso-ling had retreated from Shanghai to the railway center of Suchowfu several hundred miles north of Tsingkiangpu. Their enemy, a combination of eastern and central generals under Wu Pei-fu, advanced north up the canal. Chang suddenly staged a counter-offensive. The opposing armies met head-on at Tsingkiangpu nine days after the death of little Nelson Junior.

The first skirmish fifteen miles north obliged Wu's troops to withdraw to a strong defensive position about two-and-a-half miles from the hospital, along the banks of the Salt Canal, a branch which runs east from the city. Hundreds of terrified countrywomen and old men streamed into the hospital compound. On Sunday night, November 1, "the din of artillery, machine guns, and rifle fire was incessant" and continued with occasional pauses throughout Monday and Tuesday. On Wednesday the attacking army began an all-out attempt to capture Tsingkiangpu, which would then be sacked. They "broke over the Salt Canal in two places," Nelson wrote, "and came so close that we could see their bullets biting the dust and hear them whine over our heads. One of their shells burst right at the back of our house, about two hundred yards away."

Nelson found it most exciting, and Virginia felt no fear either. Nelson wrote, "I can truthfully say that we were not scared. We realized that our work was here and that it was our duty to stick by it. We were seeing, too, before our very eyes the fulfillment of the promises of the Ninety-first Psalm. It was wonderful to feel His protecting care." Nelson saw eight shell bursts within a few minutes, "but there was only the feeling of pity for those who were being killed and wounded, and no personal fear." The new, deeper inner peace which had followed the death of Nelson Junior remained unruffled, and the two girls took their cue from the parents.

On Thursday night General Chang made a flank march and assaulted the city from the south the next morning. He shelled it too, rather inefficiently: several canal boats were sunk, several houses hit, shrapnel burst over the Talbots' home, and a stray bullet broke a window in the girls' school. The infantry, however, reached the walls before being repulsed at noon. Saturday's attack was even more savage but again unsuccessful, and Chang's baffled army withdrew north, leaving a battlefield strewn with many hundreds of dead and wounded soldiers and unfortunate peasants caught in the cross fire.

The hospital took about a hundred seriously wounded. Nelson amputated or saved shattered limbs, sewed up bayonet stabs, and extracted bullets or shrapnel. Abdominal cases were complicated because the metal scattered intestinal worms. Soon the lesser wounded were at the gates begging to be taken in because the military "hospital" in the city did little except stuff wounds with gauze and wonder why they became infected. One of the "surgeons" had been a weaver at the mission's former orphanage.

The hospital was crammed. The multitude of refugees and wounded presented "wonderful evangelistic opportunities.... It is also a great hindrance to the regular work."

*   *   *   *   *

Throughout 1926 the political crisis in China grew more explosive. As the tide rose from the south, bitter hatred of foreigners spread into many parts of China. One missionary of the China Inland Mission wrote of being "misunderstood by those we seek to serve, drinking the cup of ingratitude, shame, humiliation, and reproach, despised by the many and hated by some. We are partakers of the fellowship of Christ's sufferings and learning when reviled not to revile again." On the other hand, Tsingkiangpu showed gratitude and appreciation. Communist agitators remained too few to have the slightest effect. The hospital was full and the patients more responsive to the gospel than ever, partly because of the success of the new Book Room and the Christian literature campaign.

In the spring of 1926 the district suffered a diphtheria epidemic. Nelson cabled Benjamin Clayton in Texas, who cabled back a generous donation which immediately was spent for antitoxin. The epidemic chiefly affected the poorest who could pay nothing toward treatment, and Nelson soon exhausted Clayton's donation; he then enlisted help from the Rockefeller Foundation in Peking and from a government organization. The hospital dispensed eight million units of antitoxin, saving hundreds of lives.

One of the wettest summers in years ruined the fall bean

crop and caused floods which prevented the wheat planting so that famine next year became a certainty. Bandits grew more cruel: they no longer sent sliced ears to warn relatives, but murdered the victims who could not pay ransom instantly—and even some who paid.

In July 1926 the Nationalist and Communist southerners launched their drive to the north and by October had conquered the vital upper Yangtze valley. The revolutionaries won battle after battle, and it was only a matter of time before the whole country would fall. On March 10, 1927 Tsingkiangpu's land and water links with Shanghai and Nanking were cut. Nelson, however, had an up-to-date superheterodyne radio in the hospital office. When he put on the earphones, tickled the crystal, endured the squeaks, and twiddled the knobs, the missionaries received the news from Shanghai.

It was always bad. Nanking fell on March 24 with the murder of foreigners, including missionaries. The American consul and vice-consul—both sons of the SPM—had rescued many others. The aged Andrew Sydenstricker, his daughter Pearl Buck, and her husband, a teacher of agriculture, were hidden by their Chinese servants in a peasant hut. One SPM doctor was pushed protesting into the hospital coal bin by his devoted Chinese staff, to emerge later sooty but safe.

Nelson twiddled the knobs again and heard that Shanghai had fallen, amid looting and carnage—the International Settlement stayed unscathed because the British had sent battalions of the Brigade of Guards.

All continued peaceful at Tsingkiangpu. Nelson's feelings were much as he expressed them at another time of crisis a few years later: "We simply live by faith not by sight. If we lived by the latter, we would leave by the first boat. As we live by faith, though, God gives a deeper blessing of peace and joy."

* * * * *

Thousands of miles away in America Nelson's mother studied the newspaper and knew more about the situation than Nelson, for correspondents were wiring their papers much which Shanghai radio did not broadcast.

As she studied and prayed, she began to realize that Nelson, the family, and all their colleagues were in growing danger since the southern armies were poised to drive north up the railway to the west and up the Grand Canal. She had a shrewd idea that Nelson did not realize the danger. She felt, too, that he would ignore a call to evacuate his beloved hospital unless he received a message from someone he trusted: she knew his opinion of timid consuls who tried to rescue their nationals from imaginary perils. Looking at the map, she decided that the person to warn him was Kerr Taylor, who had been temporarily at Taichow to the south and was listed among those evacuated by American gunboat to Shanghai.

Mrs. Bell prayed, urgently, trustfully.

There is a twelve-hour difference between Waynesboro and Shanghai, and at precisely the time Mrs. Bell lay praying on her bed at night, the American vice-consul in Shanghai was having a hectic morning that Tuesday, March 29, 1927. The British and American Ministers in Peking had ordered a total evacuation of missionaries from the interior. He decided to enlist the help of missionaries already in Shanghai to contact their colleagues.

At Waynesboro it was nearly midnight and Mrs. Bell still prayed. At Tsingkiangpu it was nearly noon. Nelson went across to the hospital office, put on the earphones, and began to tune in for the midday news.

Through the static he heard the announcer say: "I have a very important message for the Southern Presbyterian missionaries listening in at Tsingkiangpu: 'It is imperative that you evacuate immediately. Travel north via Haichow and Tsingtao. A U.S. destroyer is waiting at Chinkiang, but travel via Yangchow is uncertain. Notify Hwaian, Sutsien, Suchowfu, and Haichow. Signed, H. Kerr Taylor.'"

This was, as Nelson said, "quite a dramatic moment for us." And very dramatic for his mother several weeks later when she read Nelson's account, checked the times, and realized that her prayer had been answered 10,000 miles away as and when she actually prayed.

But it took more than Kerr Taylor to shift Tsingkiangpu folk. They wanted to stay; they felt they should stay. However, they duly sent Kerr Taylor's message to other stations, and Aunt Sophie hired a special messenger to go by canal boat to warn their son, James Graham, Jr., his family, and SPM colleagues at Yencheng. Then they sat tight.

Into Nelson Bell's earphones squawked a message from the consul at Tsingtao and then from the American Minister himself, "insisting that we leave." The decisive factor, however, was a frank acceptance that to stay might increase the difficulties of Chinese Christians when the victorious revolutionary army poured into North Kiangsu.

The missionary staff took their time; they were not going to flee, but withdraw. Six days passed while they arranged the work of the hospital and advised on problems raised by Pastor Kao and his venerable father, the hospital evangelist, who might never see his dear friends again. Virginia and Nelson stored their few valuables in the attic. This operation was continually, though touchingly, interrupted when caller after caller gravely expressed his or her sorrow at the leaving of Dr. "Lover of the Chinese People" and his wife and daughters. Church members, past patients, shopkeepers, traders, and lawyers—particularly encouraging were callers who had no connection with church or hospital, yet walked or came by rickshaw up Ten Li Street to show their desire that the foreigners should soon return.

Early on April 5, with heavy hearts, wondering what terrors their city would suffer before they saw it again, Rosa and Ruth, their parents, and all their missionary "aunts" and "uncles" embarked on a small boat which carried them to Haichow; Ma Er, the ex-soldier whose ears had been chopped off, insisted on coming as an escort. At Haichow they took passage on a little Japanese steamer, in odiferous company with eight hundred emigrating laborers, to Tsingtao, the German-style coastal resort, where they were reunited with friends from all the other northern stations. Only James Graham, Jr. and the Yencheng party were missing. The consul at length ordered a gunboat upriver to search for them, when they arrived by sea in a junk, having found all land routes blocked by battles or by defeated and

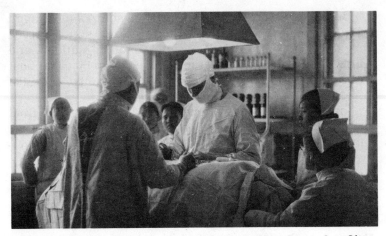

An operation—Dr. Bell assisted by Dr. Ch'ien; Miss Cassie Lee Oliver, R.N., anesthetist

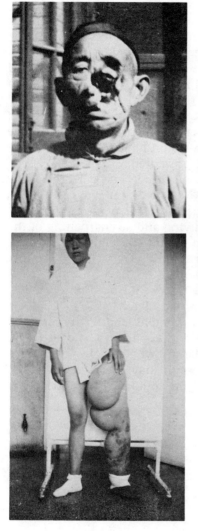

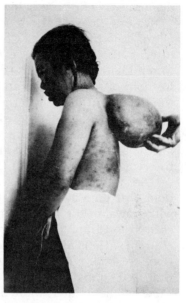

The hospital treated almost every conceivable medical problem, from tumors to war wounds.

demoralized northern soldiers.

No one knew if the Nationalists and their Communist allies, soon to control all China, would permit return to the interior, though the new government could be in no position to repudiate treaties with the Great Powers which included freedom of travel, trade, and lawful activity. From Tsingtao the Bells went to the International Settlement at Shanghai. They were not due for furlough, but Virginia was seven months pregnant, and the sensible course was to go home for the birth, returning in four months if possible or taking the remainder of furlough if prevented.

"Are we discouraged?" wrote Nelson on board the *President Taft* on May 4, 1927. "No! God is already using this withdrawal of the missionaries and this persecution of the church in China for the purifying and strengthening of the church....He is only going to permit the trials and persecutions to go far enough to purify the church." Bell's certainty that God's providence is sovereign enabled him to feel the same in the greater, more lasting withdrawal and persecution which began twenty-two years later.

As to the Bells themselves, when at length they returned to Tsingkiangpu, Ray Womeldorf's gateman said to them: "You would have been quite all right when the revolutionaries arrived. Of course, you all would have been killed in the first three days, but after that you would have been all right!"

Part Three
THE WALL OF FIRE
1928 - 1941

14
Happy Return

PASTOR KAO sat composing a letter. Each brush stroke carried a prayer as the characters lengthened down the paper.

"My dearly beloved Dr. Bell," he wrote. "We have not seen each other's faces for six months, and during this time I have thought of you and each member of your family and longed for you. In my mind's eye I constantly see your smiling face and talk with you, and in my ears I hear the sound of your voice singing hymns. Come back! I want you to quickly come back."

Tsingkiangpu had been terrorized by the Nationalist-Communists and Pastor Kao had suffered some persecution. The hospital compound had been occupied by troops nine times and looted: the X-ray machine was the only serious equipment casualty, but the boys' and girls' schools were stripped from top to bottom. After the first looting of the Bell home, friends and servants removed the heavy furniture to safety, then plastered over the access to the attic, where the valuables were stored, and hid the stairs by sections. Further looters were puzzled because the house appeared to have a top story; the Bells' wily old gateman, who was not a Christian, looked innocent and shook his head: "I have been here a very long time, and I have never heard or seen anything about an attic."

He rescued the doorknobs which had been thrown around the grounds, while a local brass-smith recognized and bought the name plate of the Bells' wood stove to keep it safe against their return. Soldiers were billeted in all the rooms because the populace had burned down the barracks.

Dr. Ts'ao being held in high esteem by even the most rabid Nationalist, the hospital was not molested further but could keep open, until the terror stopped patients from coming to the clinic and the beds were requisitioned for wounded soldiers. As soon as conditions improved, Drs. Ts'ao and Ch'ien resumed the clinic and took ward patients. Unlike some hospital staffs after missionaries withdrew, the two were scrupulous in handling the finances. In the church, regular services never stopped, although attendance dropped off and for a few months the pastor received no financial help. However, congregations were once again increasing and Pastor Kao had been given a raise in salary.

As 1927 passed into 1928, war continued in both North and South China, and Western powers would not permit their nationals to go inland. Back in the United States the Bells had stayed in Waynesboro until the birth of Virginia Bell in June 1927: they nicknamed her MaiMai (pronounced *Mamie*), meaning "little sister."

They spent six months at Houston, Texas. Nelson served as assistant pastor (lay) at First Presbyterian, thus binding even closer the ties between Houston and Tsingkiangpu. He became celebrated for his lunch hour talks to the business community. Though carefully prepared, these seemed impromptu: "He got up in the pulpit and just began to talk," recalled Benjamin Clayton. The Southern Presbyterians offered ordination, but Nelson Bell remained convinced "that a layman who had dedicated his life to Jesus Christ, plus the fact that he was a surgeon, carried a certain testimony that an ordained minister couldn't have." Bell also spent a day each week at the Herman Hospital gaining further experience.

For four months, while waiting for China to reopen, they lived at Holden, West Virginia, where Nelson headed the surgical department at the hospital while the chief surgeon went to Europe. "It was a most satisfactory experience, financially, as well as to demonstrate that one can take the experience of the mission hospital and use it to great advantage at home," Bell wrote.

When inland China at last reopened in the fall of 1928,

the Bells, after a holiday at Waynesboro, returned to Houston for weekend services on their way to the Pacific coast early in November. "It looked like almost the entire congregation came up and filed by and spoke to us....The people just cannot do enough for us." Money for a new X-ray machine was subscribed by the church, and Benjamin Clayton added a substantial donation for Nelson to use as he wished. The Bells were given the best rooms at the hotel and left Houston loaded with love and goodies. MaiMai, nearly eighteen months old, had a cold and Ruth mild flu, but both recovered on the ship. The baby celebrated by throwing her pillow into the Pacific.

*   *   *   *   *

Old Elder Kao, the hospital evangelist, lay dying, surrounded by his numerous children and grandchildren, all Christians through his example and teaching.

He knew the Bells were on their way back to China. "Only one prayer is unanswered," murmured Elder Kao. "I did so want to see their beloved faces again." A long silence. Then his family heard him stir. "It is for the best," he whispered. "We shall meet just a little later." He beckoned to his eldest son, the pastor: "Live by the Bible always. Preach by it. Never depart from it in the least particular." He closed his eyes and soon afterward his breathing stopped.

A few weeks later, on his little farm south of Tsingkiangpu, Ma Er crammed his cap over the place where his ears had been, took his savings from the hiding place in the wall, counted out enough coin to get him the whole way down the Grand Canal and across the Yangtze, and hurried into the city. The Bells had arrived in Shanghai, and Ma Er was determined to be the first to greet them up-country.

Addison Talbot, who with the Jimmy Grahams and other missionaries waiting in Shanghai had returned immediately on the ending of the ban on inland residence and had begun itinerating, was told confidently by a peasant that Dr. "Lover of the Chinese People" had already arrived. They came on the Shanghai Express to Chinkiang—with twenty-two boxes of groceries and a new Baby Austin—where they were greeted by Ray Womeldorf, who had brought the Bells' houseboy Yang Er, "and to our surprise, Ma Er, the boy who had his ears cut off." They crossed the Yangtze, a large party including the Montgomerys, the Womeldorfs, and their families, Wang NaiNai, who had come from Shanghai with the Bells, and Cassie Lee Oliver, the missionary head nurse who had returned from America with them.

Water on the Grand Canal being too low to reach the city without long delay, Nelson wired the hospital to hire the local bus (a Ford truck with wooden seats) to meet them at Kaoyu, eighty miles south, which the party did not reach until next afternoon in drizzling rain because the launch had gone aground for six hours. One of the hospital boys "came on the boat just bubbling with excitement and seemed so glad to see us." All the party except the Bells transferred to the bus while fifteen boatmen manhandled the Baby Austin off the launch and up a long flight of stone steps. Then, with Virginia and the baby in front and Ruth and Rosa squeezed in the back, Nelson drove along the canal bank—four feet wide, no more—until he reached the so-called motor road and could speed up to twenty miles an hour in the rain behind the bus. But the bus became stuck at a bridge, and they all spent the night in a Chinese inn after tacking newspaper around the wall to keep their bedding from touching the accumulation of years of filth. A good hot Chinese supper helped.

They reached Hwaian in the early afternoon in December 1928 where the Montgomerys and Womeldorfs left them. Bell relates, "And we came on to Tsingkiangpu. We were surprised to meet some of the hospital boys out quite a way from the city. They had stayed out until dark the day before and were waiting for us. When we got to the end of the street that leads into our part of the city, a big crowd was waiting with long strings of firecrackers. We got out and spoke to them all and then drove on slowly to the hospital. Here we found the front gatehouse and dispensary courtyard crowded with people waiting to meet us—a lot more firecrackers too. Again we got out and spoke to all and we walked across the main hospital courtyard and on back to our house, all the way escorted by the crowd, with firecrackers popping, some of the strings hanging from hospital windows. The boy who met us in Kaoyu had told us they had cleaned up our house so we could go in it, and after the night in the inn, we were sure we could.

"We were totally unprepared, though, for this welcome, and the people seemed so genuinely glad to see us. I was completely taken by surprise, and it was plain that they really meant it."

* * * * *

"The day after our arrival carpenters, masons, painters, paperhangers, etc., started work, and after three weeks of hard work, in which Virginia led, the house came out looking like new, the furniture all refinished at the same time."

The family quickly settled into their old China ways, every day exciting, busy, and jolly from morn to night. Rosa recalled an evening when she and Ruth were being put to bed when the house was still topsy-turvy and the curtains not up.

"Daddy came into the room in his pajamas and said to Mother: 'Tuck them in and come on to bed.' 'Don't be in such a hurry,' she replied. Mother had been reading aloud about King Arthur and the Round Table, and Daddy picked up a curtain rod from the window sill and lunged with it like a sword, pretending he was a knight of the Round Table. So Mother picked up a slipper and tossed it at him; he ducked and it went through the window with a great shattering of glass.

"All the servants came rushing to see what had happened, and Daddy called out the window, 'It's all right; go on back to bed.' And the next morning they all had wry grins on their faces."

Though civil conditions were quieter and bandits no longer roamed the district in hordes, the Bells were soon reminded that life had not changed much. "Last Monday while we were at supper, we heard quite a bit of firing which sounded quite close. After supper I went out and found some bandits had tried to carry off an old man who owns a grain store near the hospital gate. He slipped and they fired at him, hitting one of their own men. When they tried to carry their own man off, he could not walk; so they shot him through the head so he could tell no tales and then they ran off. We often remark that the children can certainly tell tales which rival the days in the old West when they grow big."

A few weeks later Ruth was playing with the Talbot boys in the Bells' yard when she found under a tree a spherical object which she thought was a weight for Chinese scales, though it had an odd piece of metal down one curve, held by a pin. She hung it on the tree by a piece of string as a marker for their little animal graveyard. The Talbots' gateman saw it when he came to take the boys home and acted swiftly. As an old soldier he realized that a hand grenade with a rusty pin, hung on a tree by an old piece of string, might fall and explode any moment. He hid this lethal relic of the northern retreat of 1927 until Dr. Bell's return from the hospital. He promptly deposited it in the lake. The Bells were all the more thankful for Ruth's escape because they remembered an incident in 1925 when a soldier traded a hand grenade for some candy. The candy peddler did not know what it was and pulled out the pin; the explosion killed him and wounded two little children who were buying candy, one so severely that the doctor could not save its life.

Nelson once described return from furlough as a movement in three stages: "First the exaltation and pleasure of seeing old friends, then the awful depression as one feels the weight of the many problems, then the return to the normal level." In the special circumstances of 1928 the level could hardly be normal, for every serious case in the region seemed to have awaited the American doctor's return, while the civil war's legacy of damage and disruption involved reorganization and improvisation. And so did, on one occasion, the new Baby Austin. It developed carburetor trouble on one of Nelson's first visits to Hwaian and had to be pushed ignominiously home while Nelson returned by rickshaw. One man pulled him, another pushed; the rare opportunity of having the doctor as passenger put them on their mettle and "they did not slack their pace of a trot for the entire ten miles," which they covered in one hour and eighteen minutes, a rate of 7.8 miles per hour. Small wonder Ruth remembered the enormous calf muscles of rickshaw men.

The new magistrate, whose wife was a Christian, invited the Bells to a feast in the city and begged the doctor to resume his weekly prison visits. He went on Sunday, December 30, 1929, a cold day with a sting in the air, "and certainly did have a warm welcome from a large number of my old friends....I found some of the men pitifully cold because of lack of clothes. One man did not even have a pair of pants. I sent over to the city this morning and bought three suits of cotton-padded clothes and will take them over late this afternoon. This has to be done in person as otherwise the right people would not receive the clothing." He recognized a head hanging over the east gate with his bandage on it and took comfort in knowing that he had ministered to the criminal's soul as well as his body.

The Bells, one and all, were delighted to be in Tsingkiangpu. "I love China *very*, very much," Ruth wrote to her grandfather. In March 1929, Nelson declared, "I was never more sure of anything in my life than I am that God called us back at this time....The way is so freely open for us to work and the people so willing to hear the gospel."

And up Ten Li Street, in among the street vendors, the mules, and the swinging shoulder-tubs of the laborers, more and more victims of a particular disease were finding their way. For a new era had opened for the hospital which would give it fame far beyond China.

15
Kala-azar

The tropical disease kala-azar (black fever) is a protozoal infection caused by a parasite in the bloodstream which enlarges the spleen until it may fill the entire left side of the abdomen. Kala-azar proves fatal if not treated, and its incidence was higher in North Kiangsu than anywhere on earth and carried off thousands of men, women, and children, generally of the poorest, every year.

The advanced stages almost always induce severe anemia, while nose and gum bleeding, dysentery, abscesses, bronchitis, and pneumonia are other complications. And whereas the carrier of malaria had been identified as the anopheles mosquito by Ross and Manston as far back as 1898, no one was sure about kala-azar until the mid-1930s when the sand fly was isolated as carrier, partly through research in Tsingkiangpu.

From 1915 the use of antimony achieved some cures in India and China, but only if highly complicated tests were followed by treatment for two or three months. In the early 1920s an Indian Medical Service doctor, and then a Chinese in Peking, simplified the test, but little could be done until scientists in Germany developed a new drug, stibosan, which also used antimony. Stibosan, or later neo-stibosan, injected intravenously three times weekly, cured all but the most advanced patients in about three weeks.

Under Nelson Bell, Dr. Ts'ao had just begun to use it at Tsingkiangpu before the evacuation of 1927. Stibosan was expensive but its results were sensational. On his return in December 1928 Bell found, as he wrote to Dr. Woods in

America, that "kala-azar had made fearful strides in this section. Whole villages are affected." He was amazed how many sufferers were prepared to pay the necessarily high cost of treatment but saw at once that tens of thousands could not afford it.

He wrote to Benjamin Clayton. In the four or five weeks of the letter's journey from the Pacific to Houston, many hundreds of kala-azar sufferers died in the Tsingkiangpu region.

On Sunday, February 3, 1929, the local Bank of China manager stepped out of a rickshaw at the Bells' front door and handed the doctor a fat check, the $1000 cabled by Clayton immediately on reading Nelson's letter.

With the money, until it should be exhausted, Bell could bring the expensive kala-azar treatment into the scheme applied to all surgical and other medical cases, whereby poor people only paid a nominal fee charged according to means. Since Bell was punctilious in the courtesy of sending thanks, he wrote a detailed description to Benjamin Clayton. On March 9, to his surprise and delight, a cable from Clayton "came absolutely unsolicited asking if I could use $2500 more for kala-azar medicine." It was now obvious that Clayton intended to undergird the kala-azar work which could be extended to a scale more in tune with the need. Nelson was in no doubt of the need. "Yesterday," he wrote to his mother, on Tuesday, March 19, "I was in the heart of the kala-azar district and they told me rarely a home but what had one or more cases. We could pick out cases standing by their homes or by the road as we drove by. All are anemic, drawn, and have a sick look; one can almost diagnose a case by their looks."

That weekend had been typically busy. On return from treatments and preaching at the jail on Sunday he found a man wanting him to come to Hwaian for a child ill with diphtheria. He drove there after midday dinner; "saw the child and also saw the Montgomery children, all of whom have been more or less sick with flu, etc. Then came back across country to another village, reaching there about a quarter of four. The people had arranged a house for me to preach in and had brought in borrowed benches. The place

is not much for looks but it is much better than the open
street, and it was crowded. They keep so much quieter and
there is so much more attention in such a place. I hope
they will be able to keep it up. There is one baptized Christian
who lives about a mile from there; he is much interested
and says he will come each afternoon. I hope the work will
go forward now on the right basis. We have not put a cent
of money into it, and it will be so much better if that plan
can continue.

"I reached home by five, in time to lead foreign service.
That night I received a letter from one of our former nurses
who lives about thirty-seven miles from here, north of the
city of Antung. He is very ill and begged me to come to see
him. He was always a good and reliable boy when here and
a real Christian, so I got up early yesterday morning and
went to see him, found him ill with kala-azar and in addition
one lung partly gone with TB. He just cried when he saw
me and held on to my hand. I had planned to bring him
back in the car but did not think he could stand the trip,
so told them to carry him on a bed in a few days if he was
better. Got home by 12:45, in time for dinner. The road
from here to Antung (twenty miles) is especially good—came
in in fifty-five minutes which is fine time for China.

"Have been operating all morning and now have a few
minutes before dinner. I have invited a number of officials
and leading men here to supper tonight; am having a first-
class Chinese feast for them and hope things will go off
well. Mr. Ts'eng, the Magistrate, the heads of the Chamber
of Commerce, Chief of Police, head of Bus Co., head of the
chief government school, etc., are all invited. They have all
been nice to me, and I am taking this chance to in some
measure repay their kindness."

The kala-azar clinic grew fast as the news of cure spread
through the thickly populated region. April 1929 was the
biggest month for admissions and receipts in the hospital's
history. But Nelson could not give his full time to kala-azar.
He was primarily a surgeon and had more than enough
cases: reversing the leg and foot of a bandit whose foot
faced backward because a bullet wound had been neglected;
repairing the thigh of a leading member of the Chamber of

Commerce who, with his automatic pistol carried for defense, had managed not only to put a bullet in himself but another into an old beggar's arm, also sent up to the hospital. On a Sunday evening, while conducting a Bible reading for the nurses, Nelson had to rush off to do a speedy tracheotomy on a child suffocating from diphtheria. He sometimes did fifteen operations in a day.

It was in 1929 that Nelson removed a ninety-four pound abdominal tumor (giant ovarian cyst) from a woman who weighed only ninety pounds herself after the operation. She had arrived supported by two friends. The operation removed so much ballast that she tended to fall over backwards when she first tried to walk.

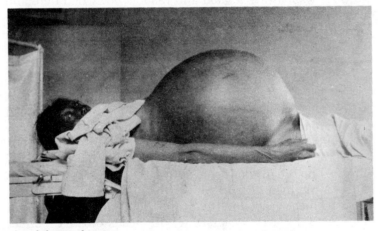

An abdominal tumor

On top of all this he must now organize the great enlargement dictated by "kala-azar patients crowding in in increasing numbers." His Chinese and American colleagues never thought of Nelson Bell as a worrier, but in May 1929 he confessed to his mother, "I find out here my big trouble is worrying about things [the Lord] is already working out for me."

The requirement of more space had been worked out already because the boys' school had closed when the new government imposed conditions which the SPM could not

accept. This Nationalist educational policy would later involve Nelson Bell in one of the hardest controversies of his
career, but at present it merely provided a fine empty building right beside the hospital. The other need was more staff.
He had already wired Dr. Woods in America: "Unprecedented
crowds, unhampered opportunities. Come." Woods had been
home since 1926 and still was not completely fit but replied
that he would return that year.

Bell now thought up a highly original scheme. Why
should not a newly qualified Christian doctor do his internship in Tsingkiangpu, without committing himself to
subsequent missionary service? Bell would choose him, the
mission board should approve him, and Benjamin Clayton
could pay his salary. Nelson Bell wrote frankly to Clayton,
who accepted this new charge without hesitation. Then Bell
cabled the intern on whom he had his eyes: Norman Patterson, son and brother of SPM missionaries.

*Patients with gunshot wounds spilled into the hospital yard one day follow-
ing civil disturbances, August 1933.*

*   *   *   *   *

"Four months' work, March—June 1929: Patients treated
in clinic, 13,545; inpatients, admitted to hospital, 736;
operations performed in hospital, 362; operations performed

in clinic, 239."

With the hospital expanding so rapidly, the Bells did not wish to leave it for the grim journey to and from their Kuling vacationland. Nelson discovered that for the price of one year's travel he could build a swimming pool in his yard.

A deep well had been dug in 1924 when the Houston Unit went up. Owing to a lack of drainage, the swimming pool had to be built above ground. It took four men six hours to pump it full. It was primitive by American standards and ice cold, but large enough for a child's dive and for adult swimming. They changed the water every week, thus providing 2000 gallons to water Virginia's flower, vegetable, and fruit beds. "The swimming pool is the greatest thing we have ever had here for making hot weather bearable," Nelson wrote in July. "When so hot and tired, a plunge and swim makes one feel like a new person, and the children simply have the time of their lives in it."

As Ruth, aged nine, wrote to her grandfather, with commendable handwriting and spelling but paucity of punctuation, on October 22: "The swimming pool has been a great pleasure to us all summer, in it I learned to dive float swim and turn the somersault and all other things that a duck can do."

This, possibly her first extant letter, prattled on: "We have the nicest doll's house you ever saw we also have lots of pets the hospital kitchen has lots of birds which we play with they also gave us two ducks one for Rosa and one for me.... The Chinese have not changed very many of their old habits women still smoke they still gamble and play cards drink and do all other things which we do not do."

After that rather prim remark, and following a paragraph about the grandparents' new home in Waynesboro, the letter ended with a bit of a barb: "Rosa says she will write when she feels like it, she's to lazy now."

*   *   *   *   *

The twenty-six-year-old Dr. Norman Patterson, Tsing-kiangpu's first intern, arrived with Dr. and Mrs. Woods, with whom he would lodge, in early September. Norman

("Uncle Doc" to the children) was son of Brown Patterson and his physician wife, who both came from Nelson's section of Virginia and had pioneered the SPM work at Sutsien on the Grand Canal, seventy miles north of Tsingkiangpu. "I am very glad he is going to have this year with you and Dr. W. at TKP," Brown Patterson had written to Nelson. "I do not know anyone, anywhere that I would rather he would be with this year."

Within a few days Nelson could report him "fitting in splendidly. He is a nice fellow, so full of fun and life, but well-trained and efficient and his Chinese is coming back to him nicely....He adds much to the life of the station." Like Nelson, he combined genuine compassion with gaiety, even more hilarious than Nelson's, and became popular with the Chinese.

Having been raised in China, Norman knew their minds: this fellow-feeling and his joviality got him out of a tight situation some years later when he turned would-be kidnappers or murderers into an escort against other brigands by the simple expedient of offering them a lift in his car.

Nelson made a point of daily tennis lest after the different world of the Medical College of Virginia the intern feel dull and lonely. He need not have worried. Young Athalie Hallum from America arrived at Hwaian, not as a missionary, but to tutor the three Montgomery girls and the three Yates girls. (With the three Bells at Tsingkiangpu there were nine girls between the two stations at this time. Six grew up to be missionaries; of the three who did not, one is a pillar of her church in New Mexico, with her scientist husband, one is the wife of a Christian professor in Grand Rapids, Michigan, and the other is the wife of Billy Graham). Athalie, who had been told by James Graham, Jr. on the ship that Norman Patterson was "a prince of a fellow," wrote, "I will never forget my first glimpse of Dr. and Mrs. Bell and Dr. Patterson. A few days after my arrival in Hwaian, they came down from Tsingkiangpu to have dinner with the Montgomerys, where I was staying. Hearing a car drive up (an event, as there were no cars in Hwaian), I glanced out my window, and there was the tiniest car I had ever seen. I could hardly believe my eyes when three adults alighted. The two men were both six feet or over. That little car fascinated me. Later on, Dr. Patterson came to see me many times in it, and my feeling was that he should have been carrying the car instead of the other way around."

Norman promptly fell head over heels in love with Athalie. The older missionaries, unlike the dragons of Ningpo in 1856 who tried to ruin the love story of Hudson Taylor and Maria, did all they could to forward the match. Athalie was invited to stay at the Bells. "They are one of the most fascinating couples I've ever met," Athalie wrote to her mother. "She is perfectly charming. He too is a vibrant personality, full of wit and charm and so completely dedicated to his Lord that service to Him is as natural as breathing. They have three precious daughters."

To Rosa and Ruth, who had never been around a courting couple, it was like a fairy tale. And, added Athalie, "There was never a dull moment when the two doctors were together. Once when I was visiting the Bells, Dr. Patterson came over to have breakfast with us. He was seated next to Dr. Bell who was serving fried eggs and passing the plates around. When Dr. Pat held out his hand for his plate, Dr. Bell plopped the egg right into his outstretched hand! I'll never forget the look on Dr. Pat's face—for once, he just seemed at a loss for words!"

The staffs and families of both stations gathered at the Bells for the Christmas dinner of 1929, the whitest Christmas in memory. Nelson had been out on a call, driving through the snow, but returned in time to change for dinner in a decorated home at a decorated table. "The youngest men all dressed in tuxedos," Athalie wrote home. "Mrs. Bell was dressed in an evening dress; I was in red velvet. There were about twenty-five of us in all, and we had a lovely time. Our 'turkey' was baked wild goose with chestnuts. We also had lye hominy, duck hash, English peas, creamed potatoes, cauliflower, baked ham, vegetable salad, homemade candy, cocoa, nuts, and fruit cake. After dinner Mr. Stevens, a widower, played the guitar and we sang all the old Southern songs." (Sometimes the "turkey" was duck or a bustard. Many years later when the girls were at college in America, Ruth was asked by Harold Lindsell what they ate for

Thanksgiving dinner in China. "*Bastards*," she replied promptly. "Bastards? O come, come, surely not," said Harold. Ruth retorted hotly: "I ought to know; I lived there and ate them!")

Norman and Athalie were married in Shanghai the following year in the middle of a thunderstorm: the bride, the consul, and the guests were delayed by flooded streets, and the electric light failed so that the ceremony was performed by the light of candles in the decorations. The day the Pattersons' first baby was born, in the Bells' home on June 12, 1931, Virginia heard Norman chase Rosa and Ruth for some prank with: "You all get away. I am used to bossing children; have been bossing one for half a day now!"

Ambulatory kala-azar patients under treatment at one time. In 1940 a total of 4717 cases were treated.

Norman and Athalie Patterson

16
The World's Largest Presbyterian Hospital

BY now, kala-azar patients were more numerous than all others. Three teams of nurses gave injections, two in the morning and the third in the afternoon, to inpatients only. Special inns had been built outside the hospital gates for the rest. In May 1930 Herr Kornatz, the Shanghai head of the German firm importing stibosan, told Nelson that Tsingkiangpu used more of the drug than any other place in China. Kornatz, a Christian and thorough anti-Nazi, came several times. "He is awfully nice with the children and they are very fond of him." He gave Ruth a young police dog (Alsatian) named Prinz, a magnificent sable who to the Chinese looked like a wolf. He was an instinctive watch dog and became an adored pet too.

When Kornatz went on leave, he carried a film of the kala-azar work at Tsingkiangpu, whose fame thus spread to Germany. Nelson Bell became a world-renowned authority on kala-azar, and provided much material with which the British expert, Professor A. W. Woodruff, wrote the standard work on the subject. The Tsingkiangpu Hospital treated more kala-azar patients than all other hospitals in China combined and was the largest kala-azar clinic on earth. It was already the largest Presbyterian hospital in China and in a few years, with 380 beds, became the largest Presbyterian mission hospital in the world.

"With all of these blessings," Nelson Bell wrote to his mother, "I just have to pray constantly that we will not set our hearts and ambitions on the physical and material side of the work. If we can only use all of these added opportunities to win more souls to Him."

Soon after his return from furlough, Nelson had written that "the best men are now in control of the Nationalist party." Chiang Kai-shek had broken with the Communists and was trying to initiate the reforms which had been the object of the 1927 revolution. To the ordinary Chinese, however, the corruption, intrigue, and dishonesty seemed entirely unchanged. By the hindsight of several years later the victory of Chiang and the Nationalists (Kuomintang) could be seen as the faint start of better times, which might have brought lasting prosperity and peace had not the Japanese attacked; but for the present, disillusion prevented optimism. "All we can do," said Dr. Ts'ao gloomily to Nelson, "is work each day, eat, go to bed, and not worry about the future."

The situation remained very Chinese. "We can have chaos and disorder right outside our own door and yet be perfectly quiet and peaceful....It's China, not America, and what may be a perfect maelstrom of disorder today may be perfectly quiet tomorrow." And a battle could rage around the mission at Suchowfu, 150 miles to the north, while all was quiet at Tsingkiangpu.

By spring of 1930 the local garrison had been reduced from 18,000 to 500 soldiers, under the leadership of a nasty-faced colonel. Some of these tried to rob a village and were badly cut up, at which the colonel declared the villagers to be bandits and set off to wipe them out; the magistrate heard in time to stop more than one or two murders, and when he came to the hospital to visit the cut-up soldiers, he asked to speak to Nelson privately. Nelson said: "There are some mighty bad tales going around about this whole matter."

"I know it," replied the magistrate, "and that is why I want to talk with you." He told Nelson the whole story, said he was determined to punish the soldiers, and asked if he was right. Nelson warmly encouraged him and "he just took my hand and held it and the tears filled his eyes. I had a good talk with him about God and Christ."

The hordes of the bandits had gone, but Dr. Ts'ao's father-in-law was abducted and not released for weeks. The

Bells never knew when a flare-up would disturb the night. During a banquet given by the magistrate for Woods and Bell and all the Chinese educational leaders of the city, they were deafened by a sudden brief gunfight outside. Bandits still sometimes blocked the road or held up the launch on the canal. Once Nelson was asked to drive the magistrate to stop a threatened battle between a division of government soldiers and the division sent to replace them—quite like old times, for in warlord days he had saved the city from a bloody assault by acting as go-between.

In June 1930 the Bells set off down the Grand Canal for a mission meeting and a short vacation in Shanghai, "the fastest trip we ever made down. All launches carry military guards (ten armed soldiers) now, but they still tie up during most of the night. We really had little fear of being held up, although there was a possibility of it, so we all planned to lie flat on the floor the minute any shooting began. Ruth was rather hoping we would be held up for the experience.... The boat was badly infested with bedbugs, fleas, mosquitoes, and rats, and we had a pretty miserable night, especially Ruth, as she is always bitten so much worse than anyone else." They arrived in Shanghai to learn that the consul had written all Americans in North Kiangsu to evacuate immediately. However, everyone sat tight, and the scare subsided quickly.

In Nelson's eyes the American consul-general was much too quick to withdraw. During one Christmas celebration, when Tsingkiangpu and all its region lay in profound peace, the station was astounded to receive a consular wire urging instant withdrawal to the coast. "China is truly in a pitiable condition," he wrote from Tsingkiangpu in August 1930, "and unless the two contending parties can come to some agreement and stop their fighting, there will probably be worse conditions yet to come....God's promises are our protection and we are in His keeping. Frankly, I cannot tell what the future holds."

On Saturday, October 18, 1930, conditions suddenly became chaotic. "People began pouring in and the roads were full of rickshaws, barrows, and people leading animals. All who could find room stopped in Tsingkiangpu, hundreds went to Hwaian. The children climbed a tree where they could watch, and MaiMai came running to me and said, 'Daddy, the Chinese are running.' Poor things, they were so pitiful and so helpless. A large throng of bandits had been seen just across the Salt Canal and the people expected them to take that place immediately.

"We had a station prayer meeting at noon to pray for guidance. We did not want to be foolhardy, nor did we want to send the women and children away unless necessary. We decided to stay on, as we are not especially afraid of bandits. However, at clinic time Drs. Ch'ien and Ts'ao were greatly disturbed, said they had heard that the bandits called themselves the 'Twenty-seventh Red Army' and were flying red flags. They urged us to get the women and children away."

Dr. Woods drove his wife to Hwaian. Nelson finished the clinic, which was lighter than usual because of the civil disturbance combined with heavily overcast skies, while Virginia and the children got ready. But when Nelson said Virginia must remain at Hwaian when he returned to Tsingkiangpu, she refused: "Absolutely not. I'm not leaving you." The children never forgot that moment. "My mother had the attitude that wherever Daddy was, she was going to be," Rosa recalled. "So she bundled us off, with Wang NaiNai to look after MaiMai, but Mother stayed with him."

As Nelson drove back to the city in the dusk, it began to rain and poured all night. "God's way of quieting the bandits down." The dampened enemy withdrew ten miles. Government reinforcements arrived on Monday, fought a battle, and shut the enemy up in a small town with mud walls. What is more, an airplane, the first ever seen at Tsingkiangpu, arrived from Nanking and, to the amazement of the citizens, landed on a field. The plane had "quite a psychological effect" on the enemy, and an airfield was leveled a week or two later.

The girls returned from Hwaian on that Monday. That night Nelson wrote to his mother: "I look at Virginia and marvel at her courage and absolute lack of any fear. For weeks she has had the plan of keeping chloroform on hand so in case she had to hide with MaiMai, she could put her to sleep and keep her quiet. She carries on her work just as usual and is an inspiration to all."

*　*　*　*　*

Virginia's work was unending.

"I do not know what I would have done without her in the clinic," Nelson had written the year before. "She has taken all the responsibility for the women patients, and I have only had the sickest ones to treat. She has seen so many sick people and worked with Dr. Woods and myself so long she has a splendid practical idea of diseases and what to do." Her sympathy and her control of the nurses made the clinic so popular that, despite their proverbial reticence in submitting for examination or treatment, women began to outnumber men. Nelson said he would rather have Virginia in that department than another doctor.

Toward the end of 1930 a tutor, Lucy Fletcher, came from America for the Bell girls and the Talbot boys. But Virginia still had little time for relaxation, for she took on the organizing of the morning kala-azar clinic. She had servants, but at times there was enough to keep each one more than busy. Nelson wrote: "I know of no one who really is busier than she is. She is always doing something and does so much sewing for the children. She is the best manager in the mission, always thinks ahead and plans ahead. All over the mission she has the reputation for efficiency. She certainly takes time with the girls, sees that they study and that they read the best books."

There was almost always at least one house guest. Yet Virginia did not share the full health which never failed her husband, apart from occasional flu, a period of indigestion caused by strong coffee, or intermittent return of trouble from a slipped disc. Virginia's migraine headaches would not yield to treatment.

"She's a precious wife and mother and homemaker," Nelson confided to his parents after a peculiarly harrowing period in national, local, and mission affairs. "The strain of the last few months has been very hard on her, and I am afraid I have not appreciated it as fully as I should. I do hope the weather and roads will permit my taking her to

Haichow in the spring. That is her ideal trip out here, and she does enjoy Elisabeth McLauchlin and her sister Gay Currie so much and the glimpse of the mountains up there."

As for Virginia's feelings for Nelson, these are neatly summed up by a comment written in busy, crowded Tsingkiangpu while he was in Shanghai: "It is indescribably lonely when he is away." Together, they could endure anything with their usual sparkle. "Don't you worry about our living under a strain," Nelson assured his mother. "God's grace is so absolutely sufficient, and He sustains and helps in such a wonderful way and makes the problems and trials roll off without leaving a lasting impression. Passages like 'Thy youth is renewed like the eagle's' (Psalm 103:5) and 'They shall mount up with wings as eagles' (Isaiah 40:31) are so literally true.": But the strain was only too evident by the sense of relief when each crisis passed.

*   *   *   *   *

Despite the unsettled conditions of the early 1930s the Tsingkiangpu Hospital forged ahead fulfilling the role implied by its Chinese name, *Love and Mercy* or *Benevolent-Compassionate*.

It now had three Chinese and three American doctors. Norman Patterson spent six months on the medical side and his other six on the surgical. Woods, with Dr. Ts'ao under him specializing in kala-azar, was medical chief. Over sixty, he had been returned for part-time work only, but "What he really does is a full day's work each half-day." He overtaxed his strength and was troubled by coughs and colds.

Nelson, now in his thirties, was surgical chief and also administrative superintendent, which included, until he delegated these duties a few years later, not only the bookkeeping, but admissions. He had to decide whether to admit a patient to a bed and judge what to charge. An outpatient merely paid three copper coins for a card of admission and no medical record was kept. An inpatient paid a single sum, however long his stay or expensive his treatment. Since this sum varied according to the patient's means, a jovial battle of wits always developed. Nelson must detect whether the old clothes and air of decay, the tales of woe or hungry children were genuine. An infallible guide was a glance at the feet. However torn or mildewy the garments worn to hoodwink the hospital, no Chinese would alter his footwear. Satin slippers were good for fifty dollars and bare feet a sure sign of poverty. But, Bell wrote to Benjamin Clayton, "the majority are so pitifully poor that it often makes one's heart ache to pry into conditions of poverty almost beyond description. I even found one patient's father had sold one child to secure the money to treat the other. Needless to say, I took immediate steps to get the child back which had been sold."

A Chinese nurse who later lived in Taiwan said that Dr. Bell would often pay the agreed charges out of his own pocket.

On the surgical side Bell was assisted by Dr. Ch'ien. "Dr. Ch'ien and Dr. Ts'ao are the backbone," he wrote in 1930. "I doubt if many hospitals in China have two men who fit in every particular as they do." Nelson recalled Ch'ien, who died after rough treatment from the Japanese during World War II, as "a brilliant man, a true intellectual who would have made a fine medical professor but stuck with us because I had put him through medical school. He read widely and kept abreast of world affairs. He became an elder of the church." Bell also had Eli Liu, a male graduate nurse, originally from the orphanage, who showed much aptitude in surgery. A third doctor, Li, who was a former postmaster, joined in 1929 but almost at once fell sick. He retired to his home in an unsettled part of China where he was caught in a siege and died within two months of leaving Tsingkiangpu. He was succeeded by the gentle Dr. Wu, an unusual choice in that though baptized, he was not a committed Christian; Wu soon became a very genuine one.

The nurses under Cassie Lee Oliver now included girls, although male nurses still predominated in the early 1930s, and the hospital's reputation insured a steady stream of applications for employment. Some were even written in English, but none so charming as a letter received by one

Medical staff at hospital, 1938; left to right: Drs. Gieser, Wu, Ts'ao, Woods, Koh, Ch'ien, and Bell

of Nelson's friends:

"*Most Honored Sir*: Understanding that there are several hands wanted in your honor's departments, I beg to offer you my hand.

"As to my adjustments, I appeared before the Matric. Exam. at _____ but failed, the reason for which I will describe. To begin with my writing was illegible, this was due to climatic reasons for having come from a warm into a cold climate found my fingers stiff and very disobedient to my wishes. Further I had received a great shock to my mental system in the shape of the death of my only fond brother.

"Besides most honored sir I beg to state that I am in a very uncomfortable circumstance, being sole support of my fond brother's seven issues, consisting of three adults and four adulteresses, the latter being the bane of my existence, owing to my having to support two of my own wives as well as their issues of which by God's misfortune the feminine gender predominate.

"If by wonderful good fortune these few lines meet with your benign kindness and favorable turn of mind, I the poor menial shall ever pray for the long life and prosperity as well as your honor's posthumous olive branches."

* * * * *

The hospital staff had the satisfaction of receiving continual expressions of gratitude. One day Nelson opened the local Chinese newspaper and saw a signed advertisement in the personal column: "In public and grateful acknowledgment to Dr. Bell of the Love and Mercy Hospital, who through the marvelous skill of his hands saved my wife's life." A brief description followed of an obstructed delivery, a rush to the hospital in the doctor's car, and a Caesarean in the nick of time. "Such virtue and skill on his part cannot be repaid, but I take this way of expressing my thanks through this paper that all may know."

A grateful patient sometimes had the story of his cure, his profound appreciation, and the virtues of the doctor painted on a *pien*, a big lacquered board five or six feet long and two feet broad. A *pien* would be presented ceremonially, the doctor making a little speech on his utter unworthiness of such kindness, with serving of refreshments. Silk scrolls or silver shields in a glass case became more common in the 1930s. A peasant who wished to emphasize his gratitude would ceremoniously present a few eggs or sweet potatoes or peanuts.

The wealthy parent of a boy who had been cured after months in the hospital thanked Bell in a particularly pleasing way. The boy had become most interested in the gospel, and his father invited Bell to drive over for a midday feast at which he should tell the assembled guests about Christ. He took Dr. Ts'ao and loaded the car with tracts, booklets, and New Testaments.

"I found the home I was invited to a very large one, and they had three rooms thrown together into one, with chairs and stools fixed in rows like a chapel and a rostrum and table for me, and they had invited in a big crowd to hear me preach, at least sixty. They all listened so well and I enjoyed it thoroughly." First he spoke of creation and the Creator, and then how Jesus Christ, the Creator of the world, came back to redeem it for Himself. "The whole process of redemption was very familiar to them," he commented, "not only because they had pawnshops, but also because many of them had had to redeem loved ones by paying ransom to bandits." He ended by explaining personal faith in Christ and urging that each should accept Him. "They were respectful," he recalled forty years later, "and unquestionably some were deeply moved." Host and guests begged the doctor to come again, often, but since their town lay near Hwaian he referred them to Jim Montgomery.

Even a surgeon as organized as Nelson Bell could not give as much time to direct evangelism as he could wish. Christopher Willis of the Shanghai Christian Bookroom later said: "I do not recall any other missionary who worked in such a systematic way, or who accomplished so much in one day, as Dr. Bell, who always knew exactly what he wanted and how he wanted it prepared. Yet, he never seemed in a hurry and always had leisure for a little chat, which made him a very welcome customer." But although he squeezed seventy seconds out of every minute, he must leave many spiritual conversations to the new hospital evangelist appointed since the Elder Kao's death. Every member of the staff was aware of responsibility for the healing of the patient's whole man, not merely his body, and Nelson was never happier than when he could give the decisive word himself: such as to the young soldier brought in with a serious abdominal condition caused by an old gunshot wound. "It was a hopeless case, but I let him stay in. I taught him how to pray, and he seemed so earnest. He died last night, and one of the nurses said he went by his bed only a short time before he died and heard him praying. I have had a most peaceful feeling about him all day."

Or there was the educated young man in his mid-twenties with sarcoma: one of his eyes stuck out like an orange.

Nelson asked him to wait in a little room, and after clinic went to see him alone: "It might have been one of the Chinese doctors or evangelists, but in this case I was the one who talked to him. I said, 'There is nothing we can do for you. This tumor has gone too far; we cannot operate on you. But, remember this: All of us are going to die. And the big question for all of us is, Where will we be after we die?' And then, as simply as I could, I told him the story of Christ, of God's Son coming and dying for our sins." The young man went home with a pile of books and a New Testament. Two months later he came back to the clinic, "and by that time the tumor was as large as his head; it was a fearful looking thing. My heart sank and I thought, *he's still coming back hoping that we can do something for him.* So we sent him to the little room, and I sat down and talked to him. And he said, 'I haven't come back here to ask you to treat me, but I have come back to tell you that I now have accepted Jesus Christ as my Savior, and I have peace in my heart. And I know I am not going to live much longer, but when I die I am going to be with Him.'"

Sometimes the seed bore remarkable harvest. In 1930 an inveterate gambler and opium smoker, despised by his neighbors as a very dreg of humanity, although he had come from a good family, entered the hospital for heart trouble. He left cured in body and saved in soul. As the years went by, news trickled in that he was always telling people about Christ. By the outbreak of the Japanese war a church of fifty met in his village, hitherto without one Christian, and in January 1938 he visited the hospital and went to the prayer meeting. "The minute he opened his mouth," wrote Bell, "I felt, 'Here is a man who is constantly talking with God.'"

Bell and his colleagues all noted an unprecedented openness to the gospel in these years of the early thirties. "The opportunity is simply wonderful and the average patient so very responsive," Bell reported in 1931. It was so in the countryside and in the jail visitation; on the Grand Canal in the spring of 1931 Bell was actually asked by the launch officials to preach to the other passengers.

Into this atmosphere of growing acceptance Bell brought the young Andrew Gih.

Virginia—age two-and-a-half

Jimmy and Sophie Graham with Chinese hospital evangelists

17
"An Interesting Mixture"

ANDREW GIH was then twenty-nine. Once virulently anti-Christian, he was already famous in China as an evangelist. Bell secured his services at short notice, and Gih brought his Bethel Band of five for a packed ten days during January 1931.

"We have fallen in love with these people," Nelson wrote. "Such evidence of complete filling of the Holy Spirit and such power in preaching and teaching." Philip Lee, only nineteen, who played the piano, cornet, and harp and sang tenor later became an assistant pastor in Honolulu. The two young women and another young man remained in China after 1949. Andrew Gih became well-known in America, Britain, and Southeast Asia for his convention ministry and for his evangelism among overseas Chinese. In 1931 Nelson Bell described him as "one of the most Spirit-filled and powerful preachers I ever heard. He simply makes people look into their hearts, see their sins, and confess them to the Lord. They are all so humble and so confident in the Lord's power....They have made a profound impression here and I hope and pray will win many souls to Christ and quicken and help all of us Christians."

Dr. Bell was so patently thrilled by the campaign's effect on the nurses that they, as Andrew Gih recalled, "were greatly surprised, and blessed God." The new doctor, Wu, confessed Christ for the first time; the Bells' old teacher, Kang, who had wandered from active loyalty to Christ, openly returned; Yang Er, now promoted to be the Bells' cook, who had attended family prayers for seven years, applied to join the church soon after and was admitted by the session that Easter.

Rosa and Ruth had "just begged and coaxed and pleaded so we could go to the meetings." Rosa was turning thirteen. "One night," related Rosa, "I felt the Lord really speaking to my heart all through Andrew Gih's message—though I don't remember the message, and it was in Chinese too. At the close of the meeting he invited any in the congregation who would like to dedicate their life to the Lord to come forward. I went forward, and that's when I really stepped out for the Lord, and that's when my battles began....As soon as Satan really knows you've stepped over on the Lord's side, he starts in with his obstacles on the path, and he's been hot and heavy with them right on down through the years." And in overcoming them, her father helped without obtruding, "primarily by being himself; just being what he was spoke a lot louder than anything else. And the things of the Lord were always first in the home and in the family."

Thus Andrew Gih had a direct influence on the Bells. The two elder girls could still scrap, but they had true *ai shin* for each other, a typical Chinese expression best translated by the phrase which Nelson often used when signing letters to his parents: "with a *heart full of love.*"

Rosa at thirteen looked more like sixteen and was the more studious of the two. "Ruth is growing fast," her mother wrote, "is still somewhat scatterbrained, but *learning.*" Ruth was sensitive and never liked to be far from her parents. She was not robust, but she had a passion for martyrdom, Rosa recalled, and "used to pray every night that the Lord would let her be a martyr before the end of the year. She wanted to be captured by bandits and beheaded, killed for Jesus' sake. And I thought, *Oh, horrid.* So every night when she prayed like that, I would pray, 'Lord, don't You listen to her.'"

Then in 1931 a young man from distant, scarcely known Tibet came to the hospital, passed on by the kala-azar research station which the government had recently set up in Tsingkiangpu. He had heard the name of Jesus but had never seen a Bible or heard a sermon. Almost the first day he bought a Bible. The result was miraculous. Nelson said he had never seen in China such complete transformation of heart and mind in so short a time. The Tibetan begged for baptism because he was returning to Tibet. The session gave him a grueling examination; he was baptized and left for Nanking and faraway, lonely, mountainous Tibet which had few Christians and no missionaries.

Ruth determined to grow up to be a pioneer to Tibet, an old-maid missionary. This was no passing whim; it became a deep, settled aim. Rosa thought her too frail, but Ruth persisted until ten years later she nearly broke off her engagement to Billy Graham, who had not received similar guidance.

*   *   *   *   *

Her father recalled the Ruth of childhood as "an interesting mixture of deep spirituality and mischievous fun." Rosa and Ruth were very much children. They swam and played pirates with the Talbot boys and had a tree house built in one of the mulberry trees. Nelson organized them into "Camp Fire Scouts." Young Bill Talbot, who had already decided to follow the profession of his hero "Uncle" Nelson (he later became a pathologist), recalled the scouting vividly. "Uncle Nelson had us memorize the Scout oath and the Scout laws. I remember especially the time when he laid out a trail to be followed. He did this by dropping small pieces of paper at intervals. This trail took us out through the farms and country villages which were nearby. We went by ourselves, and this was a completely new experience, inasmuch as we had always been accompanied by an adult whenever we left the mission compounds."

The girls kept pigeons, magpies, and "a pair of canaries," and Ruth was given a baby turtle which soon outwitted her. But best of all was Tar Baby.

Tar Baby, or T. B. for short, was a black puppy, one of two born to the Montgomery dog. "It is only a mongrel, but as far as Ruth is concerned it is the most beautiful dog in the world," Nelson related. Unfortunately T. B. did not grow up missionary hearted. She was inclined to chase the Chinese, and Prinz would run and catch her by the scruff of the neck. Not that young Prinz was blameless at that time himself: "One of his favorite pastimes is to grab hold of the clothes of some bound-foot woman and drag her off the walk. We are rushing out of the door all during the day rescuing someone."

After some months Ruth noticed that T. B. was fatter and less fierce and suddenly, intense excitement: "We have ten dogs. T. B. added eight puppies to the family this morning," Virginia told her mother-in-law. "MaiMai and Ruth are spellbound with delight; I am spellbound, but not with delight." Nelson added: "The children just hang around the box and watch them. Virginia says she never expected to have a dog farm."

A month later T. B. bit the housewoman's grown-up son, the first real bite. In that particular instance Virginia found it "hard to feel other than indifferent, as I have always detested her son. The dog has had anti-rabies treatment so I guess the man will soon be all right."

But T. B. was becoming a menace, and on February 22, 1931, Nelson had to put her to sleep with chloroform; if he gave her away, she would be mistreated. "I did not tell Ruth until it was all over, and she was awfully sweet about it; said she was glad I had done it. She wants her buried here in the yard where she can put flowers on the grave. She is such a tender-hearted little thing."

But, as Ruth later commented, children see the same thing differently from grownups. "When T. B. died it was my first real heartbreak. I doubt if there is any suffering more intense than a child's. T. B. was my first great love, and to me she was the most beautiful dog in the whole world. I used to tell her my troubles and she would listen intently, her brown eyes full of sympathetic interest, and she never betrayed a confidence. I was aware of the hostility toward her on the part of some of the Chinese and even some of the missionaries, and I overheard from time to time disparaging remarks about her. But it only made me love her the more. My love for her and hers for me was a very important thing at that time of my life."

As for Prinz, Ruth had resented him at first, the handsome, sweet-tempered thoroughbred whom everyone contrasted favorably with the nondescript T. B., but she soon loved him deeply also. He grew up the devoted friend and protector of all the household, fierce only to intruders. Ruth was his primary loyalty. "When we played tag, he would chase whoever was chasing me, grab them by the arm, and pull them to the ground. On one occasion when Mother sent the nurse out to the sand pile to get MaiMai, who did not happen to want to come in, Prinz got between her and the nurse and would not let the nurse get near her."

When the Bells returned to Tsingkiangpu after a trip of lengthy absence, as soon as they entered the yard the well-scrubbed Prinz would "run nearly wild, jumping up and kissing one and all, then would run wildly around the yard, yelping and jumping, then back again to jump up on someone." He lived until 1938, longer than most foreign dogs do in China, dying after a short illness. "We all feel like a member of the family has gone."

18
Reinforcement and Tragedy, 1931

A T the end of Norman Patterson's year of internship he and Athalie were accepted by the SPM for permanent service and assigned to his parents' station, Sutsien, where the American doctor had died. Colleagues who had been a trifle green-eyed when Tsingkiangpu acquired an intern admired Bell's willingness to finance and train a man yet not hang on to him.

Nelson's next proposed intern withdrew on health grounds, though the gap was partially closed by the arrival of a laboratory technician in April 1931, Elinor Myers, who afterward married Dr. Woods's son, Russell. Her salary and travel expenses were met by Mr. Clayton. Then, in late August 1931, the young, newly qualified Dr. Kirk Mosley of New Orleans and his bride, Corinne, a trained nurse, reached China on a three-year contract under the Benjamin Clayton Fund.

Dr. Mosley soon had to revise his ideas of missionaries and mission hospitals. "The North Kiangsu Mission was having its annual meeting in Shanghai," he recalled. "I was awestruck, not only by Dr. Bell, but by all of the missionaries for their deep conviction, often at cross-purpose with one another, on the vital issues of the day. I wondered how the mission could be a cohesive force with the missionaries in what seemed to be such profound disagreement. I soon discovered that though they spoke openly and frankly and with deep feeling, it was never with rudeness or in a vindictive manner. After a session ended there was a spirit of brotherly love and fellowship among the whole group which was more obvious and abiding than their sharp criticism of each others' views."

That particular mission meeting had to deal with a serious crisis of principle which will be discussed in the next chapter. Dr. Mosley could know nothing of the situation but admired his new colleagues' firm belief in heart and mind "about their service for the Lord and what was right in their understanding of God's will; and their willingness, even among their peers, to be singled out and be subject to criticism. This readiness to champion and proclaim his deep conviction about God's work and God's purpose characterizes Nelson Bell."

Dr. Mosley continued: "After leaving Shanghai, we began our journey to Tsingkiangpu with the Bell family—Nelson, Virginia, Rosa, Ruth, and MaiMai. While crossing the Yangtze River, Dr. Bell pointed out that the dangers of a small boat in such a mighty stream crowded with sampans, junks of all descriptions, boats, large ships, and ocean freighters might be compared to the way of life. There were recognizable dangers on all sides, as well as hidden dangers from partially submerged logs and debris. Nelson reminded us that the dangers in life are just as great, numerous, and threatening; only God's love can protect us in carrying out God's purpose in our lives. This complete trust in God's purpose for his life characterizes Nelson Bell and accounts for his confident attitude toward life."

Tsingkiangpu Hospital was a shock to the young physician who had just completed his medical training at one of the outstanding medical institutions where all the equipment, facilities, and services were available for the best possible modern medical care of patients. His initial impression was of a badly equipped and meagerly furnished hospital which did not seem capable of rendering much in the way of medical care, good or bad. This impression quickly and completely changed. "I discovered the high quality of medical care given to patients, and more important, the outstanding quality of care from the sociological and psychological point of view. All this care was undergirded by a spiritual concern which made the sick person not simply a patient but a fellow human being with a soul in need of healing. The management and administration of the hospital, with its large outpatient service, were most remarkable. It was here that I became keenly aware of Nelson as a surgeon. Sound judgment blended with skill, ingenuity, and imagination replaced most adequately the sophisticated equipment and the modernized facilities found in hospitals in the United States. The surgical service was heavy and included a large variety of cases, and the surgical skill of Dr. Bell was well-known throughout the region."

Writing nearly forty years later, Dr. Mosley described the mission stations as unusual "because of the unusual people there, particularly the senior missionaries: the James Woodses, the James Grahams, and the Talbots. The unique experience of working closely with this inspired group was a spiritual stimulation rarely found today. They were gentle yet determined, friendly, firm, and steadfast, generous yet careful and conservative, dedicated yet fun-loving. The tennis games, Rook parties, long walks in the countryside, dips in the pool, birthday parties, daily family prayers, and weekly prayer meetings were a way of life and living of this community of people who truly enjoyed their work in the name of the Lord and felt secure and content in His love and care."

Bell and the other missionaries were equally impressed with the Mosleys. "An *unusually* nice boy, a real Christian. He has such a nice face and is rather quiet; he is studious and also has lots of fun in him," Bell wrote, soon finding him a good, careful doctor as well. "She is just as lively as you please and very attractive and will be a hard worker."

The Mosleys had hardly arrived when the mission station was rocked by tragedies.

The summer of 1931 had been appalling for China because of floods after heavy rains. The Yangtze had overflowed at Hankow, in central China, creating a disaster area which brought international aid. Nearer home the banks of the Grand Canal broke at Sutsien, and by early August the two ancient bridges at Tsingkiangpu were under water and the new foreign-built bridge awash. When the whole Bell family started down the canal for Shanghai on August 24, the west bank was already partially flooded, yet crowded with refugees. A typhoon whirled in the neighborhood, and four hours after the Bells had passed, the bank broke in thirteen places. They knew nothing of this at the time, but four hours later they would all have drowned, for nothing could have saved a launch in such a catastrophe: the force of the water created a lake 150 miles long and 100 miles wide.

Seven million people were homeless in North Kiangsu, and in Kirk Mosley's early days the Tsingkiangpu Hospital undertook relief work planned by Woods and equipped by Bell with a hired steam launch.

"The cabin on the launch is small," Bell wrote, "and I found to my sorrow last night that it is also infested with bedbugs. Our plan is to go down the canal for fifty miles or so, putting out notices each three or four miles that we will stop there on our return, then come back and treat all sick. Malaria and dysentery will probably be the chief things we will find. It will also be a wonderful opportunity for preaching and giving away tracts and selling Gospel portions. These people come from sections of the back country along the canal where there is practically no Christian work being done, and I feel this opportunity is really a God-sent one."

Soon the disasters became more personal as tragedy piled on tragedy that fall of 1931. Cassie Lee Oliver, the head nurse, developed tuberculosis. The Bells rigged up a place for her on a summer sleeping porch, and thanks to her indomitable spirit and Virginia's care, she recovered; but the tuberculosis infected one of the Bells, though not disclosing itself for two years.

On Monday, October 26, when Nelson was thoroughly enjoying himself operating, using a new spinal anesthetic, a code wire came which, when decoded, told that a friend from another mission station, who was loved by the mission workers and Chinese alike was critically ill. Two days later her stricken husband wired that she had died. As soon as he could get away he left to console his friend. As Nelson's friend put it: "Nelson, more than a hundred miles away, dropped his medical work and rushed down through dangerous ways; he came to wrap his arms of love about his brother and close friend. You don't forget such understanding. Here was Christian fellowship beyond its mere conventional expression. A good physician and friend *would* be there at such a time, not just with his medical kit, but with his love."

Then one of the male nurses came running from the other compound with news that Uncle Jimmy Graham's house, empty during furlough, had been surrounded by soldiers and three kidnapped children discovered. Another nurse followed hard on the heels of the first to say that hordes of angry citizens were looting.

Bell sent his card by a nurse, who was a fast runner, to the nearest police station and went up there the back way. "The back gate was locked," he wrote, "but I could see through the cracks that there were hundreds of people inside. I kicked the hinges off the gate and went in and chased the entire lot out and fastened the front gate. By that time police were there in force. It seems that a few days ago several bandits were caught here by Hwaian militia, and under the thumbscrews they told of these three children hidden. These Hwaian police came here without warrant and took the place and found the three children buried in a hole inside a small outhouse in the Grahams' yard." The gateman was plainly guilty of harboring and his son-in-law was suspected as a bandit.

The house had not, in fact, been entered by the crowds, only by the police, and the Grahams sustained no loss except a broken window. But any Chinese owning a house where hostages were discovered could normally expect to be tortured by the police, if not executed, and for a few days the missionaries were a little nervous of repercussions. Their reputation, however, was solid. Even anti-foreign agitators did not attempt to whip up feeling, and the magistrate contented himself with lopping off the heads of the Graham gateman and two accomplices.

In the middle of a night that same week another wire arrived: "Jack Vinson carried off by bandits."

"Uncle Jack" of Haichow, a widower, was a great favorite throughout the mission and among the Chinese, not the least because he never let constant pain interfere with his itinerating. He had intended coming to the Bells for the previous Christmas until prevented by an unexpected claim of duty. "You are *all* such a sweet happy lot," he wrote, when sending the little presents he had intended to bring, "you and those three sweet daughters of yours....I am very, very fond of each one of you."

Vinson, only three weeks out of the hospital after an operation, had been visiting his country churches when he was caught in a bandit raid and carried off with the Christians and other townsfolk after the place had been sacked. A government force chased the bandits. Besieged in another small town, they offered Vinson his freedom if he would persuade this force to withdraw. When they would not promise to release every captive, he refused. The bandits tried to break out and many were killed. The survivors fled with Vinson and a few other captives, but Vinson could not run because of his operation, so one bandit shot him and another beheaded him.

Among the townsfolk rescued by government troops was the small daughter of a Chinese pastor. She told how earlier she had seen Vinson threatened by a bandit with a revolver: "I'm going to kill you! Aren't you afraid?"

"No, I am not afraid," Vinson had replied. "If you kill me, I will go right to God."

The death of a missionary who had refused to save himself created a great impression among pagans and Christians alike, and when E. H. Hamilton ("Ham") heard the story after emerging from another bandit-infested area, he wrote his well-known poem, "Afraid? Of What?" which was later to strengthen John and Betty Stam before their martyrdom and encourage many others facing death. The poem has been translated into Chinese and other languages and set to music:

Afraid? Of What?
To feel the spirit's glad release?
To pass from pain to perfect peace,
The strife and strain of life to cease?
Afraid—of that?

Afraid? Of What?
Afraid to see the Savior's face

To hear his welcome, and to trace
The glory gleam from wounds of grace?
Afraid—of that?

Afraid? Of What?
A flash, a crash, a pierced heart;
Darkness, light, O Heaven's art!
A wound of His a counterpart!
Afraid—of that?

Afraid? Of What?
To do by death what life could not—
Baptize with blood a stony plot,
Till souls shall blossom from the spot?
Afraid—of that?

Nelson wrote on December 30, 1931: "Truly, we have been hit hard this fall, but we still have the assurance that God only permits these things in love, and we know that *all* things work together for those who love the Lord." At the next mission meeting Nelson Bell was one of those who spoke at the memorial services held for the two who had died suddenly that November. He sought to show how the one was a martyr as much as the other: "He, a victim of the dangers all itinerating missionaries face; she, the victim of the dangers of all who stay at home, surrounded by heathenism in all its awful aspects."

* * * * *

The remarkable progress at Tsingkiangpu, like that of other Christian missions and the whole church in China, was now threatened from several directions, including political turmoil that gripped the country.

The defeated Communists had not abandoned their aim of gaining the country. Their most successful thrusts came through agitation among students who in many parts of China were behaving like the Red Guards of the 1960s, taking over schools, forcing their wishes on magistrates, and even toppling Chiang Kai-shek for a brief period.

The long-term plans of the Communist opposition could be offset if Generalissimo Chiang succeeded in stabilizing and reforming the country, removing the abuses and inequalities which bred Communism. He had been baptized a Christian in October 1931, a courageous step which did him no good politically. But Chiang's hope of remaking China was imperiled by the Japanese.

In September 1931 the Japanese occupied Manchuria on a trumped-up excuse. "Naturally, the Chinese are much worked up over the affair," Nelson wrote, "and there is great indignation. As is usual, when they get in trouble, they turn to America and look for help, and they are now making a great capital of America's friendship. Some of them said the other day, if England or America had done this, they would not worry, as they knew we had hearts and consciences, but they feared Japan. Dr. Woods remarked that they look on England and America as two old women they can bulldoze, but they know Japan is a rough customer." England, America, and the League of Nations responded to China's pleas by the first of the supine appeasements which were to lead to the Second World War.

China saved herself by her own exertions during the next Japanese aggression, the brutal attack in Shanghai in February 1932, which for a short while looked like the start of a full-scale Sino-Japanese war. Some of the SPM stations had to evacuate, but the missionaries of Tsingkiangpu, after full discussion, stayed where they were. Corinne Mosley said to Virginia, "You all know much more about conditions than we do, and when we see you are not disturbed, why should we be?"

Nelson was certain that fighting would break out again and that Japanese pressure "may throw China into more and more chaos." Indeed, the chaos seemed unending. One summer evening in 1932, after a mutiny at nearby Hwaian and news of the Communist capture of faraway Changsha, Virginia and Nelson were sitting out on the porch after supper. Virginia said: "It is hard to realize, with the peace and quiet here in our own yard, how completely surrounded we are by chaos and general lawlessness." As Nelson commented to his mother: "Humanly speaking, this is no place to be in now, but when we look at God's promise and when He so plainly leads us here and opens the way for us to carry on our work as He is, why should we be fearful and afraid? It is wonderful how peaceful He permits us to feel."

And there were other, more subtle dangers. One was a loss of nerve among supporters in America which was sliding deeper into the Great Depression. Cuts in stipend and appropriations were partially offset by a more favorable rate of exchange, but the SPM board ordered furloughs to be postponed, which Nelson considered a danger to health and efficiency. And they stopped sending out new missionaries just when the response to Christianity in China was warmer than ever before.

A greater danger came from a movement to alter the entire purpose of Christian missions. Between 1931 and 1933 Nelson Bell found himself engaged in two controversies. The principles debated remain extraordinarily relevant, for they go to the root of matters which do not change in substance, however much they may change in detail. The actual issues in North Kiangsu are a matter of history, but the principles behind them concern the eternal purpose of Christian evangelism.

There were two controversies, one local and one more general and spread over a longer period. They are best considered together.

Kirk and Corinne Mosley

19
What Is the
Missionary Aim?

THE new Nationalist government had laid down a new educational policy. To qualify as an accredited institution which could award degrees, diplomas, or certificates, every college and school must register with the Ministry of Education. Once registered, its constitution could be altered at will by the government, regardless of the aims and principles of founders or supporters.

Almost all such institutions in China were missionary foundations, yet the new decree stated categorically that a registered school must not teach the Bible or the Christian religion except as an optional extra. And every Monday morning all students and staff must hold a ceremony before a portrait of Dr. Sun Yat-sen, the late president. It was this requirement, more than any other, which bothered strong Chinese Christians. Nelson Bell explained in a letter to his mother: "I can conceive of intelligent Chinese going through the ceremony with only thoughts of honoring a great national hero; but the trouble is that the background of the Chinese people as a whole is one of idolatry, and to most of them they are actually worshiping his picture—just as they worship the picture or tablets of their ancestors. It is closely allied with ancestor worship." (The same issue later brought persecution to Japanese Christians who would not bow to the emperor's picture.)

These anti-Christian conditions produced a dilemma for Christian missions. Some of them registered their schools; some closed them. Some withdrew support from institutions of higher education which were virtually compelled to register or disappear. The SPM decided not to register: their missionaries were in China not merely to educate but to evangelize and to train Christian leaders. The SPM's Mid-China Mission, however, had a share in a college which registered, and also voted to register one of their own high schools.

The North Kiangsu Mission, on the other hand, deplored the Mid-China actions and warmly approved the policy of the parent body in Nashville. The Tsingkiangpu schools shut down, giving Bell his providential space for kala-azar patients. At one SPM station the schools managed to continue unregistered and unhindered until the government ordered that every secondary school in the land must register, with all that this implied, or close by July 31, 1931.

This order brought a new crisis.

The Chinese pastor and elders in this particular station proposed to register, but they could not do so without a majority vote of the North Kiangsu Mission.

Tsingkiangpu was up in arms at once. "If," Bell stated, "we must relegate the worship of God and the teaching of His Word to a secondary place, what justification do we have for running these schools? It is not our duty to bring secular education to the Chinese." The Tsingkiangpu Chinese were right behind their Americans. Pastor Kao said he would rather his son be a mason or carpenter "than go to a school where Dr. Sun is worshiped and the Bible put out." Dr. Ch'ien, whose own brother was one of the agitators for registration at the station in question, said: "The arguments against registration of our schools under present conditions are simply unanswerable. There is only one thing to do: close the schools; then open institutions for one purpose only—the teaching of characters and the Bible."

Nelson Bell was determined not to compromise, even at the cost of hard feelings. "I had rather resign from the mission than permit such a thing to be, for it means denying God and His Word as the primary motive of our educational work." He sent a long personal reply to the leading American exponent of registration: "I don't think that in my whole life I have ever prayed more earnestly and continually than I have since receiving your letter Saturday night. . . . You urge strongly the need felt by the Chinese for Christian schools to which they may send their children. No one sympathizes with them in this more than I do. But compromising the very foundations of our school work to make possible a continuation of these schools can never be justified because of the need. Not only so, but I firmly believe that such a school will prove a *menace* to the future of the church, and to the very parents who now desire it for their children, because it will be founded on a denial of God and His Word as the primary aim of Christian education. Far better to send their children to an avowedly heathen institution than to heathen schools posing in the guise of Christian."

Bell's letter did not change its recipient's mind, but the schools closed on July 31. The matter was placed on the agenda for the September meeting of the North Kiangsu Mission of the SPM. Nelson, as he wrote to a colleague on August 12, felt "we are facing the crisis of our mission and we must stand firm or start in for chaos and futility." Even the most ardent advocates of registration admitted that registered colleges and high schools soon lost their distinctive Christian character, yet money was poured into them while countryside evangelism was cut back through lack of funds. "It seems to many of us a direct misappropriation of funds."

The Bells traveled to Shanghai in September 1931—it was the time they just missed being drowned by the bursting of the canal banks—and the matter was fully debated, with no holds barred, at the mission meeting which so impressed the newly arrived Kirk Mosley. The dissenting station lost its case, but by no means accepted defeat. At the next mission meeting, held in May 1932 at Tsingkiangpu because communications with Shanghai were disrupted, thirteen Chinese of its presbytery's school board came too. They and their missionary backers wanted the mission to donate the buildings, staff, and the annual grant from America to the presbytery. The presbytery would then found a new school which would register, and the SPM would save face because the registered school did not belong to them.

This suggested a typical Chinese compromise, put up with a blandness which ignored a previous refusal at Shanghai to grant that very request.

Bell and his colleagues dealt with it in a way the Chinese could understand. Bell announced a feast, and the delegates knew that at the end of a long morning's session they would be served a delicious meal. In this atmosphere of hospitality they presented their argument to those who must vote on it. Then Bell made a long speech on "Why I cannot agree to your proposition."

This talk in Chinese in a faraway city in 1932 has not lost its point, for in the light of subsequent history a strong case may be made that Christian missions which compromised on education did a grave disservice to China or to any country.

He began: "I cannot agree because, first, the church in all nations is now being tested, and God is using this particular test in China. To agree would be to follow the way of the world, away from Him. Secondly, because the Bible, the Sword of the Spirit, should be in front of us as our active agent for Christian warfare. In a registered school not only is it forbidden in front, it must be *behind,* and not only behind, but it must be *hidden.* Thirdly, because the name of Christ must be excluded from the school in every way. This is of Satan, as he hates that Name above all others."

Bell next mentioned the Sun Yat-sen ceremony and the other snags which entangled a registered school. "Church history shows that each age has its testing and that whenever the church has compromised with the world, it has suffered loss of power and usefulness, but wherever it has resisted, even to persecution and death, it has been blessed of God."

He concluded: "Most of your arguments are based on the statement, *Muh yu fah tse* ('There is nothing else to do'). You will ask me, 'If we do not register, what can we do? How can we educate our children?' My answer is that I do not know. But this I do know: when we commit our way to God, He opens the way for us; and when we open our own way, it is the wrong way. God is able to provide for you, if you will trust Him. The children of Israel came to the Red Sea and their cause looked hopeless, with the hosts of Egypt behind, the mountains on the side, and the sea in front, but 'God opened the way.'"

Bell's gift of putting strong arguments in a spirit of love, so that clarity did not extinguish charity, won the day. During the silence which pervades a Chinese feast, except for the sound of chopsticks speeding from bowl to mouth, the dissenting delegates grew content. They withdrew their petitions with genuine courtesy and went away happy.

*   *   *   *   *

Behind this crisis lay a second problem: whether missionary buildings and funds should be turned over to the Chinese. A National Christian Council pamphlet had already made such a demand of all missions, even adding that Chinese would be sent to America and Britain to sit on home committees or boards.

Nelson Bell believed that to keep a church subsidized from foreign funds was to keep it weak. He was all for an indigenous church, self-supporting and self-propagating under national leadership. He had written in May 1931 that the real trouble was that the Chinese would not be able to take hold "as fast as we are willing to let go." The indigenous program had proved highly effective in Korea and was the SPM aim, though around Tsingkiangpu the mission still paid and chose many of the country preachers. Some of them, in Bell's view, were not chosen by the Holy Spirit: they thus proved failures. The church in Tsingkiangpu had supported itself for years and was self-governing; it set such a high spiritual value on membership that in April 1932 nearly one hundred applied but only eight were admitted after oral examination by the session. Even the gentle Dr. Wu had to apply several times.

But to hand over Western-built hospitals and schools to Chinese control seemed a sure way to ruin the church and squander the resources. A missionary hospital had been founded for the benefit of all the people in its region, not to provide income and power for local Christians. Moreover, when Bell had gone on long vacations to Kuling in earlier days, the work had dropped, and although he now had a devoted staff, they worked best under Western leadership, especially in any crisis. The Great Evacuation had proved them steadfast; yet when Bell returned in 1928 they were only too thankful.

Bell's policy certainly paid off, for Tsingkiangpu survived when several hospitals failed after the missionaries were interned or expelled by the Japanese in 1941. His policy cannot be judged by attitudes of independence which arose throughout Asia during World War II. In the 1930s, when the West still ruled India and much of Asia, when the "White Man's Burden" was an accepted political doctrine, and when China still struggled in chaos, Bell was right.

*   *   *   *   *

However, a far wider controversy agitated Christian missions at this time.

A commission of American laymen, under the chairmanship of the eminent Harvard philosopher, William E. Hocking, decided to investigate American overseas missions. The members of this Laymen's Foreign Missions Inquiry were theologically liberal, rather than conservative, and most were modernists, at a period when modernism leaned toward extreme doctrines of human goodness which proved untenable in the upheavals and horrors of World War II.

First they sent out a fact-finding group. Medical missions in China were the responsibility of Dr. William G. Lennox, whom Bell described as "a capable and experienced physician and statistician." He did this work responsibly but was allowed too short a time: he visited only some thirty out of over two hundred hospitals. Tsingkiangpu was not one of them. His report, however, was fair.

Next a Commission of Appraisal swept into Shanghai in November 1930. It included two well-known physicians, one of whom had previous experience with China. These sent out a voluminous questionnaire, but many of the questions were loaded or required more work than busy doctors could give in the brief time permitted. They visited several hospitals on the coast between Canton and Shanghai, a few in the Yangtze valley, and some on the railway between Nanking and Peking.

The Laymen's report, *Rethinking Missions,* appeared with much sensational press publicity in the fall of 1932 and went through ten editions in six months. Missionary doctors were astonished and distressed to read: "The impression gained from our study of the clinical work of American missions in the Orient was in general one of disappointment." The book offered, as "the story of a typical American mission hospital," a highly imaginative and fictional account of a foolish do-gooder who single-handedly sees "five hundred or even a thousand outpatients in one morning, too many of whom leave with a good Bible text and the wrong medicine. Correct diagnoses are not attempted; important early diseases—cancer, tuberculosis, and the like—are overlooked."

To read such rubbish while sitting in a highly organized office of a very efficient hospital like Tsingkiangpu would have been amusing were it not for the certainty that uninformed people in America would assume a basis in fact, since the book was issued by men of prestige. Medical missions appeared to be a poor use of money in the Great Depression.

Nelson Bell took up his pen on behalf of less articulate brethren.

He wrote to the two medical members of the Commission of Appraisal to ask how many mission hospitals they had seen in China. Dr. Emerson replied that while he had no list at hand, "Dr. Lennox, Dr. Houghton, or myself visited every American-supported hospital in China, as well as many others." Since Tsingkiangpu had seen nothing of them, Bell decided to do a little research. He sent out a questionnaire and made the surprising discovery that a maximum of forty out of a possible 220 hospitals had been investigated and that visits by Houghton or Emerson were hurried, sometimes even a quick half-hour between trains. Nor did the generalizations of *Rethinking Missions* represent the findings of Dr. Lennox. In instance after instance (which would be wearisome to give in detail over half a century later) Bell was able to show that Lennox's accuracies had been ignored in favor of wild statements. Bell concluded that the medical section of the book "was not scientifically prepared, nor was it factually based."

By pamphlet and article Bell made his point that the commission had come out to the Orient with its mind made up, determined not to be confused with facts. The members deplored evangelical Christianity and did not extend to it the tolerance they urged for non-Christian religions. They deplored evangelism. One of their four principles ran: "The use of medical or other professional service as a direct means of making converts, or public services in wards and dispensaries from which patients cannot escape, is subtly coercive and improper." Bell's private comments on that principle had to be wrapped in asbestos lest they set his paper on fire, while even the Chinese Medical Association, which included all shades of Christian opinion, was surprised to find the report "harking back to a view rapidly becoming discredited that healing methods should in most cases be purely physical ones."

In a letter to the *North China Daily News* (signed "Upcountry"), Bell pointed out that the commissioners were, in effect, urging missionaries merely to feed the prodigal son in the far country, disinfect his hogs, and whitewash the sty.

The Laymen's Foreign Missions Inquiry claimed that the chief concern of missions should be humanitarian since "man is not eternally lost because he knows not Christ." This philosophy grew out of a low view of the Bible, a high view of the great non-Christian religions, and a thorough distaste for the cross of Christ except as a deathless example.

Bell had already fought hard against such modernism, which had its echoes in some other missions, though not in North Kiangsu, where the SPM members held to a common sense conservatism, true to Scripture but free from the harsh rigidity of some of the conservatives of the day in America. Bell did not side-step personal controversy. Indeed, one of his friends feared Bell grilled a suspected modernist too vigorously; the man seemed visibly embarrassed. But the friend discovered that his fears were groundless: "Nelson could criticize a person to his face and show him where he was wrong but do it in such a loving way that there was no feeling of bitterness."

Bell followed closely the course of the modernist-conservative controversy which was shaking America. He was particularly impressed with the scholarly stand of a new paper called *Christianity Today.* The original magazine of that name did not exist for long, but Bell stored the title in his mind for future use.

He was also strengthened in his own convictions by a visit to Korea.

The Bells had decided not to send Rosa to the American high school in Shanghai, feeling some of its faculty were infected by too-liberal views. They chose instead the foreign school run by Presbyterians at Pyengyang (now Pyongyang) in northern Korea. The Bells all went down to Shanghai, and Nelson took Rosa via Japan in September 1932, returning by train through Japanese-occupied Manchuria. Pyengyang was then one of the world's most Christian cities. The tragedy of North Korea lay fourteen years in the future. No one knew in 1932 that the Red Army would pour across the frontier a few days before the Japanese surrender of 1945 to create a Communist state of North Korea, which ruthlessly exterminated, exiled, or drove underground the faithful Korean church and made Pyengyang the atheist capital.

Nelson and Rosa, leaving for her high school in Pyengyang, Korea

"The grip the gospel has gotten on that nation is simply wonderful," Bell wrote. "The Korean is generous and anxious to tell others of the Savior, and the development of their churches shows how their faithfulness is blessed." Bell returned all the more opposed to the Laymen's report and its view that the primary missionary aim is to improve the bodily and temporal conditions of the underprivileged.

Discussing the report with Benjamin Clayton, he wrote: "I am now in my seventeenth year in China, and I have seen with my own eyes the power of the gospel of Christ changing the hearts and lives of thousands of people. I see it every day and I know that it works. . . .

"It is our constant aim to help the bodies of these people all we can, using all the skill we possess and also trying to keep up with the latest developments in medicine and surgery, but we still believe the soul of the patient is infinitely precious, and it is our constant prayer that God will help us to do the best job we can on their bodies, that through this we may point them to Christ who saved us and who is so willing to save them."

*   *   *   *   *

As if the report was not enough bombardment, Christian missions in China received another broadside in the later months of 1932.

Pearl Buck had become famous for her novel *The Good Earth* in 1931. The Southern Presbyterian Mission, not realizing she no longer sympathized with her father's colleagues, sought to honor her. By her own account, she understood she was to meet a few SPM leaders at the Waldorf-Astoria in New York and therefore prepared an uncompromising, hard-hitting speech. When she discovered four hundred guests who had paid luncheon tickets to hear her in the ballroom, Mrs. Buck kept to her script and caused a sensation. She expressed the view that missionaries were ignorant, arrogant, superstitious, and crude. The speech was published in the *Literary Digest* as "Is There a Place for Foreign Missions?"

In the controversy that followed, Nelson Bell wrote an

article answering one particular point. Pearl Buck had called for an end to preaching and urged that the spirit of Christ be manifested solely by mode of life. Her sensational speech has long been forgotten, but Bell's words remain timely, especially now that church aid to underdeveloped countries is often considered to be evangelism in itself, and the beliefs of those who dispense the aid are looked upon not only as irrelevant but unmentionable.

"It is unthinkable," Bell's article runs, "that one should go as a missionary and have in one's heart the knowledge of God, His Son our Savior, and the offer which He makes of eternal life to all who believe, and then remain silent. Nor can I imagine greater conceit than to imagine that one, by one's own force of personality and attractiveness, could win one soul to Christ. God uses the witness of the Christ-like life, and there is not a missionary in China who is not praying and daily striving, by God's grace, to so live and act that He may be glorified, but the fact remains that we are told that it is the *preaching* of the Cross, the gospel of redemption from sin through faith in the shed blood of the Savior, which is the 'power of God.'"

20
Ruth Hears
a Tiny Cry

O N Tuesday, October 18, 1932, the twelve-year-old
Ruth set out with her best friend Catherine
("Sandy") Yates and their tutor Lucy Fletcher on
the daily walk along the high mud wall to the other compound, a half mile away, where lessons were held at the
girls' school building (which is still in use as a primary
school).

It was the year of the cholera which followed the famine
which followed the floods of 1931. From June to September
the Tsingkiangpu staff had been inundated with cholera
cases. They also set up an emergency hospital with a full-time
doctor at Hwaian, a prefectural city of 200,000. When Nelson
drove to and from Hwaian, people continually stopped the
Baby Austin begging him to come to their homes. In one
he found a father, mother, and a little boy at death's door;
only the daughter who had called him was well. Working in
the appalling stench inevitable in such circumstances, he
set up three sets of saline containers and valves for simul-
taneous transfusions. One of the patients needed seven
quarts of saline, taking more than two hours; meanwhile
nurses were giving transfusions in other homes. The saline
solution saved thousands of lives in the region.

The Bell children knew how much misery the epidemic
had caused, but on this October day Ruth came face to face
with a different kind of suffering.

She happened to be the first up the steep incline, and
as she stepped onto the pathway which ran along the wall,
she glanced down to the moat some fifteen or twenty feet

The school for the mission's children

below. She saw a tiny baby boy lying naked in the mud, and, Ruth wrote to Rosa at high school, "A woman standing near called to us saying, 'Alive.' So I scrambled down to where it lay and saw it breathe, then give a tiny cry, so I ran for Dr. Woods (Mother and Daddy were in Hwaian) and then came back, and Miss F. went to hurry things up a little, while I stood and fanned off the huge green flies that had settled on it by the fifties. Its eyes were open and filled with pus so that all you could see was yellow. A few rags lying by were all it had and its tiny naked body was blue from the cold." The weather had turned frosty enough for the water buffalo's hoofprints to be iced over.

"A crowd had gathered around it and as soon as Miss Fletcher came back we had to leave for school, but when we came from school we went over to the hospital to see it, and honestly! you could hardly recognize it it was so very clean, only pitifully white and thin. When it ate or drank milk it gave a wheezy cough.

"The parents were found and had evidently thrown it out as it was having convulsions and they were sure it would die, but it did not. We hoped and prayed God to let it live and yet, on the other hand, I pled with Him to take it home out of this vale of sin and tears (where the only mother it had did not care for it more than to throw it away before it died!), and He did. Friday night it fell asleep."

The pagan Chinese had a superstition that if they buried a child who had died before cutting his teeth, the evil spirits would come back and take another child. Therefore, dead babies were thrown out, a custom so common that Ruth had been very small when she saw her first dead baby. She said, "I will never forget the absolute horror of it. I couldn't sleep that night." The daily walk along the wall to school took Miss Fletcher, Sandy, and Ruth near a favorite place for throwing out dead babies, and later the children even had names for the scavenger dogs which ate the corpses: Hitler, Gorgon, and Mussolini. Another time they saw the wife of the Christian cemetery keeper feeding a baby girl she had found alive by pressing milk from her breasts into a little shell and pouring it into a mouth too weak to suck. The children took the baby to the hospital. Both parents were found to be inpatients; when the baby fell sick, too, they had supposed the hospital would turn them all out, so they threw the baby away. Rescued, it survived.

But what impressed Ruth deepest was that heathendom, in stark contrast to the kindliness of the Chinese Christians, should force parents to such action. "The parents suffer when their children die. It's not easy to take your baby out and leave it to be eaten by dogs." Once on the walk to school they passed a father carrying his child in a curious way: "We watched him, and he went down outside across the moat and out into the fields where there were grave mounds. He laid the little body down and stood beside it for awhile, then turned and walked away. That afternoon as we came back from school, the dogs were devouring the body, and we children were so angry that we yelled and shouted at the dogs. One picked up the head and went in one direction and the others dragged the body in another direction. These are among the things that stood out in my mind as a child. They help to illustrate what the Bible says: 'The tender mercies of the wicked are cruel.' I remember one time seeing a crowd of Chinese beating a mad dog to death and laughing while they did it. It contrasted so with the kindness of the Christians I knew, and it made a deep impression."

*   *   *   *   *

Hsi Si-fu had been head carpenter at the hospital for years. He was dependable, thorough, and courteous and had the abilities more of a building contractor than a mere carpenter. At present he was directing a team of assistants, including his own son, in building a house for the Mosleys, which Virginia had designed and Nelson supervised in his spare time as a relaxing hobby.

Hsi had made furniture for the Bells and was always "so interested in us and all we do...such a genuine help and blessing to us." He attended chapel and understood the preaching, but he was not a Christian. He declined, with Confucian courtesy, every suggestion of personal commitment. He lit joss sticks, performed the annual ceremony of returning the kitchen god to heaven to insure the prosperity of the home, and fulfilled his obligations to the spirits of his ancestors. At any relative's death he was punctilious in burning incense, paper money, and paper furniture to ease entrance into the afterlife.

One day in 1932 he was working near the clinic and remarked casually as he passed Dr. Bell: "You know, Doctor, a dog bit me on the hand a while ago as I was coming from lunch."

"Was it mad?"

"No, just a neighbor's dog. I flipped my hand at him and he bit me."

"I wonder if we hadn't better give you the anti-rabies treatments?"

"No, Doctor. That dog's not mad; I know it." Bell did not press the matter since Hsi Si-fu understood well the dangers of rabies; like any Chinese of the day he had seen men and children die of a mad dog's bite.

Two weeks later Nelson came downstairs first thing on Monday morning and found Hsi Si-fu standing at the foot of the steps.

"Doctor, I can't swallow! I can't swallow!"

At that moment Bell was certain the man had rabies. Unless the diagnosis was mercifully wrong, Hsi Si-fu lay under sentence of a painful death within twenty-four hours, and he knew it.

Bell put him in an isolation ward and carried out tests. By ten o'clock the symptoms were only too certain. He told the carpenter gently but frankly that he would die. During the morning while Bell was doing operations, Hsi's son stayed with him; many friends called to sympathize, and several sought to prepare his mind and soul for death. Nelson Bell went across immediately after lunch, and the son withdrew to stand in the doorway.

"Hsi Si-fu," Nelson said as he sat beside the bed, "you have rabies, and you know it. And you are going to die. All these years you have heard the gospel yet you have never accepted Christ as your Savior."

As Hsi listened, all that he had heard and courteously rejected suddenly clicked. As Nelson wrote three days later: "He had never made a public profession of faith, but he did then; of his own volition he knelt down and prayed, made such a clear, unequivocal confession of sin and profession of faith in Jesus as his Savior. Then he got up and turned to his son and said, 'Son, I have accepted Christ as my Savior and I want you to, too; and when I die, I don't want you to burn incense and paper money or carry out any heathen practices, as they are false.'"

Hsi could have given no surer proof of genuine conversion. Had his confession and prayer been lip service to please his friend the doctor, he would have ignored the subject of the funeral; the order to the son to omit the ancestral customs was an act of faith and courage, rejecting his life's deepest superstitions.

When his wife came in, Hsi repeated his instructions about the funeral. He then told his son to order a rickshaw; he wanted to die at home. Nelson warned him to be careful when the paroxysms came not to bite others in his agony and infect them. He promised and said, "I want to go back by your house and tell Mrs. Bell good-by."

Nelson went to see him after supper. Hsi's house had quite a substantial courtyard, halfway up Ten Li Street, which had filled with neighbors whom Hsi was telling, between bouts of pain and choking, that he had become a Christian and that they must accept Christ too.

Next morning at about six Nelson went again. The family and neighbors told how Hsi had prayed and preached all night between the paroxysms. Nelson found him weaker now, but "so thoughtful and gentle and courteous up to the very last, and so very appreciative. He said he felt so badly not to have finished the new house, and when I asked him about the continuation of his work, he turned it over to his son and the son of a former carpenter who worked for him."

He died at 7:00 a.m. The family, none of whom had been believers, loyally obeyed his wishes for a Christian funeral.

Nelson wrote to Cassie Lee Oliver at Kuling, "We all feel so badly about Hsi Si-fu that I just don't feel like writing about it. It was so sudden and unexpected, but we are happy and thankful he made such a clear confession of sin and faith in Christ as his Savior. His family have all been just fine. He is to be buried tomorrow morning."

*   *   *   *   *

One morning in March 1933 Nelson was supervising kala-azar admissions when the hospital accountant and registrar, Kao Mei-hong, brought him evidence that someone had tampered with one of the charts issued to patients. Each chart had a passport-style photograph, taken on the spot, for identification and to prevent fraud because the stibosan drug fetched high prices on the black market. This chart had a young man's photograph and a child's statistics.

It was traced to a country peasant who had agreed in his ignorance to hand his card to one of the innkeepers, the clever, disreputable son of the local sheriff, for sale to a healthy man who wanted supplies of the drug. Nelson gave Innkeeper Fang, in front of his father, a tongue-lashing which lost him much face.

Kao Mei-hong (known as Kao Er, which means "Kao the Second") thought no more about it. Kao was the brother of the pastor and son of the dear old elder who had died in 1928, and though once wild, he had exuberant faith and a great booming laugh. He adored his wife and their two small children, a girl of eighteen months and a boy of eight whom Nelson considered "an exceptionally brilliant child and a very lovable one. In any gathering where questions on the Bible were asked, he would be the first one to answer and always right to the point."

Nearly three months after this incident, Nelson and the Kao brothers were ending a Bible class for nurses when a man rushed in with news that bandits had broken into Kao Er's house brandishing automatics and had kidnapped the two children.

Even if Kao paid a ransom—and he was not rich—they might never be returned. Moreover the little girl had barely recovered from whooping cough; she was too frail to survive captivity more than a day or two. The class dissolved in consternation and sorrow. Suddenly they heard Kao's booming voice: "Don't worry! God has some good purpose in all this."

Troops scoured the country. At that time an average three hundred people were kidnapped every night in the regions of the SPM North Kiangsu Mission, but Kao's children touched a special chord in the authorities, who made every effort, to no avail. All Christians of Tsingkiangpu held special prayer meetings. "We children," recalled Ruth, "were so concerned because we knew what bandits were like, and here were a little boy and a baby girl in their hands. And we prayed."

Two long weeks passed. Kao began to receive anonymous letters implicating this or that person or offering information at a price, and ransom demands, some of them bogus. One note demanded $60,000; at least no finger or ear came with it.

Kao and his wife reached a decision. He posted a notice in Ten Li Street near the hospital gate: "I am not a rich man and could not pay even $50. God gave me these children, and He will return them to me. I will not pay ransom. I leave the matter in the hands of God."

The neighbors laughed! No ransom, no child. None laughed with more ribaldry than Innkeeper Fang.

There was not only laughter. Kirk Mosley recalled: "Kao's decision brought a sharp and critical response from his non-Christian friends and neighbors. How could he trust in the Lord who was unable to protect his children from being kidnapped in the first place? How could he risk the lives of these two innocent children by refusing to pay the ransom for their return? Kao and his Christian friends had daily prayer meetings with petitions to God for the safe return of the children. After a number of days and weeks when the children had not yet been returned, the non-Christians began to be even more critical and tried to raise real doubt in his mind about the effectiveness of prayer and trust in the Lord. Kao's faith and confidence in the Lord never wavered." Dr. Mosley felt that Nelson Bell's own "utter dependence upon and his great confidence in the promise of the Lord" played a considerable part. "The paradox of Nelson is that his dependency generates a supreme confidence in his daily way of life. The confidence is carried over to his friends and colleagues. A fine example of this is Kao's story."

Kao carried on his office duties and continued to lead his share of chapel services. His laugh was heard no less. His wife did not falter either, though the days seemed longer and longer.

Thirty-three days after the abduction, a fast messenger pedaled into the hospital from Antung, twenty miles away. Government soldiers had captured a bandit chief whose wife was nursing two babies. Under questioning, she had confessed that one was a hostage. An old crone had then volunteered that this little girl came from Tsingkiangpu. Nelson had the hospital driver take Kao to Antung at once. As was the custom, the soldiers had to be given a present, though they grudgingly accepted less "squeeze" than they demanded, and the girl was home that night. What is more, she was in bouncing health because the bandit's wife had plenty of milk for both babies. Kao said: "I could not afford a wet nurse, but the Lord provided one."

Kao's critics were not impressed.

"They pointed out, with a great deal of credibility," Mosley recalled, "that a baby girl had little value, and the bandits had found it not worth the worry of taking care of her. The non-Christian neighbors were certain that the boy would never be returned without the ransom being paid. But Kao and his friends continued in prayers with unshaken faith in God's love and with complete confidence in God's promise to hear His servants."

The soldiers were angry at the small "squeeze" and would not exert themselves to find the boy. The captured bandit, however, told the militia that this particular abduction had been at the suggestion of "an innkeeper named Fang, near the Benevolent Compassionate Hospital." Confronted by the police with their thumbscrews and leg-crusher, Fang hastily confessed, saying the crime had been his revenge on Kao for loss of face. But Fang swore he had no idea of the boy's whereabouts.

Seven days later Nelson was up at the hospital when a male nurse who had gone home on vacation rushed in breathless and excited. Nelson saw that whatever the news might be, it was good, and at length the nurse could tell his story. Militia had brushed with some bandits near his village, about eighteen miles from Tsingkiangpu. As the bandits retreated, they had thrown a small boy in a ditch. The militia heard a weak shout and found him. The boy told them he was Mr. Kao's son. He was too weak to walk for he had been kept underground in a hole, gagged, and covered with corn. They carried him to the village tea shop where the nurse, walking down the street, found him. "And when we saw each other we just cried—we were so happy."

Once again Kao bumped along the dirt lanes in the hospital car. At the village he had only to sign his name on the back of his visiting card; no cash was requested.

The sensation was tremendous. Never before in all North Kiangsu had a child been recovered without a ransom, except when soldiers caught up with the kidnappers immediately. Forty days, yet the child was safe and well. That evening hundreds of citizens visited the Kao home, until at last he mounted a box with the children to tell the crowd "how God had brought about their release." A non-Christian assured Bell that all up and down the street that night people were saying, "Truly, God did hear those prayers."

The next Sunday, as Mrs. Billy Graham often told the story to her own children, Ruth saw "Mr. Kao Er and his

wife stand up in the church to give public thanks to God
for what He had done. Mr. Kao was carrying the little boy
who still couldn't walk, and his wife was carrying the little
girl. And they stood up before the whole congregation to
give God the glory."

The Billy Graham children would then pray for Kao Er's
son and daughter who would have been twenty-four and
seventeen at the Communist revolution of 1949. Many years
later Ruth received a photograph of the son from Shanghai
with a personal inscription.

*   *   *   *   *

As a postscript to these incidents of 1932-33 comes the
tale of the plank bridge and the bullet.

On December 11, 1932, Virginia had another son. Rosa,
Ruth, and five-year-old MaiMai had prayed hard for a boy
because as good Chinese they were sorry for their parents
being saddled with girls; and they were abashed to discover
that their parents had prayed for another girl. The new Bell
arrived nicely on time so that his father could meet Rosa
at Shanghai on her return from Korea for Christmas; he
was named Benjamin Clayton after Tsingkiangpu's benefac-
tor.

Clayton, or DiDi (meaning "brother") as he was known
when small, was still an infant in arms when Nelson was
invited to survey and advise Haichow SPM Hospital. John
Reed, who as a boy had hero-worshiped him in Richmond,
Virginia, had recently arrived there as missionary doctor,
together with his vivacious wife Sally. The Bell family went,
enjoying what was virtually a vacation.

When the time came for the ninety-mile drive back to
Tsingkiangpu, the local military commander insisted they
take an escort of an officer and three soldiers because of
the bandits. Since even Nelson's Baby Austin could not hold
six Bells and four soldiers, the Haichow station arranged a
convoy. James Graham, Jr. drove his Model A Ford carrying
Virginia, Clayton, and the three girls. Next came the Austin
driven by the TKP hospital driver (always known as "Varnish"

because the sound was the same in Chinese) with Nelson beside him and two extremely young soldiers behind them. John Reed in his Ford, with Sally and the other two escorts, brought up the rear.

The road required slow driving, and the soldiers in the Baby Austin were soon comfortably asleep, their pistols on their laps. The convoy reached a canal where, whenever a car came by, a couple of planks making a ramshackle bridge, twelve feet by eight feet, were placed across. This would take time, so Nelson stepped out of the car to stretch his legs.

At that instant a loud gunshot made everybody jump.

Nelson looked around. Through the back of the seat where a moment earlier he had been sitting, he saw a bullet hole. And a frightened soldier in the back seat was holding a smoking gun.

"*Buh t'sai i!*" blubbered the soldier. "I wasn't thinking what I was doing!"

The officer hurried over, profuse in apologies. "He is very new. It is the first time he has ever had a pistol in his hands!"

Clayton Bell, May, 1934

21
Ken and Kay

KEN AND KAY GIESER were Northerners. Ken, almost twenty-six, was soon to qualify for his M.D. from Northwestern University and had arranged an internship at a Chicago hospital. Kay, slightly younger, was daughter of Vice-President Kirk of Wheaton College in Wheaton, Illinois. They were missionary volunteers who aimed to serve in Africa. But the Depression caused mission after mission to reply gloomily to their inquiries: No recruits until further notice.

In April 1934 Ken Gieser read an article by a Southern Presbyterian medical missionary in Africa whom they remembered hearing when students at Wheaton. Northerners though they were, Ken wrote to Nashville. By return post Dr. Darby Fulton, executive secretary, replied: No recruits for Africa until further notice—but he had just received a cable from China where one of their missionaries had a "Benjamin Clayton Fund" which was unaffected by the Depression. He needed another young doctor, preferably one who had not done his internship, for a three-year contract.

Dr. Fulton continued: "Dr. Bell, the man under whom you will work, is an exceptionally fine surgeon and physician, but he never forgets to carry a strong evangelistic emphasis through his work. He is constantly endeavoring to bring men face to face with Christ as their Savior, and this aim is paramount in all of his missionary activities." The Giesers liked the tone of the letter this Dr. Bell had prepared for possible interns, which after detailing medical opportunities continued: "What we want primarily is a doctor with a real

Ken and Kay Gieser

Christian motive. Without that, he would be unhappy and injure the work, too."

The Illinois State Board of Medical Examiners approved the internship—a tribute to the hospital in China and its surgeon. The SPM board approved the two candidates, and five months later, at about midnight on September 6, 1934, their Japanese liner docked in Shanghai. Shipboard life had been fun and the food delicious, but now, kept awake in their cabin by the shouts and clatter of unloading, they steeled themselves for the rigors ahead and donned their best behavior to meet the doctor whom they knew only from letters and snapshots.

Early next morning Kay looked out of the porthole and spotted him on the dockside: tall, younger looking than his forty years except for slightly graying hair, and obviously enjoying himself. "A man of strength and warmth." Beside him stood a tall, sixteen-year-old girl (Rosa had developed tuberculosis at high school in Korea and had been seriously ill; she was spending the year at home. Ruth had sailed for the fall term at Pyengyang a few days before the Giesers reached Shanghai).

The Giesers waved and the Bells yelled back, but the Giesers went through customs still feeling that hardships were around the corner. They met Dr. Bell outside the customs shed. "Well, Ken and Kay, how would you like a chocolate sundae?"

The Giesers recalled their amazement. "We thought we had left such things behind in America. We knew right away we were with a man who had a very understanding heart." They were soon at Shanghai's famous Chocolate Shop, where Mrs. Campbell, the manager, served ice cream which had been brought in barrels from America to be refrozen and topped with ingredients to produce the most succulent sundaes in China, "Oh, Dr. Bell!" exclaimed Kay.

"Call me Nelson; don't call me Dr. Bell." And another preconception subsided, for the Giesers had understood that senior missionaries were stiff and gloried in keeping recruits in their place.

Eventually they reached Tsingkiangpu, and as the Baby Austin squeezed through the gate into the hospital compound, the old squint-eyed gatekeeper danced about waving a big string of popping firecrackers on a long stick. The Giesers were not too sure whether this was a Chinese welcome or one imported from south of the Mason-Dixon Line.

A large German shepherd dog dashed out, barking and leaping to lick Nelson and Rosa and run around in circles, and then came Mrs. Bell, "with her arms wide-open, just welcoming us in such a way we felt like we had known her for a long time." Soon, again to the astonishment of a couple expecting the iron rations of a mission station as they had imagined it, they were sitting down to a meal of hot biscuits, fried chicken, and iced tea with mint.

The Giesers lived with the Bells for nearly a year because the home built for the Mosleys, who were now fully accredited missionaries at another station, had been needed for one of the evangelistic staff and a new house would not be available until spring.

Ken proved to be an excellent doctor. Both of them were found to be characterized by spirituality, exuberance, balance, and humor. Ken played chess and tennis, and it was at his suggestion that they laid out a miniature golf course across the yards. He played the piano, cornet, and organ and had a movie camera. The young Bells took to these new grown-ups who refused to be called "Uncle" and "Aunt," but rather were plain Ken and Kay, and Nelson wrote three months after their arrival: "The Giesers are so happy, and today remarked at the dinner table that every day they found out something new which made them happier than ever that they were here."

The Giesers' diary and their memories provide a vivid insight into the thriving medical mission in its prime in the years immediately before the Japanese war: the chapel at morning worship crowded with male nurses in white coats and female nurses in smart uniforms; the motley crush of walking-patients and their families wrapped against the winter cold, who wore "queer little black hats, some with red buttons on the top, and drab-colored outer cloaks, their hands stuffed in the opposite sleeves."

The offices and wards seemed a mixture of clinical efficiency and clever improvisation. Nelson's rows of steel filing cabinets might have been wafted straight from an American hospital, but the knot of relatives around each bed, spitting on the floor whenever they felt the need, could only be Asia.

Kenneth Gieser later became one of America's distinguished surgeons, and it was Tsingkiangpu which stimulated his interest in eyes. Bell had sent Dr. Ts'ao to Peking for training, and since 1932 he had run a much-needed eye clinic. The medical side remained in the charge of Dr. Woods, but at sixty-seven he was growing deaf, a fact the patients could not comprehend. In his spare time, instead of tennis, Woods went for walks or read a detective story from the enormous stack of paperbacks behind his door. Nelson's love for detection had not waned either (He quoted the wag who said: "I like a nice, clean murder, nothing immoral in it.").

Woods retained his intense concern for the hospital. The young Giesers used "to shudder sometimes" at the heated discussions between Woods and Bell. On two or three occasions, "the sparks flew like mad as they argued back and forth. It seemed to us Nelson would give more than Dr. Woods. Woods was a ramrod. They both had their minds and tongues under control, but they would be very heated." Twice, over subjects long forgotten, the difference was sharp enough to split any other station that the Giesers afterwards knew. But the moment discussion was over, Woods and Bell were "warm friends right away again. No rancor, or any sign of it after the meeting. No grudge. They would go along one path and it was so peaceful, you would never know they had had an argument. It was amazing."

Ken Gieser loved surgery with Nelson Bell day after day. "We would operate together every morning from about 8:30 until 12:00 or 12:30. We would be standing across from each other at the operating table, and coming right from school, it was my privilege to be his assistant. He was an excellent teacher. He was a general surgeon; he knew his limitations and stayed within them, but what he did, he did well. If he had had more training, he would have perhaps done a little more extensive chest surgery and things like this, but he did gastrectomies, intestinal mastinosis, and such things very well.

"He was an astute man when it came to physical diagnosis. Out there we didn't have all of the diagnostic accessories that one has in America; you had to make your diagnosis pretty much by what you could see and what you could feel—decide what you were going to do by what you figured the patient could take. And Nelson was clever at being able to feel a pulse and listen to a heart and determine what a patient could tolerate in the way of surgical procedures. We were up against many, many situations where if the patient were not operated on, we knew he or she would die, and lots of times it was a question of whether the patient could stand the operation. This was a matter of judgment, and Nelson was excellent at it.

"He operated quickly, as he did everything. He used to say: 'I talk fast; I eat fast; I do everything fast.' Virginia used to get after him for eating fast. He could do a tremendous amount of work in three or four hours at the operating table."

Between operations, and even while finishing up a case, he would send for the hospital secretary and records keeper, Lina Bradley, a middle-aged former SPM missionary who had afterward been secretary to the governor of South Carolina; Bell had heard of her "as an outstanding Christian" and invited her to Tsingkiangpu in 1934 under the Benjamin Clayton Fund. Miss Lina would take a seat near the operating table, and when routine displaced decisions, when the complicated part of an operation was over and the routine of closing up the patient had begun, Bell's fingers would be deftly sewing gut while his mind and lips were dictating notes on the operation or answering business letters. When he had used spinal anesthesia and the patient was conscious, the apparent normality of such procedure encouraged a therapeutic relaxation.

Nelson had been keeping careful records of his cases, and in 1934 he submitted a representative one hundred to the American College of Surgeons to earn the coveted rank of Fellow of the American College of Surgeons (F.A.C.S.). The reviewer appointed by the college, a well-qualified teacher of surgery, reported that they constituted "excellent work, done under obviously difficult conditions. There is a great variety of material, well-handled and with good results."

On October 19, 1934, at convocation in Boston Symphony Hall, President Robert B. Greenburgh conferred a fellowship on Dr. L. Nelson Bell *in absentia.*

* * * * *

The worthy regents of the American College of Surgeons would have been intrigued to see how L. Nelson Bell, M.D., F.A.C.S. spent part of that particular evening (or it may have been a few days later). The incident might be called "The Melon Seed Story."

About 4:30 p.m. Bell brought Ken Gieser to the operating theater where a five-year-old girl lay breathing painfully. A dried melon seed had gone down the wrong way five days before and lodged in her trachea (windpipe). The frightened parents did nothing until nearly too late. Bell gave her ether and tried to reach the seed with a special bronchoscope, but the seed was too low and the tiny windpipe too narrow, so he told the parents that an immediate operation was the only hope. The father replied that he could not possibly give permission—he must ask the grandfather; the parents set off into the city to find him. The hours ticked by with the little girl fighting for breath.

At 9:30 p.m., more than five hours after the girl's admission, the parents and the grandfather arrived at the hospital anxious for surgery at once. The doctors returned to surgery, and "we could plainly see that the child was putting every ounce of strength into getting enough air to keep alive. Its color was bad." This terrible strain could not last much longer.

Ken gave her a plastic doll sent across by Kay; dolls had long been used to cheer or quiet children, and grown women sometimes begged for them too. The child was pleased but too uncomfortable and weary to do more than hold it limply. In the presence of the family Bell "asked the Lord to help me." He gave a local anesthetic above the breastbone and began a deep incision down the trachea, intending to reach the seed with small instruments, the risk being that a long operation might strain the heart.

The moment he finished the incision, the child coughed and, to the doctors' amazement, the seed flew out, nearly hitting the ceiling. Soon the incision was sewed up and the child was playing happily with the doll.

"One chance in a hundred," Bell told the family, "but God worked it out that way." He went on to tell "of Him and how He had helped."

*   *   *   *   *

These months were packed with incidents for Ken and Kay Gieser—such as watching the Tsingkiangpu fire brigade answering an alarm.

The Giesers had been invited with Dr. Woods to a feast near the canal bank. The restaurant was a ramshackle timber building like a toothpick sticking up in the air. They entered through the kitchen which was open to the street with cats and dogs running in and out, fly-blown raw meat hanging from grease-encrusted walls, and dried fish and fowls dangling from the ceiling. Cooks, stripped to the waist, dashed to and fro. The Americans climbed creaking stairs to join the Chinese host and guests on the third floor. The windows gave a good view of the city, but during the hour's pause after the waiters had shouted the orders down to the kitchen, the Giesers did not dare lean against the rickety wall. The house creaked and groaned in the strong wind.

Just as a dirty waiter brought two large greasy dishes, they heard "a tremendous pounding and clashing of cymbals" and saw smoke pouring from mud huts a quarter of a mile away. With infinite dignity a man in a brass helmet, short yellow raincoat, blue tights, and grass sandals pranced across the canal bridge carrying a tall white banner with black characters proclaiming "Fire Brigade." He was followed by men with long hooked poles and others with blue wooden tubs. Four men in brass helmets, blowing whistles, pulled the fire engine which four men pushed. It was merely a frame on four wheels containing two pumps and a huge brass bell which another man clanged with all his might.

A pause, and then the second division marched by. Their equipment included a twelve-foot bamboo ladder and a hose rolled up neatly in a big basket carried between two men who almost allowed themselves to trot.

The huts burned to the ground.

Perhaps more effective than the fire brigade was the local custom of publicly flogging the owner of any building that burned down.

A very different experience was Ken's first sermon in China—to the prisoners in the jail. He had heard of an ex-convict, in the hospital as a patient shortly after release from a prison farm, who had told Nelson that he and six other "alumni" of Tsingkiangpu jail had met regularly for prayer all the six years of their sentence. Nelson could cite scores of cases of evident conversion and considered the jail one of his most fruitful spheres. This Sunday morning Ken stood on a box beside Nelson who was ready to interpret.

"I was soon glad Dr. Bell had placed me on the box with him, for the men crowded in on us until the little yard was packed. Here and there stragglers came out of their cells. They hobbled slowly. Heavy iron shackles dangled noisily from their ankles." Ken noticed as he preached that none wore prison garb, merely tattered fragments. Some of the bodies had crude paper patches over open sores; others had itch. "Their faces were unshaven and dirty. Scars and cynical grooves seemed to characterize these uninviting countenances.

"Yet every man stood motionless. There was no whispering or jittering. A stillness which spoke of dead earnestness prevailed. Each sentence seemed to be devoured." Ken knew "that this same Jesus who saved me from a life of sin could also save even the most notorious Chinese bandit."

When Ken stopped, Nelson continued. Next there was much nudging and shoving until somehow they had all knelt down and bowed their heads: "It seemed no easy task to get on one's knees when both ankles were bound with iron." When the clanking ceased, Bell led them in prayer after him. Ken "could not understand all he said, but I could sense the very Spirit of God in this dismal place."

*   *   *   *   *

Bell was called from prayer meeting one evening. He did not come back for a long time, and the Giesers could see a milling crowd around the hospital office. Suddenly six heavily armed detectives in black uniforms emerged and ran—actually ran—toward the gate, hustling a handcuffed young man dressed in smart brown silk.

The hospital, it seemed, had come under police suspicion for gun-running, a capital offense. The staff already suspected the elegant young stranger and asked detectives who were lurking outside the gate to arrest him; he in turn accused Dr. Bell of selling him two guns. Detectives searched the man at Bell's request and found a most polite letter signed by twenty-five country folk and addressed to "The Hospital Superintendent" which offered thanks for his benevolence in supplying arms for protection against bandits, promised the arms would never be misused, and praised him for such pity on poor defenseless countrymen.

The young man, named Gold, was hurried to the police station. Bell went to the *yamen* and considered the matter serious enough to inform the American consul-general, the first time he had ever reported any incident, for it could have most damaging repercussions.

He assumed the fellow was a crook ready to disappear when the deluded country folk had paid in advance for the guns they would never see. But the plot when unraveled proved to be an attempt at revenge by a dismissed female nurse. The elegant Gold and his wife were her dupes. The matter was eventually closed by the insertion of a newspaper notice in which the Golds apologized to Bell and to the hospital and identified the fraudulent nurse.

Bandits did not erupt into Tsingkiangpu as much as formerly, and they certainly did not worry the children. One hot night the previous summer when Nelson, Ruth, and small Clayton were sleeping on the attic porch under the open sky, a gun fight started outside the hospital compound.

Virginia called out of her window below: "Nelson! You and the children get down here."

"Oh, Mother," Ruth called back above the firing, "let us stay up here, please."

*   *   *   *   *

Every day Ken Gieser returned from his cases and Kay from her evangelism to the security and affection of the Bell home. They had no problems of adjustment to a foreign land; Nelson and Virginia made everything easy. The home was attractive, the food tasty and varied. Ken thought his first birthday in China, soon after arrival, would be dull because none but his wife knew the date. He came down to breakfast to find not only presents but an invitation to his birthday party. All the missionaries came, led by Uncle Jimmy and a frail Aunt Sophie who were both now over seventy; the SPM had granted their request to spend their retirement at Tsingkiangpu.

"There was such a warm, homelike atmosphere," the

Giesers recalled. Virginia inspired them by her thoughtfulness and love, Nelson by his "wonderful sense of humor and great capacity for showing his affection." If Virginia was not at the clinic, or teaching MaiMai, or playing with Clayton, or dispensing hospitality, she would be tending the roses and chrysanthemums in her garden or canning fruit. "Nelson would rush in from the hospital to his office at home and you'd hear him typing away vigorously as could be; then he would be off to something else. It was amazing how both were so efficient. And it was amazing that two people with such strong personalities could be so happy, really happy. There was an unusually close relationship between husband and wife."

The Giesers were amused that Virginia liked to be the first to read any new books sent from America for the station's use. If she thought them improper, she threw them into the fire. *Gone With the Wind* (1936) went into the flames, and *The Grapes of Wrath* (1939) went even quicker. The Giesers enjoyed the reading aloud, and the Bible games and quizzes on Sunday night, though Kay was occasionally reduced to tears by her low marks for memory verses, at which the Bell children excelled. Clayton was, of course, too young as yet, and once at family prayers when his father said, "Shall we pray," he convulsed them all by retorting in Chinese, "I don't want to pray; I want to eat!"

Bits from Ruth's letters were sometimes read aloud at the table. She had hated leaving home for Korea and often said that being a missionary child was her best preparation for a lifetime of good-bys. But she enjoyed school. A remark in a letter stuck in her father's mind for years: "I am praying like working does no good, and working like praying does no good." She had already developed her habit of accumulating pithy sayings read or heard, though Ruth cannot trace the origin of this one.

That Christmas in the exceptionally mild winter of 1934 the Giesers found Ruth "just part of one happy family. None of them were aware especially of leadership ability—they just enjoyed life. They studied, they played hard, they had much of the attitude toward life that their parents had. . . .It is exciting to see how God has blessed each of those children now. But in their growing-up stage they just seemed like regular, normal, healthy, happy American children."

If for the Giesers Tsingkiangpu began lifelong friendships, the Bells found the Giesers the most appreciative of guests. And the Giesers had profound influence on the story of the Bells because they clinched the decision to send the girls to Wheaton College.

Rosa had already heard of Wheaton and was determined to go there. As early as October 23, 1932, Nelson wrote to his mother that if they went on furlough in 1935, they intended to place Rosa at college. "We much prefer a Southern school, but if necessary we will send her to Wheaton, near Chicago. It is a good college and stands unswervingly, even aggressively for the truth. I am convinced that in these days an institution cannot simply *stand* for the truth or try to take a neutral position. Satan is actively fighting through men and women unfaithful to God and His Word, and we must fight back, in His power." When the Giesers, both Wheaton alumni (one being the daughter of the Wheaton vice-president) lived in their home for eight months, the Bells became certain it was a college with the high academic standards and balanced spiritual atmosphere which they sought for their daughters.

By the time they left for furlough in June 1935, the Bells knew that Wheaton would come into their lives.

The entire family together, Christmas 1934

Embarking on overland trip by rickshaw

Travel by barge on the Grand Canal, 1935

22
A Wide-Open Door

HOME again, home again, and O how grand it seems, the thrill of being home," wrote Virginia on August 30, 1936—not in America but back in Tsingkiangpu. The Bells had spent much of their third furlough in Montreat, the Presbyterian mountain resort and conference center in North Carolina, where Rosa and Ruth attended Montreat High School. Ruth found her Pyengyang training had put her a year ahead of her class. Upon returning to China, they left Rosa to start at Wheaton in the fall, and Ruth at Yokohama on her way to Korea for an additional year of study. Sixteen, they felt, was too young for college.

When the new Bell car neared Tsingkiangpu, as Virginia wrote to the two girls, with another carbon for Mother Bell, "All the sights, sounds, and smells along the way were so familiar—we felt so at home and had to take stock of ourselves to realize we had ever been away. The canal banks were covered with drying rushes, threshed wheat also drying, families eating their noon meal under the shade of a matting roof, strings of people towing boats, water buffalo cooling in some mud hole, acres of lotus, donkeys laden with bags of grain, peddlers with various kinds of wares, and rickshaws with their various passengers, many of them young fellows on their way to school for the fall. We did not hear the familiar title of 'foreign devil' any more than usual, did not hear it at all south of Chinkiang, so possibly they will learn better someday up in this neck of the woods.

"We reached here about a quarter of four. Daddy didn't honk his horn coming down the street so they would not

On furlough with the Bell family in Virginia. Left to right: James McKim Bell, James H. Bell, Norma Bell Norris, Ruth Lee McCue Bell, and Nelson Bell

know we were coming, but it did no good; they had someone stationed at the corner, and as soon as he spied the car, off he went with the word; a man was standing there with the usual long bamboo pole and a great string of firecrackers which he got started by the time we reached the corner.

"When we got to the hospital gate, there was another long string; you couldn't hear yourself think. When we turned into the compound, there was a crowd of people in front of the chapel with another string of firecrackers, and when we got into our yard there was another. The noise was deafening and the smoke blinding and the whole mob, at least two hundred, came right on in after us, so I guess you would call it a right big homecoming. The mob didn't tarry long, thanks to a little help from the gateman who kept reminding them to 'Walk Slowly.' The next thing was to see Prinz; Cassie Lee had him locked up in the Giesers' yard because he is afraid of firecrackers and also because of the mob—we didn't want to offend them. He was overjoyed to see us and has been sticking close to MaiMai and Clayton ever since. He won't budge one step with either Nelson or me if Clayton doesn't come. Clayton is not afraid of him but is apprehensive of Prinz's affection; he is too demonstrative."

They were soon back in the swim, with Nelson doing

more surgery "than I could catch up with. However, it is the sort of work I love." Ken Gieser was temporarily at Kuling recovering from illness; Dr. Woods was on holiday; and though Dr. Ts'ao proved a tower of strength medically and spiritually, the hospital had declined with the absence of leadership. Nelson smoothed out a squabble between nurses, negotiated with the government which wanted nurses' schools to register, and encouraged the pastor to arrange a special week for spiritual renewal. Nelson preached frequently in the hospital chapel, as previously, and sang a solo at the church on the next Communion Sunday. "Many, many times since our return," he wrote to Benjamin Clayton, whose munificence continued unabated, "we have thanked God for permitting us to come back here....Where would I rather be? I want to be right here, where I am."

That fall of 1936 a young American couple, the Ernest Carlburgs, came to Tsingkiangpu city from West China. They replaced the English maiden ladies of the China Inland Mission (one had died and the other retired) who had worked the CIM segment of the region for many years and, coincidentally, had initiated Ruth into the mysteries of brewing an English cup of tea, decidedly different from Chinese or American. The Carlburgs later worked with the Overseas Missionary Fellowship (formerly CIM) in Taiwan, and Mrs. Carlburg recalled how in 1936, "We arrived in Tsingkiangpu just three weeks before the birth of a baby. The loving welcome given to us, who were hardly more than strangers, was most typical of the warm-hearted group there. I very much suspect that it was Virginia who planned a 'baby shower' which supplied me with such nice home-side things for the new baby. He was our third, but the first to have much of anything in the way of American baby clothes. I also remember that they had just received a large shipment of layettes for Chinese babies, and I was allowed to look these over and choose what I wished.

"So from the first day, though we well might have been considered poor country cousins, we were accepted into their warm fellowship. There was a weekly prayer meeting that was the highlight of the week for us.

"To us, who had not seen what might be called an American home for six years, the Bells' home was like heaven on earth. I remember being there for Thanksgiving dinner, with all that goes to make it an American holiday occasion. But the thing that stands out most from that or similar dinners is the fact that it was an absolutely first-class social time, but on the dot of 9:00 p.m., even in the middle of a game, things closed and the party dispersed for everyone was working at top production and could not afford late nights, even for Thanksgiving. But their compound, this little bit of America, and heaven on earth, did not hold priority in their hearts. The work, whether in the hospital or country, was what the Lord's call had been to them, and He had all their hearts and strength."

Virginia was never too busy to show kindness to other people's children, as the small Carlburgs found. Their son Cliff, aged two, became the special care of nine-year-old MaiMai.

Nelson had bought a small bicycle in Japan for Clayton, who at less than four years astonished them by learning to ride it in an hour; he would speed around the yard to his heart's content. He also played golf with Nelson and Ken on the miniature course, using a cut-down club, "and Nelson said he often made better shots than they."

One of the earliest memories of the Reverend Dr. Clayton Bell comes from April 1937 when Nelson received news that his father had died of pneumonia on March 4 at the age of 83. Mrs. Bell wisely had not cabled, but her letter was delayed by a shipping strike, followed by the collision of the liner *President Coolidge*, and arrived with 103 other postal packets. Clayton remembers "that Dad was in a rather reflective mood, and I asked him something about it. I don't remember his exact answer, but I remember the reassurance that came through his answers—that Grandfather Bell was with the Lord and I didn't have to be upset by this." As Nelson wrote to his mother, "Faith in Christ surely does take the sting out of death."

*   *   *   *   *

By 1937 China showed unmistakable signs of progress.

The bandits had gone completely from the Tsingkiangpu region for the first time in the Bells' entire experience. A hard-surfaced road, part of a network of new strategic highways, now ran right to the Yangtze, and a thirty-two span concrete bridge replaced one of the worst ferries. Nelson's was the first car across because he persuaded the engineer to let him drive over before the surface was ready. Tsingkiangpu had an improved airfield, plans for a wide street leading to a new modern bridge to be built by the north gate, and was now linked by telephone to Shanghai. The great Yellow River Project had been nearly completed: thousands of conscript peasants were digging out the old bed to relieve flooding up-country and to provide an alternate waterway should Japan capture the main river in the north. They looked like ants, toiling as far as the eye could see.

The people accepted Western medicine more readily, and the government had started an obstetrical clinic in the city and had enlarged their kala-azar research center. The mission hospital and the country evangelists, both American and Chinese, found steadily increasing response to the Christian message: the people's willingness to listen, which had been so noticeable in the early 1930s, had proved no passing phase. It was much strengthened by the popular Chiang Kai-shek after his sensational kidnapping at Sian. Nelson wrote on January 3, 1937: "We are all rejoicing over General Chiang's Christian testimony since his release. Tuesday morning he had it broadcasted over the Chinese radio, thanking the Christians for their prayers on his behalf, and the papers say he sent his personal secretary to the Union Church in Nanking to thank the people and that this man said that...General Chiang's courage and peace of heart had resulted from constant Bible reading and prayer during his detention. I wonder if the leader of any other large nation today would have taken similar steps in time of stress?"

Chiang's government had a long way to go to make China a modern democracy. The personally incorruptible Generalissimo had not yet eradicated graft, even in his entourage, nor had he ended the rapacities of landlords or lessened the extremes of poverty and wealth. But a start had been made. Nelson commented: "The progress is remarkable, and the people are of one heart and one purpose now, probably for the first time in centuries." The Communists had completed the long march around the western provinces to seize a northern area which would be a strategic base should the international situation offer them a new opportunity to seize power.

Left to itself Chiang's government eventually might have created a modern state in friendly equality with the Western world. The Japanese, however, would not leave the Chinese alone. China grew stronger, but war with Japan became inevitable.

Throughout the spring and summer of 1937 Nelson Bell accumulated essential foodstuffs and medical supplies.

23
Japan Attacks, 1937

L ATE in June 1937 the Bells drove home from a happy visit to Shanghai where Ruth had arrived from her last term at high school in Korea. The situation at the hospital could hardly have been better. The Nurses Training School problem had been settled with the government without compromise; a serious situation in the hospital kitchen had resolved itself; the Bells had a new and more efficient refrigerator; and patients poured in from the peaceful countryside and city. Nelson wrote: "In all of our trip, going and coming and in Shanghai, God has been so good to us, and we feel the change did us good. The opportunities of the work are almost unlimited and God's good hand is on us. How I do pray that He will keep us humble and the open channels through which He can bless many."

The one shadow on the family horizon was the impending departure of Ruth, having just celebrated her seventeenth birthday, for America and Wheaton College.

She had been happy, popular, and hard-working at Pyeng-yang, though not of marked academic record except in Bible. She had developed in spiritual perception and was a leader in student spiritual activities, while showing understanding and sympathy with the difficulties of Korean Christians under the Japanese. "Ruth is so happy to be home," Nelson wrote on June 27, "and it is so nice to have her here. She is a precious child and still a child, and going home will be hard for her. It is certainly the one hard thing missionaries have to do—have their children so far away during these important years. I am asking the Lord to open the way, if it is His will, to have them come out for the summer two years from now. Summer round-trip rates third class are very reasonable, and the two together could come that way if the right steamers are running. Or, they might come three years from now (1940) when the Olympic Games are being played in Japan and special rates are sure to be in effect. This is just a dream, if it is the Lord's will."

Then the Japanese attacked China.

At first it was not clear whether the incidents near Peking early in July 1937 would lead to full-scale war. The Chinese could hardly accede to Japanese demands without Chiang losing such face that he must resign; the great powers, however, could force Japan to climb down. But Europe, practicing appeasement, merely called a conference, which America, practicing isolation, sabotaged by staying away.

Nelson laid in a six months' supply of fuel. He had the roof painted with "American Hospital" in characters (equally recognizable by Japanese and Chinese airmen) and "U.S.A." in English letters. He sent the Japanese Foreign Ministry, through a friend high up in the State Department, exact plans of the hospital, giving no excuse for "mistakes." He ran up the American flag which normally did not fly because missionaries had no wish to flaunt their foreignness.

Early on August 1, Tsingkiangpu felt three earthquake shocks, one strong enough to wake Nelson. Even the Chinese Christians were filled with superstitious gloom at such a sign of impending evil. Little Clayton (DiDi) Bell, impervious to war or earthquake, delighted his parents by learning to swim that week, at the age of four-and-a-half.

The Bells planned to send Ruth's baggage by launch a few days ahead and to start by road on Monday, August 16, going as far as the Yangtze, and then by ferry and train to Shanghai to see her off to America. But Mother Bell back at Waynesboro was studying the newspapers. She estimated the family's likely departure date and, sure the crisis would erupt into war just when they were traveling, she prayed decidedly that they should wait.

On the morning the baggage was due for dispatch, reports were coming in on Nelson's radio that refugees were fleeing from Shanghai and other big cities and that the Yangtze ferries could not tie up at the Chinkiang jetty for fear of being swamped by terrified Chinese. A message from the launch company asked the doctor to get the baggage down at once ahead of schedule. He hurried into the room where Virginia and Ruth were packing. They could not oblige: the laundry was still to come, nor had the tailor delivered. Nelson "came back in a few minutes," recorded Virginia, "and said it didn't make any difference for the launches were not running and nothing was allowed to cross the Yangtze. Ruth and I were just finishing up our last mending, etc., so we got to work and cleaned our rooms and settled back to relax and enjoy ourselves and revise our thinking. She is jubilant over the prospect of staying. Nelson wired the treasurer in Shanghai to cancel her steamer ticket. The next day we heard you could cross the river, but no trains, so Nelson had the bright idea of getting on a British river steamer at Chinkiang and taking Ruth to Shanghai that way, but the next radio broadcast said that Whangpoo was blocked, and the next broadcast said the river below Chinkiang was blocked and that they were fighting in Shanghai, so we feel there is nothing left for us to decide; it is just impossible to go. We feel like we are on a holiday. Everything is in order, and Ruth has a lot of pretty new clothes, nothing elaborate, mostly prints. We are enjoying the feeling—the Lord seems doubly near at a time like this. And we know we are where we should be. We are pretty well blocked in, but feel we are as safe here as anywhere."

On August 13, 1937, the radio suddenly reported that Japanese planes were bombing the Chinese city at Shanghai and Japanese marines were landing. Moment by moment reports dramatically described fierce fighting and Chinese attempts to bomb the Japanese ships, bringing heavy casualties to foreigners in the International Settlement. To complicate matters, a typhoon approached the China coast; the Monday when the Bells would have started their journey brought terrific wind and rain. Nelson sent Mother Bell and Rosa a cable: "Undisturbed. Ruth staying."

Tuesday, August 17, Tsingkiangpu had its first air raid. Three Japanese planes flew over and dropped three or four bombs at the airport. The Bells left their dinner and rushed upstairs to look: by going to the open attic porch they could get a bird's-eye view of the countryside. Explosions, flashes, dust—and soon came reports of the damage: one cow killed, one training plane damaged, and a third bomb which fell near the north gate did not explode. But no one expected this farcical raid to be typical. "The Chinese are terrified," Virginia wrote, "and every time we leave the compound, they think we are evacuating; just our being here means a lot to their peace of mind, and it is a fine opportunity to witness to them, the peace we have in our own hearts that comes from faith and trust in an all-powerful and all-loving and all-wise God."

Meanwhile, to Nelson's disgust, American consuls throughout eastern China, where the Japanese might advance, bombarded American missionaries with orders to evacuate. News of evacuation "makes me mad," Nelson wrote, especially as British consuls displayed the traditional stiff upper lip and declined to interfere with the lawful pursuits of British subjects merely because Japanese scrapped with Chinese. Nelson ignored the American consular message.

On the Thursday after the war really began the clinic was small. "The people in the city are simply petrified with fear as a radio message has come saying twenty-two Japanese planes are flying into North Kiangsu now and another raid here is expected. Poor people, with no knowledge of God and utter lack of preparation and defense, it is pitiful. This is a bright clear afternoon and vision is perfect. If they hit this hospital, it will be intentional. All stores in the city are closed and doors and windows up." The alarm proved false, and the city settled down unhappily, living on its nerves.

In early September the American ambassador in Nanking personally and persistently urged Bell and the others to get out of Tsingkiangpu; American mission hospitals had already been bombed ("by mistake") elsewhere, the Japanese might advance swiftly and start shelling the place, or Chinese Communists might loot it. Either way, American blood could be spilled. The ambassador himself fled from Nanking on the direct orders of President Roosevelt—to the

Evacuating Tsingkiangpu in September, 1937

detriment of American prestige.

The embassy's repeated warnings that to stay would be stubborn (President Roosevelt's own word for missionaries), disobedient, and would forfeit consular protection, were prayed about earnestly at station prayers and in private devotions. Nelson, as always, tried to follow his motto: "Trust in the Lord with all thine heart; and lean not unto thine own understanding. In all thy ways acknowledge him and he shall direct thy paths."

This guidance, as Nelson commented, "may not be what I hope; it may not be what I expect. And, again, I think of that verse: 'Thine ears shall hear a word behind thee, saying, This is the way, walk ye in it, when ye turn to the right hand, and when ye turn to the left.' There are many turnings in the life of a Christian. The thing is to be so sensitive to the leading of God's Holy Spirit that when you seemingly have come up against a stone wall, just wait, don't try to climb over it. He will show you whether to turn to the right hand or to the left."

The decisive factor was not the children's safety but the feeble physical state of the elderly Sophie Graham, virtually bedridden since a stroke the previous December, and of Uncle Jimmy. Nor could the Bells dispatch the rest to the coast while remaining themselves, for Dr. Woods and Ken Gieser had been caught at Kuling by the outbreak of war, and though Ken made his way back at once, he had taken Nelson's advice to collect Kay and sail home for furlough early. On September 11, Bell wired the consul that they would all evacuate though not considering it either necessary or advisable.

Ruth, indeed, though she loyally said nothing, thought it positively wrong; she was probably influenced subconsciously by the hope that they would soon be blockaded in Tsingkiangpu where she could remain happily, Japanese or no, until old enough to be a missionary in Tibet.

At daybreak on September 17, with the house closed and shuttered, the Bells gathered with the servants for last family prayers. Ruth has never forgotten that early morning singing of "God Be With You Till We Meet Again."

The sad party went northward by launch. They reached the railway and, despite delays due to air raids farther up the line, arrived in Haichow, from which an American destroyer took them to Tsingtao, the foreign-style port to which they had been evacuated in 1927, where they joined nearly all their Southern Presbyterian colleagues, evacuated from North Kiangsu where war now raged.

*   *   *   *   *

Tsingtao is a beautiful place with its views of mountains beyond the bay. John Reed, who had come on the same destroyer from Haichow, loaned the Bells one of his cottages which was right on the sea. With tennis for Nelson, a hired bicycle for Clayton, the American school for MaiMai, and innumerable happy friendships to renew, Tsingtao was an excellent vacation and rest. But from the moment they arrived, they began to pray about returning. "The Carlburgs are still there, and we feel mighty bad being away when we are needed so much," Nelson wrote on October 1.

They recognized that the ambassador's pressure had allowed them no option and that evacuation was the providential way of getting Ruth to America; she sailed, reluctantly, on October 22 for Wheaton and her destiny. But even before she left, they had been "praying very definitely for guidance. Our prayer has been, first, that we might be willing to do God's will and, secondly, that He would make His will plain." They recognized that it would be one of the most crucial decisions of their lives. "We are praying many times daily for leading, and I am absolutely sure that God will show His will and lead us when the time comes."

Once back at Tsingkiangpu the family would be all right, for letters reported the air raids had been confined so far to the airfield and to some harmless machine-gunning over the hospital to frighten nurses. The journey, on the other hand, could be dangerous. Nelson proposed to go back alone.

Virginia would have none of it. Should the way open, they would all go home to Tsingkiangpu together. She would not be separated from Nelson in wartime regardless of what the other wives might feel led to do. Lina Bradley (the hospital secretary) also volunteered to return. She said it did not look right to run away and leave the Chinese to do all the trusting and suffering.

On the day after Ruth's departure, Nelson received a letter from Tsingkiangpu from Dr. Koh, the junior of the four Chinese doctors, written in English: "After you leave from the hospital we all work very happily and harmoniously. Now we are all well and all of us heartily hope you will come back very soon—not for a while only but to live with us forever and forever." It made Nelson feel even more strongly that "Of all times, this is the time we should be on the job. Personally, I feel the mission work may be irreparably harmed if we missionaries do not rise to help meet this dire need. Some will say this is China's war, not ours, but we are missionaries to China and, like the wedding vows, we should be here 'for better or for worse, in health and in sickness.' We are praying earnestly for God's leading, and He will show what His will is and guide and protect when we are found in the line of His will."

That same day Nelson wired Carlburg for a report on conditions. Carlburg wired back: "BRIEF VISIT INADVIS-ABLE PROTRACTED STAY SEEMS FEASIBLE LOCAL CONDITIONS GOOD DOCTORS ADVOCATE RETURN YOU BEST INFORMED REGARDING TRAVEL HAZARD."

By the end of that week the feeling grew stronger and stronger that "God wants us to return." The travel agent who a few days earlier had vetoed the journey as too dangerous now said that the rail journey would be safe at night. On returning from the travel agency, Nelson found two Chinese officers, one of them a former patient, who had just arrived from Tsingkiangpu and had hurried around to report that the journey was feasible. To Nelson and Virginia "the leading seemed unmistakably clear." And if they had mistaken the guidance, one barrier remained by which God could stop them: the Chinese authorities required a consular letter before issuing passes to the interior, yet the American consul would certainly not recommend them for Virginia and the children; no missionary children, and only one married woman, remained at SPM stations. And of the few unmarried women, one was already reported, erroneously, a nervous wreck from bombing.

Nelson went straight to the head Chinese official responsible for passes. He found him "so cordial and so deeply appreciative of our desire to go back. He said our passports were all that were necessary for evidence, and on giving him two copies of our pictures, he fixed up the necessary passes."

That clinched it. They realized that even their best friends would criticize them for taking two young children into the war zone. No one would bother much if Nelson went back alone. Dr. Woods himself planned to return from Kuling for at least long enough to settle his affairs. But to take a girl of ten and a boy not yet five to a city already bombed, which soon might be a battlefield and then a shambles with looting and rape! Yet the Bells were not rushing blindly into danger.

"More and more clearly," Nelson wrote to his mother, sister, and the girls on October 31, "it has been shown us this week that He wants us to return. It is hard to explain this so it would seem like sense at home, and yet we do feel He is making it so plain that our station and work is the place for us. If that is true, it would be foolish and wrong and dangerous to stay away." Indeed, as he wrote a few weeks later, "The safe place is where He wants us to be."

To the SPM executive in Nashville he wrote: "If missionaries stay out now, they will miss the grandest chance

God ever gave them for winning the confidence and love of the people. It will be a sad day for Christian missions if Communists come to the aid of China and we Christian missionaries leave them flat." And to the American ambassador, after explaining the grounds of their decision and emphasizing that neither Mrs. Bell nor the children were in the least nervous, he added some home truths: "It is possible that someday the American government may be thankful for the American missionaries who have carried on in the interior of China in spite of strong advice to the contrary. This tie of Sino-American friendship may aid very materially in salvaging the friendship of the two nations, so seriously endangered by our present policy."

Nelson Bell concluded: "In returning at this time we understand that we are forfeiting the right to further assistance on the part of the government, in case of forced evacuation. We also, of course, assume full personal responsibility for this course."

The ambassador did not reply.

Bell sent a courtesy copy to the U.S. destroyer captain who had taken such trouble rescuing them from a situation into which they now were plunging back. Commander Patterson replied: "I respect and admire your motives in returning to your post of duty, and I salute the fine spirit of courage, fidelity, and humanity which has prompted you to do this. Would that there were more like you and that company of Christian gentlemen and gentlewomen whom I met on our trip to Haichow. The world is sorely in need of such. Were it not for them, one could become a hardened cynic."

Early on November 2, 1937, Nelson, Virginia, Miss Lina, MaiMai, and Clayton left Tsingtao for the battle zone.

*1937—Passport picture: Dr. Bell, Virginia, Mrs. Bell, Ruth, and Clayton.
(Rosa was at Wheaton College in America.)*

Roof of Bells' home draped with American flag to avoid Japanese bombing of Chinese buildings

Sandbagged dugout for use during time of Japanese bombing

24
The Safe Place

MAIMAI AND DIDI sat beside the blown-out windows of the diner and listened breathlessly as waiters described narrow escapes on their previous journey. DiDi hoped the antiaircraft guns next to the engine would open fire. To the children it was pure excitement, and they knew how much they were envied by Ruth, who was now on the Pacific with a splinter of shrapnel from Tsingkiangpu's first bombing, kindly donated by a Chinese officer, safe in her baggage.

Their parents took a more realistic view: when the clear early November weather gave way to an unseasonably heavy fog as they neared Suchowfu and they heard bombers pass overhead without spotting the train, Nelson and Virginia felt "a tremendous sense of God's protecting hand." Two stations were bombed a few hours after the train had passed. At Suchowfu, where the sixty-year-old Dr. McFadyen and an elderly couple, the Browns, had stoutly refused to evacuate, they watched the bombers approach and only took to the dugout when the planes droned overhead—harmlessly, because their target lay farther west.

That night, the Bells and Miss Lina stepped off their next train in the blacked-out station of the town where the line crossed the Grand Canal. A police officer recognized them. Delighted at the direction they were heading, he arranged their baggage transfer and sent soldiers to conduct them the mile of pitch darkness to the boats, where Nelson woke up boatmen and bargained a price for all-night travel. The three missionaries and two children were soon asleep in the tiny, evil-smelling cabin of a small houseboat while rain pattered on the matting which formed the absurdly low ceiling.

The homecoming on November 5 was naturally their quietest, but Nelson wrote the next day, "The Chinese were simply carried away with delight at having us back and showed their pleasure in so many ways." A Chinese general who had known Bell for three years said, with tears in his eyes: "God may protect this whole city for your sakes."

Nelson's letter continued: "We feel so definitely led to return that we have absolute peace as to what we have done. What the future holds we do not know, but the same God who is guiding and protecting us now will go on with us in the future. It takes experiences like this to make us realize how near and how dear our heavenly Father really is."

They quickly proved the rightness of their decision. Nelson wrote to his mother: "There is no way to humanly explain the peace we have in our hearts here and the joy it is to be on the job." Their spiritual development reached a higher plateau of warmth and sensitivity; their work was infused with a new power. Six months later Nelson wrote: "How we do thank Him for having called us back here and for the privileges He has given. It has been a great lesson in faith. The great fundamental blessing came when we were willing to come back, regardless of the consequences, for we felt that His special blessing started then."

*   *   *   *   *

Nelson fixed up a family air-raid shelter out of a concrete water cistern, which would be proof against all but a direct hit, for the blast of a 1937 bomb was slight compared with the blockbusters of World War II. The hospital already had trenches and shelters for staff and patients, and Nelson worked out a system of telephone warnings to all departments. At an alert he allowed no one to be in the yards, lest a pilot be tempted to use his machine gun, and would hasten out, "with a terribly empty feeling in my tummy," to check that all outer gates were shut to prevent refugees from flooding in wildly.

When Virginia shepherded the children into the dugout, they never felt the slightest fear. She often had to pull them away from watching the bombers fly in. Even when the novelty had worn off, and they had seen casualties carried in on doors or stretchers and could sense the panic in the city, the children remained unafraid. "I recall no fear whatsoever," Clayton Bell said. "I don't remember any feeling of fear of the Japanese. Mother never showed any tension that I remember." To Nelson it was further evidence of Virginia's courage: he knew that inside she felt as much fear as any.

Nelson had the same courage. Routine surgery was now performed early in the morning since bombers had never arrived before nine, but he was often in the middle of an emergency operation when he heard the drone of approaching planes. The operation could not stop. Nelson's natural fear did not convey itself to his scalpel, let alone to the nurses and assistants; even "Varnish," the hospital technician who was the most scared of all the senior staff, felt a little braver when near Nelson.

The number of patients had dropped with the first raids. Many citizens fled to the country, and the country people kept away from the city, for the Japanese were expected to bomb Tsingkiangpu heavily as a prelude to its capture before Christmas. But when Christmas passed, while the enemy concentrated on the railway further west, kala-azar and routine work increased again, together with air-raid casualties and wounded soldiers. Nelson had Psalms 91 and 34 written out on scrolls in the main hall. Special evangelistic meetings were packed by citizens as well as patients, and a mid-morning prayer meeting was held for the staff, snatching a pause from work.

Nelson sometimes drove into the country on calls. Unable to hear bombers when in his car, he kept a weather eye on people in fields or streets; if they looked up at the sky, he knew it was time to jump out and take cover. Worse than bombers were bandits; old miseries had returned with a vengeance. "When I got to the home to which I was going," he wrote in mid-January 1938, "I found things in indescribable confusion and found that during the night forty or fifty bandits had looted the place, burning the arms and legs of the man to force him to tell where his money was. Banditry is simply sweeping this section of the country now as prisons have been opened and arms and ammunitions are being sold to all who will buy them. The future in this connection almost beggars description."

*   *   *   *   *

The missionaries at Tsingkiangpu, once the largest of SPM stations, now consisted of the Bell family, Lina Bradley, and one other middle-aged lady, Jess Hall, who had resumed her work among the countrywomen of the region. Dr. Woods had returned from Kuling, but he was seventy years of age and increasingly deaf: the Bells fully approved his decision not to remain for the coming battle. The Carlburgs, to Nelson's sorrow, had been ordered by the CIM to take their furlough early and had left the city a few days after welcoming back the Bells.

Late in February 1938 the Japanese resumed their drives. Tsingkiangpu—now designated provincial capital of Kiangsu since Chinkiang had fallen—lay in the center of the only remaining area in eastern China still held by the Chinese. The enemy advanced remorselessly from all four directions. Older missionaries in Shanghai sent urgent pleas to Nelson to send Virginia and the children to safety before too late. MaiMai and Clayton were the only foreign children remaining inland in North Kiangsu and several other provinces, and the Bells were told it was monstrous they should be submitted to the horrors of possible siege and certain conquest. Even the Japanese formally requested the American ambassador to remove this obstinate family.

Nelson and Virginia saw it as a crisis of faith, even more than their decision to return the previous November. They knew by now the beastliness of the invading army after capturing a city. In Nelson's words: "The reason we dread the conquest of our area is the destruction of life and property, unbridled lust, rape, murder, and looting; we also dread the new regime setup, using the dregs of local humanity as the pawns through which they govern and then the bringing in and establishing of brothels and opium dens and everything else they can think of to enslave the people." And the Japanese were already showing their contempt for Americans by slapping faces and looting homes. Yet the hospital was full, the medical and evangelistic opportunities were unprecedented, and the Chinese staff kept together; Tsingkiangpu was the only SPM hospital unaffected by staff desertions. "If you stay," they said, "we will stay."

Nelson had been studying Psalms, Proverbs, Isaiah, and other parts of the Bible, marking the scores of divine promises of protection, guidance, and power, and had been overwhelmingly impressed by one verse: "The promise is unto you *and to your children.*"

Virginia not only sympathized; she urged him to stay. She refused to leave. She quoted a couplet from a poem by Ralph Waldo Emerson:

> If for truth he should die
> 'Tis man's perdition to be safe.

"The children are just as happy as can be," she wrote to Mother Bell on March 6, "and if things come to the worst here, I'm going to stick right with them and keep them happily engaged. Our God is *able,* and that 'Restraining Hand' is all-loving and all-powerful."

A colleague returned, leaving his wife in Shanghai. He was, she wrote, "full of rumors and lurid tales. *Insists* on my leaving and taking the children. We went to bed very depressed, but the next morning in came Mr. Carlburg right back from Chinkiang with many good and encouraging reports. I know the Lord sent him to cheer us up."

At no time did Nelson admire his wife more than in her determination to stand by him and their beloved Chinese. She only wished more missionaries could leave rumor-ridden, expensive Shanghai, where the waves looked so much higher than in the war zone, and return to undermanned or closed stations at this hour of opportunity.

The decision to stand fast, Nelson Bell testifies, "deepened and confirmed our sense of the closeness of God. He was right there with us. Underneath with everlasting arms, over us with overshadowing wings—we were con-

scious of His peace and presence in a way that I don't think
we would ever have been otherwise. There was prayer, constant prayer, in our heart. And also constant thanksgiving
and praise for the consciousness of His presence. You had
no one else to depend on. It was a sense of safety within
His keeping."

The last escape route was blocked. With a crowded hospital and people begging for admission when every bed was
full, March passed into April. The Japanese were only a few
score miles away, yet still they did not come, hindered by
stiff resistance and by strategic considerations elsewhere.
Nelson said he felt like the dog whose master removed its
tail by cutting off an inch each day.

*   *   *   *   *

By now Gus Craig and the Rev. Bird Talbot, Addison
Talbot's eldest son, were working as evangelists at
Tsingkiangpu. About 8:30 a.m. on Saturday, May 21, 1938,
the air-raid warning sounded, "And in just a little while,"

*Left to right: Mary Alice and Bird Talbot (with Wade), and Ken and Kay
Gieser (with Richard).*

runs Virginia's vivid description, "we heard them, ten planes, the heavy roar that denotes a bomber. They flew around for nearly an hour and dropped fourteen bombs; it was no joke for they were quite close. A large piece of shrapnel fell in the compound, two bombs hit that big old temple near the coal yard, one bomb fell near the 'Pig Hotel'; they power-dived so close that even in the dugout we could hear the wind whining through the struts, and of course the horrible zooming as they rose again, but their dirty work has been done. It is when they are coming down that you hold your breath. A fire started in the city at once. Bird and I walked down to the temple; we heard they were digging people out, but it was an exaggeration—only one was killed there. We all felt sort of tired and exhausted when it was over, but so thankful we and all the Christians were safe. We were counting over our defenses, while waiting in the dugout. Overhead are the overshadowing wings, Psalm 91:4; underneath are the everlasting arms, Deuteronomy 33:27; all around, 'the angel of the Lord encampeth round about them that fear him, and delivereth them,' Psalm 34:7; inside, that 'peace which passeth all understanding,' Philippians 4:7; also, 'Thou wilt keep him in perfect peace, whose mind is stayed on thee: because he trusteth in thee,' Isaiah 26:3."

Between raids the Bells could hear continuous artillery duels from the southwest. "We feel pretty sure the enemy is approaching," Virginia wrote to the girls on Sunday, May 22. "The poor people are terrified and have left town by the thousands. We had church this a.m. at six o'clock, pretty good crowd, Bird Talbot preached—splendid message! We passed rickshaw after rickshaw loaded to the hilt, and people carrying things, leaving town; most doors were boarded up; looked like a real Sunday street, only you knew that behind the doors one or two had been left to look after the property."

The aged Dr. Woods had bravely insisted on returning after all and assumed oversight of the civilian and military wounded: "A great horde of wounded and defeated soldiers have retreated from the Suchowfu section. When a raid began, Nelson would lead singing in the dugout ('Under His wings I am safely abiding,' a duet by Nelson and Jess Hall was particularly memorable), and thus turned a nightmare into a party. One evening—after we had emerged—Virginia served a full-style American birthday supper for eleven in honor of Lillian Wells, one of the Hwaian staff whom Nelson had brought back for the night."

The next week the bombs smashed and burned out the quarter of Tsingkiangpu's inner walled city which lay nearest to the hospital. Virginia wrote to the girls in America: "It is impossible to know yet how many are killed; we are thankful so many had fled to the country the last two days—the city was almost deserted. Daddy had to amputate three legs before supper. It is all so pitiful, and the poor people are so frightened. They are huddled in the chapel and on the hospital porches, and the pastor and evangelists are talking to them and singing with them. It hasn't been a restful experience; we all feel tired and weary."

The same night Hwaian had an even worse raid. The SPM girls' school was wrecked and that birthday supper's guest of honor covered with plaster and dirt but unharmed.

Then, sixty miles to the north, a big battle ended in Chinese victory, one of their few real victories of the war. Over six hundred casualties reached Tsingkiangpu on a single day.

In mid-June the Bells had the eerie experience of waiting for raids that never came, except for one reconnaissance plane which flew so low that the Stars and Stripes blew taut in its slipstream. Each sunlit morning they wondered how many bombers would be over, and each hour seemed a reprieve; relief flooded in at dusk, and they only wished the night could last longer. A whole week passed without incident. For a time the Bells could hardly get used to the quiet, but as week succeeded week that summer the songbirds under the silent, strangely empty sky seemed sweeter and more numerous than anyone could remember.

The city returned almost to normal, the hospital busier than ever. In fact, 1938 broke all records for hospital admissions and outpatients.

*   *   *   *   *

Thirty-two years later a Chinese woman living in Taiwan,

Mrs. Chen Li Hsiu-ling, told James Graham, Jr. two stories
from this period. Hsiu-ling had been one of Dr. Bell's nurses.
Shortly before the war she had entered medical college at
Chinkiang, intending to be a doctor, but after its capture
she fell ill with suspected tuberculosis "and knew not which
way to turn." Bell heard of her plight, and she came through
the Japanese lines to be under his care. "I did not know
certainly when I went back to Tsingkiangpu that I had TB.
I only knew I was ill and devoid of all strength. Dr. Bell
himself was not sure either, at first, because the sure and
simple way of a lung X-ray was denied to him, a means that
he had used for years." For a vital part in the X-ray equipment
had failed, and it was not until February 1939 that Nelson
Bell could secure a replacement.

Bell treated her case as TB, and Hsiu-ling improved
rapidly. By then TB was reaching epidemic proportions in
Kiangsu because of wartime undernourishment and the
impossibility of X-ray investigation. Hsiu-ling continued:
"There were many deaths from this disease to which the
Chinese people seem easily susceptible. Even the nurses in
the hospital were brought down with it, one after another,
and soon became desperately ill and needed blood transfusions to save their lives. But the blood bank was exhausted,
and it is terribly difficult to get the Chinese to give their
blood. At the critical point the unexpected happened. The
doctor, who daily gave his life in service to others, now came
forth to have blood drawn from his own veins to transfuse
into the bloodstreams of the nurses. He had type O blood,
which will serve in the majority of cases. I can never forget
this act of love."

Nelson Bell did not recall the incident. On several occasions he gave blood, but this particular one "certainly did
not make any impression on me at the time."

Hsiu-ling's other story concerned a manual worker
named Chou, whom she saw in 1969 on the campus of a
Christian college in Taiwan doing his job with a vigor beyond
his years. When she commented on this, he replied that
were it not for a foreign doctor on the mainland long ago
he would have been one-legged and useless. Chou told her
that a major accident had wrecked one of his legs and those

of several fellow workers.

"There was some delay," she related, "before the men were taken to a Chinese hospital, and gangrene had already set in. The Chinese doctors ruled that to save their lives, the legs would have to be amputated. But Chou was not willing to be a one-legged man the rest of his life until there was consultation with other doctors. He demanded to be taken to a certain hospital that had a fabulous reputation, the Love and Mercy Hospital. They took him there, and soon his leg was being examined by the legendary 'Chong Ai Hua' (Dr. Bell). The good doctor shook his head ruefully over the fact that there was already gangrene in the wound and admitted to grave fears that amputation might be necessary, but he would first take him into the operating room and remove the gangrenous portion and treat the wound with all the means he had at hand to make an attempt to save the leg. This was done, and doubtless with a large ingredient of the therapy of prayer, the leg was saved. All of Chou's former co-workers lost their legs. Chou affirmed that when he emerged from the Love and Mercy Hospital, his leg was as good as ever. He became a Christian and is a member of the Christian assembly in the town of Chung Li, Taiwan."

Hsiu-ling retained an emphatic memory of the staff's devotion to Bell. "The thing above all others that he put into the hospital was *love*. He communicated to the others a spirit of mutual concern for the well-being of the patients, all based upon the example and Spirit of Christ. Even when he retired to his home, he was *still not off duty*. When the national doctors and staff were off duty, they were *really* off duty, and no nocturnal emergency would or could disturb their slumbers. But it seemed that Dr. Bell was never more than half asleep, for as soon as there was the slightest disturbance in any part of the hospital, as of a late emergency case, he would be out of his bed and out on the upstairs porch of his house calling for an explanation of the commotion, and if it was an emergency, what was the nature of it and how serious. If he could not feel sure that the nationals had the case well in hand, he would be over there in a wink, taking charge of things himself.

"This kind of dedication to duty, though they could not

match it, challenged their highest admiration, inspired them to more faithful service, and made them proud to be working for such a man."

25
The Fall of Tsingkiangpu

B OTH MaiMai and Clayton," wrote Nelson on July 17, 1938, "have come through these months in fine shape, and I am sure no harm has been done to their nervous systems, as so many people have feared. Day after day I prayed they might be kept from fear, danger, and shock, and God has answered that prayer."

The strain lay more heavily on their parents. Bird Talbot had arrived from rumor-ridden Shanghai expecting to see two, thin, nervous wrecks. Sitting in the dugout during an air raid and taking a good look at the happy and healthy Bells, he burst out laughing: "And they talk about *skeleton* forces!" But strain there was. As Nelson wrote some months later, "The more I see of Virginia and think of the staunch way she has stood by, making a home, doing her work, keeping up her courage and that of others, the more I realize she is one in a million. She has the stuff not seen so often today, and I do thank the Lord for all she has meant to me and us all this past year. Of course it has been a strain, and sometimes we just long to be out of it, but at the same time God has shown His wonderful love and power to restore and refresh and strengthen His children."

They began to dream of going home for special leave during the next summer, 1939, at their own expense, for they were not due for furlough until 1943. A special rate would allow seven weeks in America. "Just how we will finance it, I do not know yet, but I am sure the Lord will open the way if it is His will." The Bells had no private means except for a few insurance policies. Their stipend only covered their own needs and not even all the education costs, with which Nelson's brother, McKim, had generously helped out. For the exceptional expense of an extra furlough Bell took the problem where he took all his problems, great and small: "Some days ago I asked the Lord to give me some leading as to His will by a gift unsolicited and from an unexpected source. This week I received such a gift from an Independent Presbyterian Church in Amarillo, Texas. The pastor is a man I met at Moody in 1923 and again in 1935. It was very small, but I feel that God sent it, and as all things belong to Him, and as we have left it in His hands to work out, He will surely provide the money if it is His will. If it is not His will, we do not want to go." Nelson booked passages for May 30, 1939. During the intervening ten months other gifts came from other sources, and Uncle Jimmy Graham in Shanghai approved the idea so warmly that he insisted on Nelson accepting one hundred dollars.

Rest and change were not the only reasons for the vacation plan. The Bells badly wanted to see the girls at Wheaton. Not only were mails too erratic, with no letters for weeks while the Chinese post office sought ways of delivering the rapidly growing piles to beleaguered Tsingkiangpu, but Rosa had been seriously ill again with a recurrence of TB. She was better and back at college on a limited schedule, but they suffered to know how ill she had been when they were so far away. They were somewhat relieved, though, that Ruth had been with her, and Mother Bell at Waynesboro helped all she could.

*   *   *   *   *

At Wheaton Ruth majored in Bible and minored in art. While Rosa had the quick mind, Ruth was more the plodder; yet Ruth was the impetuous character, Rosa the cautious. Nelson would laugh and say that one showed the Irish, the other the Scotch side of their ancestry. "We thank God for their spiritual lives and surrender to Him," he wrote. And again: "Ruth has a mighty clear understanding of things spiritual....If ever a person has surrendered completely to the Lord, she has." She had not reached spiritual maturity at eighteen, however: she longed to quit college and set off for the far west of China, the Tibetan border. Her father also had to urge her to "remember all of us need and must have some recreation and relaxation, and God wants His children to be happy and have a good time." As she grew older, she approved this sentiment to the full.

In the early months of 1938 Ken Gieser, on furlough at Wheaton, wrote gaily to the Bells: "Everybody seems plum crazy about the girls—and of course we cannot understand it very well, knowing their mother and dad as we do. As far as I can tell, their girlfriends are many and their boyfriends are not a few. Neither of them seems to be thick with anyone but each seems to be gracefully moving around in a mighty fine group of Christian boys." Billy Graham was not among them: at nineteen, he was enjoying the stimulating freedom of the Florida Bible Institute and soon would have his momentous spiritual experience, walking alone at night near the eighteenth green of the Tampa golf course, which led him to be an evangelist.

*   *   *   *   *

In January 1939 Ken and Kay Gieser, with their baby, returned to Tsingkiangpu. They had been back in China since the fall, but Nelson reluctantly had been obliged to lend them to another station. Ken's return made the Bells' furlough plans realistic. "We have never had anything like the number of patients at this time of year before," Nelson wrote on February 10, 1939, and without Ken he could not leave.

Nor could the Bells expect to go until after what they euphemistically called the "turnover," the Japanese occupation. It was inevitable; indeed, the year of freedom had been a wholly unexpected boon which more than justified the decision to return to Tsingkiangpu in defiance of the American government's policy of evacuation.

In November 1938 Sutsien, their neighbor station seventy miles north on the Grand Canal, had fallen. The SPM compound had been in the middle of the battle, but first rumors of missionary casualties proved unfounded.

Tsingkiangpu's four-month respite from air raids ended abruptly, and the sound of distant gunfire suggested that its hour would come soon. Then the Japanese thrust eastward instead. On Christmas Day, 1938, which had been celebrated in the old style despite shortages and improvisions, Nelson had written to his mother: "This past Thursday it was my time to lead foreign prayer meeting, and I talked about the place of physical fear in the life of the Christian. Last week it dawned on me that our Lord, tempted in all points like as we are, yet without sin, hungered, thirsted, was tired, became angry, and gave every evidence of his humanity, but *He was never fearful.* Fear, therefore, must come from lack of faith—sin. Just as we never become sinless, so we never entirely lose fear, but it surely is His will for His children to live with peace in their hearts, trusting in Him and His promises."

At last, late in February, the Japanese were ready to strike at Tsingkiangpu: to smash all resistance, if need be, by bombardment from ground and air; then to turn the ruined streets into a horror of bayoneting and rape.

A verse kept running through Nelson's mind, from Paul's shipwreck: "Fear not, Paul...God hath given thee all them that sail with thee." Fifteen months earlier when the Bells had returned from Tsingtao, General Li had said: "God may protect this whole city for your sakes."

*   *   *   *   *

Monday, February 27, had begun much as usual, with air-raid warnings soon after early morning surgery. Planes passed and repassed without dropping bombs. Explosions and gunfire could be heard to the north, and the Bells were worried because three missionaries were out in that direction, at a town of Siyang eighteen miles away, for a country preachers' conference. About noon Nelson heard that Siyang had been badly bombed; he decided to rescue them in the Austin Seven.

Rumors flooded Tsingkiangpu that a big battle was being fought beyond Siyang; all available troops had been rushed north to stem the Japanese thrust. Nelson drove first to the bus station to see if he could pick up news and learned that three foreigners in rickshaws had been passed near the north gate. He returned to the hospital and found they had arrived safely—their conference had faded out the previous night because of the battle and they had left Siyang at first light before the bombing.

Next morning, Tuesday, February 28, dawned drizzly and cloudy. Far away in peaceful Wheaton Rosa celebrated her twenty-first birthday. Her father's day began with news that Siyang had fallen and the Chinese were retreating to make a last stand at Tsingkiangpu, whose citizens began to pour toward the hospital where they instinctively felt they would be safe: an unusually large number of minor ailments were brought to the clinic that day. Japanese planes passed over again and again. They did not drop bombs, but explosions could be heard to the south in the direction of Hwaian and two neighboring towns. As Nelson walked back from clinic, he saw a plane swoop down and machine-gun the crowd outside the hospital—mercifully the casualties were light.

Another plane scattered leaflets urging civilians to leave before the battle. Over the hospital it dropped warnings that "Nationals of third powers" should leave or the Japanese would take no responsibility for what might happen to them. "Not pleasant," Nelson commented, "but we felt God had permitted it to show the Chinese we were staying here because of our faith in Him and not because of our trust in the American flag."

The gate was locked at 5:00 p.m. At 7:00 p.m. when Ken Gieser made his rounds, he found some twenty people locked in who wanted to get out—mostly wounded soldiers who didn't want to be captured. He wrote in his diary: "I opened the high gate, and immediately there was a pushing and crowding of people outside trying to get in. I planted myself in the middle of the gate and finally stemmed the tide, keeping out all who are not actually patients. We do not want refugees in until there is actual danger outside."

Even then, to avoid chaos in the compound, refugee admissions were to be strictly controlled—any hospital staff and their families and then women and children—first the Christians carrying passes from Pastor Kao, afterward non-

Christians; Nelson knew that he must, if possible, account for everyone or risk the lot being slaughtered if the city fell by assault.

All that night the road past the hospital was noisy with cars, wheelbarrows, and rickshaws, as the provincial government fled the city.

At 6:30 a.m. on Wednesday, March 1, another drizzly day, refugees were admitted according to plan. In Ken Gieser's words: "Carrying beds and bedding, flour and rice, pictures and the possessions of a lifetime, the steady stream of anxious people continued. Their tense, gray faces told of a sleepless night; their nervous glances and jittery movements betrayed a fear almost unto death. Suddenly, the already rapidly moving column increased its pace to the point of confusion. Terror seized them as the word was passed along, 'The planes are coming.'

"For the safety of all, the big outer gate has been closed during all air raids, but this morning by the time we got to the gate, a regular stampede was on. A frantic, hysterical mob rushed that gate, and yet slowly and deliberately it had to be closed."

The crowded compound emptied rapidly as everyone sought cover. Six planes in perfect formation, so low that the bombs could be seen in the racks, were right overhead when Ken Gieser saw Kay, carrying Dickie, running out in the open toward the dugout. Ken was in agony lest a trigger-happy pilot try a little machine gun practice.

Kay gained cover, and a few moments later the ground shook as heavy bombs pounded to the south. Hour after hour the planes came and went; bomb explosions could be heard in the near distance, but not on the city itself. Eleven-year-old MaiMai, at the telephone to pass on warnings to the departments, counted eighty-four bomb blasts and numerous machine gun bursts. Not a single antiaircraft gun retaliated from Tsingkiangpu, though the sound of big guns was incessant to the northwest.

Every staff member had a duty. Virginia's included keeping an eye on six-year-old Clayton, but he was not in the least afraid: His favorite verse was, "The angel of the Lord encampeth round about them that fear him, and delivereth them." Nelson and Ken stayed at the gate most of the day. The doctors accepted such refugees as they could; strict control was essential to prevent mob rule. It was a hectic day, and Nelson was in pain and wearing a brace after a recurrence of his old back trouble. "Strange to say, none of us were nervous or scared in the least. God gave a sense of complete detachment, Psalm 91:7-8 being actually fulfilled—and the children were kept just as the rest of us. All day long not one of us went into the dugout we have had to use so often in the past."

Virginia's servants had hurried to the city to buy food before shopkeepers fled. At supper two enormous explosions shook the table and a great fire blazed from the city: the Chinese had blown up a canal bridge and the electric light plant (the hospital had its own).

A milling crowd swirled about the hospital gate that night, but Nelson would not permit a general admission until the Japanese had reached the next town to the north. When he and Ken left the gate and went to bed, Nelson was absolutely sure the enemy was still miles away.

About 1:30 a.m. Ken was awakened by commotion in the compound. He dressed and found Nelson up a ladder against the eight-foot wall in the middle of panic-stricken people climbing over—regarded in China as the act of a thief and a robber. He was banging the wall with a piece of wood in one hand while pushing at the intruders with the other.

"Nelson, what in the world are you doing up there?"

"I'm practicing muscular Christianity!"

With Ken's help he rounded up a hundred intruders and put them out. The panic had begun with a rumor that the Japanese army had already arrived. Nelson thought it a trick to get them inside the compound.

Neither doctor returned to bed. At first light Nelson went to the gate and announced that no more refugees would be admitted until the Japanese were in the suburbs: he still thought they were miles away. "However, planes started coming over almost immediately, and the people were so pitiful that we went to the gate and let in all who wanted to come, making them crowd in the men's and women's chapels of the clinic building."

Rumors persisted that the Japanese had entered—from the south, not the north as expected. Someone said a Rising Sun flag was flying over the east gate beyond the canal. Nelson went up to the attic porch and saw the flag through binoculars but supposed it the act of a traitor. Yet planes droned overhead, bomb racks visible, not dropping their loads. Since the validity or falseness of the rumors had a direct bearing on the refugee problem, Nelson proposed to drive to the east gate and discover the true situation.

"Virginia was dead set against my going, but while we were still looking, we saw eight soldiers riding down the big road back of the compound carrying a Japanese flag. Then we knew it was true. Then I saw two planes flying low over the city and signaling with their wings and that was significant. Immediately we foreign men went to the front gate to man the gate and, of course, told all refugees we would keep them as long as necessary. I also put up the consular and other papers, prepared over a year ago and carefully framed to protect from the weather, on the front gate."

The astonishing, merciful anticlimax had been the culmination of a brilliant strategy. The Japanese had made a feint in the north, drawing away almost the entire Chinese strength, and then swept massive armored and cavalry forces around by an undefended flank to take Tsingkiangpu from the south. They did not bomb the city itself because they wanted it undamaged as their headquarters. Nelson and Virginia felt "dazed and relieved beyond expression and thankful to the great God who had so wonderfully kept us and the city. Despite what losses the people may sustain, their houses have not been destroyed by bombing or shellfire or burning. How we did and do praise Him too for keeping the children from fear, danger, and shock of every kind."

"Clayton!" Nelson called. "You can go and pull down the dugout if you like!"

26
Under the Japanese

THE streets were deserted. At 2:30 p.m. Nelson piled Ken Gieser and Dr. Woods into the Austin Seven to go into the city and call on the Japanese commanding general. Sympathies lay totally with the Chinese, but Americans could best help through strict neutrality: by the aggressor's whim alone could the hospital function.

Nelson told little Clayton to hop in too. With shrewd understanding of Oriental psychology he sensed that a child would warm the heart of the general and prove the innocence of their activities.

When the car reached the main road, the Japanese troops were marching by. The Americans alighted and watched for a full half-hour the passing of an army of at least three thousand men. Infantry, cavalry, guns, in perfect order and discipline, and fifteen tanks to Clayton's delight, all in stark contrast to the ramshackle Chinese forces who had gone down to defeat. The missionaries politely lifted their hats as officers rode by and received salutes in return. The little Austin Seven gave them "face" in the eyes of the Japanese, and when upon reaching headquarters at last they were met at the door by the general himself, their prestige soared. Bowing to the aggressor was gall and wormwood to Nelson and Ken, but they did so for the hospital's sake. The general looked surprised and delighted at the sight of Clayton and asked them to return the next day at noon.

Again Nelson took Clayton, who retains a dim memory of the general presenting him with Japanese candy. Nelson told the general firmly that the Americans were neutrals who lived in Tsingkiangpu to preach the gospel and heal the sick. They planned to continue to do so ("I did not ask him if we could; I said we would. It was essential to show I was not afraid of him"). They had nothing to hide and would welcome the general's representatives and show them everything.

The general was courteous and friendly.

The next day Japanese military police, the dreaded Kempeitei, arrived. Nelson received them as he would any guest. The captain began the first round of the interminable interrogations which the occupying power inflicted on the busy staff over the next weeks and then asked to see each room. Nelson's heart was in his boots because one ward held badly wounded Chinese soldiers. Nelson already knew of a horror which American and British forces would discover in World War II—the Japanese bayoneting of wounded prisoners.

Nelson prayed silently. As he and the Kempeitei entered the ward, "I felt the presence of God in a most amazing way."

The Japanese paused at the door. They looked up at the ceiling; they looked around the upper part of the walls; then they turned on their heels and walked out.

*   *   *   *   *

A few nights later a Japanese soldier raped a woman outside the gates of the hospital and bayoneted her husband to death. The next morning Nelson went to headquarters and reported it. The head of the military police asked him to have the widow traced and the following day came to the hospital. Nelson reported two more rapes. The police chief spoke kindly to the widow and asked the insignia on the soldier's tunic, but she had been too distressed to notice. He expressed the army's deep regret and gave her the considerable sum of twenty dollars, either from genuine compassion or to gain face with Nelson. He visited the homes of the other two women and after inquiry gave each five dollars.

The incident was typical. Women were raped, or stripped by soldiers for amusement, and looting was not uncommon, though Tsingkiangpu experienced nothing like the plundering of the rich city of Hwaian, where the entire contents of houses were emptied into trucks. Yet the Japanese went out of their way to please Nelson and his colleagues and put no restriction on the work of the hospital, whereas another SPM hospital had been brought virtually to a standstill.

Outside the compound the days—and especially the nights—were unpredictable. Chinese troops still operated in the countryside: gunfire could be heard at night, and after one battle a Chinese told of seeing Japanese burn a pile of their dead with the badly wounded thrown on top. Peasants were brought in daily, horribly burned by bandits of their own race. The gateman's boy was kidnapped for ransom.

Tsingkiangpu Christians raised money among themselves to relieve destitution among neighbors hit by the war. The occupation warmed previously lukewarm hearts. On the first Communion Sunday, April 2, the church was packed, with some standing. But of 213 who had applied to be received into full membership, the elders admitted only eight women and four men, one being "Mr. Dirty Country," the chief hirer of laborers, whose men carried out the corpses through the hospital's back gate. He had been examined no less than twenty times. "Every precaution," Ken Gieser wrote, "is taken that the people accepted understand the gospel and live consistently in keeping with the Christian standards of the church."

Ken was a tower of strength to Nelson. "He is a fine worker, has such a nice way with the Chinese and with the Japanese, and his being here is a boon beyond words"—because it made possible the summer in the States. The thought of getting out for a while, as he wrote to Uncle Jimmy in Shanghai, was "like a tonic. Don't think these past eighteen months have taken much out of us, for God has renewed our strength and given us such joy in His continued presence. However, He knows that rest and change are needful at times and recommended it for His own disciples, so a vacation will be in line with what He approves."

Late in April the Bells left by Japanese truck convoy with the widowed Addison Talbot and nurse Cassie Lee Oliver who, to everyone's pleasure, were to be married in Shanghai. The Bells sailed on the *Empress of Japan* on May 14, 1939.

The seven weeks in America were a refreshment without which the Bells could hardly have stood the strains of the next eighteen months. Every financial need was met—humanly speaking by a combination of unsolicited gifts, general hospitality, and Nelsonic shrewdness. He bought a new Ford in Detroit, and at the end of their leave he sold it in the eastern states at a profit; totaling up his car accounts Nelson found that in effect they had ridden 4500 miles at no cost and had fifteen dollars in hand. He wrote to his mother from the train as it drew near Chicago: "This whole experience of going home has increased our faith in God and made us realize as never before how wonderfully He provides *all* when we are following His will. I just pray this experience may carry on through the years and enable us to be a greater blessing to others."

What is more, they were able to take Rosa with them as tutor for MaiMai and Clayton: the doctors said that a year in China would restore her strength before she completed her Wheaton studies. Only Ruth remained in America.

The Bells sailed back on the same ship in August 1939. When asked why they were foolish enough to return to war-stricken China at a time of world crisis, "The only answer we can give is this—we believe God wants us to be there. That being true, we would be utterly miserable in any other place."

They were still in Shanghai when England and France declared war on Nazi Germany. Nelson accumulated all the medical stores he could, and they set out for the interior with ninety-four boxes of freight weighing five tons. They had to take a roundabout route requiring twelve days of travel because guerrillas had closed the Grand Canal. Nelson's blend of authority and humor unraveled each strand of Japanese red tape, and at Suchowfu they agreed to put all his freight on a military convoy; an astonished Chinese official of the occupying power said: "You have a lot of face. They never would have done that for anyone else." To Nelson the reason lay deeper. "There were seven times in Suchowfu alone when I was up against a stone wall, and each time

God provided a man who was in a position to help. This happened elsewhere too. These evidences, again and again, of His presence and help could strengthen our faith immeasurably and make us continually to praise Him."

They arrived in Tsingkiangpu on September 12. "How good it is to be home again," wrote twelve-year-old MaiMai to her grandmother. "Even if America is a nice place to live in for a while, I still think China better."

* * * * *

Rosa's health improved in the atmosphere of home, though she still had some pleuritic pain. The familiar Bell way of life continued unaffected by the war, from family prayers in the morning until the games and reading at night, and when one of their milk goats had triplets, Rosa stayed up all night to keep the two survivors warm and fed. "By the next day," Virginia wrote, "she was so sleepy and so stiff from squatting down that she wished they had died too, which they did by noon. They had barely been disposed of when another goat had triplets."

Rosa's fluency in Chinese returned quickly, and she soon took women's classes in the city chapel twice a week, and a Sunday school. The Japanese insisted that a sentry accompany her, and once when the children were naughty the sentry came forward, shook his finger, and said in broken Chinese, "You must listen; you must listen!"

The Japanese sentry was probably genuinely—if unnecessarily—for protection, but Nelson wrote: "It is almost impossible for folks at home to realize the strain of present conditions. I believe the greatest part is that of being under constant suspicion by a people who have not the remotest idea of what we are out here to do. This causes some bizarre ideas which make it hard."

It was thus with Clayton's pigeons. They were supposed to be pets, though Clayton remembered he "never did a very good job of keeping them clean or getting close to them. I was too young to be tender and kind to them." The Japanese decided they were carrier pigeons and took much convincing that this six-year-old American was not a link in a spy chain.

On the other hand, when Nelson reported that sentries at Hwaian had turned him back despite his official pass, the military police chief put on Chinese clothes, watched while the Japanese sentries roughly waved Nelson away, then disclosed himself and dressed them down loudly before all passers-by until the soldiers wilted. Again, when Bell reported that Japanese soldiers sent to draw drinking water from the lake were chasing local women, the police chief went to the lake, found the trucks empty, and waited until the men returned. Nelson's Chinese clerk reported that the confrontation was delicious.

The basic friendliness of the Japanese toward the hospital was the result of a most fortunate choice of commanding officer, General Hori. At Hori's departure upon his promotion to major-general in March 1940, Nelson, with the approval of the Chinese doctors, followed Oriental custom by sending him a specially baked cake and the next day, with Ken, attended the departure parade. When the little general jumped down from his tall horse to thank him for the cake, Nelson gained much face in the eyes of Chinese, who in the strange atmosphere of the undeclared Sino-Japanese war did not regard such relationships as collaboration with a hated enemy but had accepted the occupation as their fate and were deeply grateful to Dr. Bell for his handling of their conquerors.

At the end of World War II Nelson inquired about Hori when visiting Tokyo and discovered that he had survived to live in retirement in a distant part of Japan.

*　*　*　*　*

"This morning," Nelson wrote on December 21, 1939, "guerrillas came in and attacked some puppet guards near the hospital gate; a regular battle went on for a half-hour but all is quiet now. We close the hospital gates the minute things start, to keep people from running in here." After the fight the Japanese wanted to search the hospital for suspicious characters but went away on learning that the gates had been closed."

A few days later Addison Talbot and his wife returned

in a Japanese convoy, following a two months' evangelistic and pastoral tour in the countryside. They endured continuous skirmishes for twenty-two hours while in a Japanese army truck; Chinese bullets whistled over their heads, and at one point a Japanese machine gunner used Cassie Lee's shoulder as a tripod. "They do not seem one bit the worse for the wear and experience." Throughout the tour the Talbots had shown splendid unconcern, even when bandits took them, and they reported "glorious opportunities in the midst of danger and destruction." They also found much fruit from the seed sown among country folk who had been refugees in the the hospital at the time of the capture of Tsingkiangpu, when the Chinese evangelists had round-the-clock services, always well-attended.

The Japanese held only the cities. Shells whizzed right over the Bells as they lay awake on the attic porch, and they would claim the promise in the Psalms: "I will both lay me down in peace, and sleep: for thou, Lord, only makest me dwell in safety." As Nelson recalled, "It was a question of either resting in God's promises for our safety and our protection, of resting in bed, or being fearful and getting out. And we chose to stay there." Rosa was equally unconcerned when daytime shellfire sent her class of older women scurrying under the benches. "This is not my war," she reflected, "so I can sit here and smile at the hilarious sight"— blissfully forgetting that shells do not discriminate.

The Bells never knew what would happen next. One day a young Chinese named Lee, chief of the puppet secret police working for the Japanese, was brought in with a ruptured appendix. While still on the critical list, lying in a private ward with his armed men outside the door, he sent for Dr. Bell. "Doctor," he whispered, "you think I'm working for the Japanese. I'm not. I'm under the orders of General Chiang Kai-shek and the Nationalist army, trying to help the Chinese. One of our strict orders is to protect missionaries and Christians."

Wary of a possible trap, Bell merely replied: "This is interesting."

A few days later Lee urged him to "get rid of your radio transmitter because the Japanese are going to search the hospital under pretense of looking for Communists." Bell said he had no transmitter, only a receiver. He explained that messages from Shanghai were kindly read out before the 1:00 p.m. news because telephone and telegraph wires were cut.

"Well, the Japanese think you have a transmitter." And they came to search.

Lee warned Bell that the Japanese were always spying on the hospital and would like to weaken its influence. But not until Lee had left the hospital—having made a profession of faith in Christ—did Bell know his true allegiance beyond doubt. A wounded guerrilla officer had been a patient for weeks. "We had been treating him right under the noses of the Japanese. Lee sent me word by one of his subordinates, 'Get rid of the man in room A-6 immediately.'"

Bell and the staff hurried the guerrilla officer out—he was nearly well—by a side door beside the morgue. A few minutes later the Japanese military police and Chinese puppet police, led by Lee, rushed up to the hospital and straight to room A-6. "Oh," said Lee "He's gone!"

They went away—the Japanese angry, Lee inscrutable.

The guerrillas, however patriotic and laudable, inevitably increased suffering. Their blockade sent prices sky-high; many businesses were ruined, and the local Christians gave unstinting relief irrespective of the creed of those they helped. During the exceptionally severe winter of 1939-40, when canals and roads were frozen and the snow-covered fields often reflected the flames of farmhouses burned by Japanese or guerrillas or by bandits, Nelson wrote: "I can see nothing but utter chaos on into the future."

In this darkness the Tsingkiangpu Hospital stood like a beacon.

Every one of the 360 beds remained full, and the average attendance at the clinics numbered four hundred a day. Kala-azar patients, especially, came in great numbers because the independent medical men who had given injections across the countryside (often after training at the hospital) could no longer obtain stibosan.

Nelson had to use continual shifts and foresight to maintain his stock of stibosan and essentials of all kinds. In

February 1940 Ray Womeldorf volunteered to go to Shanghai to bring up fresh supplies. It took him two whole months. He arrived at last with seventy-eight boxes, two tons of fuel oil, and sixty tons of kerosene. Many of the boxes had been sent by the White Cross, the Southern Presbyterian women's organization in America. Benjamin Clayton's continued munificence "means more to us than ever before" because of inflation in China. He had already given $58,500 since 1924, with unfailing regularity, and by the end his tally would reach nearly $75,000 (which would equal roughly a million dollars in 1988 terms).

Medical aid and evangelism continued hand in hand. A Chinese woman evangelist, Miss Feng, told Nelson in April 1940: "Time and again I have met people in the country who have put away their idols and who believe the gospel and who say they first heard it while a patient in this hospital." She added: "It looks like the Lord is using this scourge of kala-azar to spread the gospel among tens of thousands of people who otherwise might not have heard it."[1] In Tsingkiangpu itself, church attendance declined because many were fearful of the Japanese, although the conquerors showed respect for Christianity and would not molest a home where they found Bible posters. In a country where arm bands were a common form of identification, a Christian would wear one with a small red cross and the characters *Chi Tuh Tu* ("Christian"). These, and the little boards by which shops announced Sunday closing, proved so often to be a protection that unbelievers sometimes would assume them. Here and in other parts of China the war brought many stories of deliverance and safety for Christians and missionaries.

The occupation with its stresses and strains deepened the faith of Chinese Christians, and eternity alone will reveal how many pagans turned to Christ. "There has been *so* much to encourage us in the hospital work," Nelson told Uncle Jimmy. "So many evidences of the working of the

[1] During Billy and Ruth Graham's visit to China in 1988, they had a joyful meeting with Miss Feng, who continues to do evangelistic work through churches.

Holy Spirit and the effectiveness of the evangelistic work. Ten days or so ago I heard of four different entire families who are now believers because of patients converted here in the hospital."

In 1988, almost half a century after she first had worked as an evangelist with Dr. Bell, Miss Feng—still active in evangelism—met Ruth and Billy Graham. At center is the vice-governor of Jiangsu Province, who hosted a reception for the Grahams in Nanjing.

27
The Guiding Hand

AT the end of March 1940 Ken Gieser fell desperately ill with central pneumonia and was not expected to live. For three-and-a-half days Nelson never undressed. Ken was saved by a new drug, sulphapyridine. "Kay has just been wonderful," Virginia wrote to Ruth on March 31. "So brave and efficient and cheerful." The Giesers' second son, Chuck, had been born at Tsingkiangpu the previous November, and for the baby's sake Virginia refused to let Kay stay up all night.

Ken's convalescence was slow, for his heart had been affected, and full strength was not yet regained when Nelson set out with Rosa on May 5 to see her aboard her liner for America—a most hazardous journey but on the first day somewhat comic.

Because the Grand Canal passed through guerrilla territory, they had to go the long way around, setting off early on a beautifully fresh morning in a straggle of six rickshaws: three for themselves and the servant and three for luggage. Rosa's trunk was full of books. At noon its rickshaw collapsed with a buckled wheel. Its puller cheerfully unloaded it, straightened the wheel, and they rearranged loads. By 5:00 p.m. the roads were a nightmare, cut up by guerrillas or ruined in the fighting. Rosa, Nelson, and the servants walked most of the time, and the pullers frequently had to manhandle the rickshaws over trenches, redoubts, and shell holes. When negotiating a high narrow path, while Nelson was walking, the axle of his rickshaw snapped: he would have been thrown six or eight feet and probably broken his neck if he had been sitting in it. They reached Iling on the canal by the aid of Nelson's flashlight, sixteen hours after starting. They were still on that journey when, far away in Europe, the Germans launched their blitzkrieg on May 10, 1940.

The *Empress of Asia* had not yet sailed when Nelson had to leave Rosa at the missionary home in Shanghai.

His return journey brought more adventures. He passed through the Chinese lines while the smoke of burning towns besmirched the horizon. He "arrived at Taichow about six and Bob Price had told his servant (he lives alone) to serve me strawberries and cream, and they surely did taste good. Taichow was a little *huang* (actual translation—'shaking') because the Japanese were only seven miles away. Owing to the uncertainty and the fear of being cut off, I was sorely tempted to go on by launch for Hsinghwa Sunday morning, but decided finally that the Lord would look after that part if I honored Him and His Day. I was asked to preach at the Northend Chapel Sunday afternoon, and just before I got there, who should I meet but the boatman who brought Rosa and me from Iling to Hsinghwa.

"He went to the chapel with me and after the service asked me to use his boat on the return trip. I told him I could save time by going on to Hsinghwa by launch and taking a sailboat from there, but he insisted he could make as good time. As it would save the trouble and transfer at Hsinghwa, I finally decided to use his boat. . . .

"After leading the foreign service Sunday night and talking a while, I went on the boat about 10:00 p.m. and we left at 4:00 a.m. They worked hard and reached Hsinghwa at 8:00 p.m. I got off and called on Mr. Koll, a German missionary there, then went back on the boat." By daylight a following wind was strengthening every hour, blowing them along at a merry pace, well ahead of schedule. But around 4:00 p.m. they approached a junction where they must turn into another canal; then this wind would be useless and they might lose all they had gained.

The moment they reached the junction "the wind veered sharply and followed us all the way in. The boatman was greatly impressed and said, 'Truly this was God's doing.'"

*   *   *   *   *

"This past week we have had 997 *women* in clinic!" wrote Virginia on July 28, 1940. "My, but it is hectic, especially when five or six children are screaming at the same time. There is so much sickness. Lots of real suffering from hunger; everything is sky-high....We have been awfully busy, no time to think about the heat. We go like mad until after clinic, then bathe or go in the pool, then take our seats on the lawn, relax a little while, and have supper out of doors....While there are not many flowers just now, the trees and grass are beautiful as we have had daily rains for days....The trees and shadows during the full moon were perfectly entrancing; we hated to go to bed. It is all so peaceful you wouldn't know you were in China, except for the servants and an occasional nurse who comes for orders."

Despite such idylls, the strain was telling on Virginia. In addition to clinic work she dispensed much extra hospitality because wives of colleagues, except Kay Gieser, were in Shanghai or America. And now the Giesers had left, posted to the Chinkiang hospital for a year; Virginia again had to teach DiDi.

The headaches returned with a vengeance. Sometimes she woke at 4:00 a.m. with a fearful migraine which lasted until after breakfast; she could have asked to be invalided out, but would not.

The headaches defied every remedy. Finally in the summer of 1940 Nelson sent Virginia's history to the Mayo Clinic. Dr. Alvarez replied that the trouble was partly cumulative sustained tension and recommended a new English drug, stilbestrol, which he feared might be difficult to obtain in China. Nelson discovered it already in stock, unused. The result was immediate. Virginia regained weight and soon could go as long as three weeks without headaches.

When Nelson traveled to Korea in September 1940 to place MaiMai at school in Pyengyang, Virginia held the fort by herself, for Dr. Woods had gone on a long holiday preparatory to retirement. The Chinese doctors came to her in any difficulty "and she rose to the occasion as she always does."

Nelson's journeys to and from Korea via Tientsin were a

Dr. and Mrs. Chalmers Vinson, the last missionaries sent to China by the Benjamin Clayton fund

saga of faith and provision as well as semi-vacation after a spell of dengue fever. Before setting out he wrote his mother: "MaiMai and I have left it entirely in God's hands, asking Him to stop our plans if it is not His plan for us. Already the local authorities have said we could of course have passes to Suchowfu and go in their trucks with baggage.... It is such a comfortable feeling to leave these things in God's hands and to know He is going to show the right way." At Tientsin during the return he could describe how once again, as on the journey from Shanghai to Tsingkiangpu the previous year, "whenever a need has arisen, God has provided the right person *every time*." Nor was this coincidence. His mother was praying with meticulous attention to detail and inexhaustible expectation of answers to prayer. "Eternity alone," Nelson told her, "will show what your prayers for us have meant."

When Nelson reached Tsingkiangpu, the staff situation had been transformed, not only by the return of Dr. Woods for a final few weeks before going to live in Shanghai, but by the arrival of a new intern under the Benjamin Clayton Fund: Chalmers Vinson—son of "Uncle Jack" Vinson who had been murdered in 1931—and Olivert his wife.

Nelson had deplored the SPM policy of depleting their

China strength because of war and financial stringency: "The mission personnel is so low it is almost at vanishing point in some places." Chal Vinson had been planning for five years to come out; so Nelson invited him to Tsingkiangpu, persuaded the mission to enroll him on permanent status at once, and planned to release him if necessary to another hospital after only one year. The Vinsons would have no light task, as Nelson wrote on September 22, 1940: "Adjustment is not easy and takes grace and courage and the real missionary call. These years have been years of sifting of the missionary body."

Chal Vinson was older and more mature than his predecessors had been on their arrival, for he had been an intern for three years at a Marine hospital. He had quiet ways and a tenor voice in contrast to his wife's alto, and the Bells found them "refreshing and inspiring." Both were utterly unconcerned about present dangers and future uncertainties; and they had not been long in China when bandits held them up on their way back from the wedding of Chal's twin brother. They lost everything except the clothes they wore and some borrowed bedding strapped unnoticed under the rickshaw seat.

Nelson, however, bore a charmed life as he sped about the countryside in his Austin Seven bedecked with Red Cross and American flags. "It is dangerous," said the Japanese police, "but the country people think too much of you—they won't hurt you." Even dear old Dr. Junkin of Sutsien said he "would not ride in Nelson's car for five hundred dollars"—the guerrillas would shoot first and identify afterwards.

The whole outlook was increasingly somber. Nelson grew sure that the World War would soon spread to the Pacific, especially as the Roosevelt administration handled Japan in the worst way. Nelson would willingly have left Tsingkiangpu temporarily while America thrashed Japan, as he believed they could and should, but Cordell Hull's policy only made her more arrogant; the Bells already had a hunch that war, when it came, would start with a shattering Japanese blow from the blue.

The local authorities continued "really friendly. I have

no illusions as to what might happen, but the fact remains that God has put men here now who are disposed to us in a friendly way," and their attitude did not change as American-Japanese relations worsened. Nelson had seen and heard too much for illusions. On visits to Japanese police headquarters he had often heard the screams of Chinese being tortured or caned; he had sewn up stomaches split by bayonets. The subsequent behavior of the Japanese to Allied prisoners in World War II came as no surprise.

Nelson and Virginia faced the future fully persuaded that what God had promised, He was able to perform. As the international scene darkened, Nelson again recounted the divine promises of protection. He concluded: "It seems to me we simply have to seek one thing—to be in the place and doing the work God wants—the rest we should leave to Him in absolute faith."

He was certain by now that his work at Tsingkiangpu would be interrupted by war, and he already knew what he wanted to do if he got out of China alive; while earning his living as a surgeon until China reopened, he would establish a journal which would rally the Southern Presbyterian church by stating clearly the basic theological issues which too rapidly were becoming fogged.

*   *   *   *   *

In October 1940 the State Department ordered the evacuation of all American women and children from the Far East, and of all males not essential to the maintenance of commerce or missions. Virginia recognized the wisdom of the decision but had no intention of complying, and the mission committee made virtue of necessity by formally authorizing her to stay. Aurie Montgomery, newly returned from furlough to Hwaian with her youngest boy, eleven-year-old Robert, also refused to budge: the SPM, therefore, sensibly asked the Montgomery family to move into the Tsingkiangpu compound; they could all survive or perish—and the two boys, Clayton and Robert, play—together.

On the 14th a radio message gave the news that MaiMai's school would evacuate en masse from Korea directly to

America, including the children from China. Two weeks later, another message said that MaiMai was being sent to Shanghai. Puzzled and upset over this new development, Nelson and Virginia wanted desperately to go to Shanghai to see MaiMai and to make arrangements to send her on to the states on the *Washington*, sailing November 20.

However, the situation in Tsingkiangpu made this impossible. On November 11, Virginia wrote that "It is going to take a lot of prayer and grace to keep me from feeling bitter over not being able to go and see our baby girl. She loves home and didn't want to go in the first place. However, we know the Lord makes no mistakes and all things work together for good to them that love Him. It may be that if we had gone to Shanghai we wouldn't have been able to come back. And we feel so definitely the Lord has not led us to go."

Six days later a Japanese officer drove up to the door, saluted, and handed over a letter from MaiMai which she had sent via "Uncle Ham" at Suchowfu (E. H. Hamilton, the author of *Afraid? Of What?*), knowing he would find a way to forward it: it was several days old, but ordinary mail would have taken weeks. Virginia tore it open. MaiMai pleaded to be allowed to come home and continue education at Tsingkiangpu rather than in America. The Japanese officer had read the letter and knew its contents. He spoke up: "Let her come. She will be safe here."

The liner would sail on Wednesday. This was Saturday. Nelson and Virginia prayed about the letter, for the possibility that MaiMai might stay in China had never occurred to them. Nelson went straight to the Japanese police who at once made out the necessary passes. He then wired MaiMai, but as wires often were never received, no time could be lost.

At first light on Sunday morning Nelson, who had just recovered from another bout of fever, set off north, driving the Austin as never before with no thought for bandits, guerrillas, potholes, or punctures; he reached Suchowfu and the railway shortly before 2:00 p.m. By Tuesday morning he was in Shanghai. By Friday he and MaiMai were on their way back.

"MaiMai is *so* happy to be going home," he wrote during

the return journey. "From the human standpoint I realize fully that it seems an utterly foolish thing to do, but we do feel God's hand has been leading and He never makes mistakes.

"I had a long talk with Mr. Stanton, vice-consul in Shanghai and a friend of some years standing. He is always so cordial and sympathetic to our missionary viewpoint and is so willing to help. He did not seem shocked at all that I was bringing MaiMai back, but he also said none of us know what may happen any time.

"Never have we needed more the guiding hand of our loving heavenly Father. We are here to do His work and we are His. In case things break loose, we would be more than useless. In case things work out all right, though, we can be the means in His hands of preserving the work and property. We live day by day, asking for the listening ear and the attentive heart to know His will and to do it, and He cannot fail us."

*   *   *   *   *

In 1941 Chinese New Year fell early, on January 27. Nelson and Virginia were determined to give their friends pleasure and relaxation, and no less than 163 Chinese called to enjoy tea, cakes, and company.

A few days earlier the Bells had entertained the hospital doctors and their wives at supper, with Jim and Aurie Montgomery who now lived in the Woodses' old home. While chopsticks picked at delicacies, Nelson looked around him and wondered, "Where in China you could find a more congenial group of doctors than we have here—not a vestige of friction between them, and they each have their strong points as well as their weak ones." Ts'ao, Ch'ien, Wu, Koh, and two others would carry on while breath and freedom lasted. The Benevolent Compassionate or Love and Mercy Hospital had served more patients in 1940 than in any previous year and must keep open until the last possible moment.

On Chinese New Year's Eve the Bells invited the Montgomerys, together with Jess Hall and Mary McCown, two indomitable evangelists whom no war could scare. While they still sat around the supper table, the postman staggered in with a big load of foreign mail. Sometimes weeks had passed without letters; at one time no mail could be received unless Bell sent a man on a two-day trip. The radio kept them abreast of world affairs and even of family matters, for the shortwave station at San Francisco read out personal messages at no charge, and they would thrill to hear an announcer in America saying, "This is for you, Dr. Bell, way out there in the interior of China, from Rosa and Ruth."

In that night's pile of letters lay one from Ruth dated as late as mid-December. And thus, "way out in the interior of China" the Bells read that Ruth had met at Wheaton the man she might one day marry. She was not in love yet, and still expected to live and die a spinster in Tibet, but if she ever married, this was the man. His name was Bill (or Billy) Graham.

Before Billy and Ruth were introduced, she had seen this lanky southern freshman dash down the steps and had thought, *There's a young man who knows where he's going!* When the students were going on Sunday mission work and prayer meetings were being held in different lounges, she had heard his voice from across the passage and thought, *That's a man who knows God in a very unusual way.*

Billy Graham was older and more mature than other freshmen, though with less formal education at that time than Ruth, and already he had a reputation among the students as a forceful preacher. On their first date Ruth discovered that "for all his terrific dedication and drive, there was a winsomeness about him and a consideration for other people, which I found very endearing."

Their first date was to the Glee Club performance of the *Messiah* on a snowy December afternoon, with a long talk afterwards beside a tree, and supper at a professor's home. That night Ruth knelt at her bedside and told God in prayer that "if I could spend the rest of my life serving Him with Bill, I would consider it the greatest privilege imaginable."

Billy Graham had fallen in love with Ruth at first sight and wrote to his mother that he had met the girl he would marry. To a friend at Wheaton, however, he confided that his cause was hopeless because he had so little to commend him.

28
Unfinished Symphony

THREE weeks after the Bells received Ruth's letter, the consul again sent urgent advice to evacuate. The Tsingkiangpu reaction was predictable. "All of us here," Nelson wrote to his mother and daughters on February 16, 1941, "are for sitting tight just as long as possible, and we have the assurance that in some way God will give us clear leading as to His will. Looking at it solely from the human standpoint, the thing to do is to get out, if there is yet time to do so. But, we *must not* look at it from the human standpoint, for we are not here at the call of man or to do the work of man." Jess Hall, to Nelson's amusement, responded to the consular call by setting off deeper into the countryside on a three-weeks' tour.

Nevertheless, the Bells were in a dilemma.

The previous fall the period of service between furloughs had been reduced from seven years to five. The Bells' furlough thus became due the very next summer, 1941, instead of 1943. Their first reaction had been to postpone this right of furlough by one year: Nelson considered that an older colleague in another station had a prior claim and both doctors should not be out of China at once. Nor could Nelson easily afford the cost of living in the States with three girls being educated.

When war in the Pacific seemed more likely, he provisionally booked passage for May 31, 1941. On March 7, however, he wrote to the family: "The more we think of going home this summer, the more we feel that it may not be God's will for us to do so. The hospital work has never been more encouraging, and God has protected and preserved it and provided for all of its needs in such a wonderful way that, unless He gives some definite leading to the contrary, we question whether we should leave. This came over me like a wave last Tuesday when we admitted fifty-four patients— the needs and opportunities just seem unlimited."

Bell did not cancel their passages but booked a provisional one for MaiMai to sail with another missionary family on her way to school at Montreat. Her parents and Clayton would take a vacation in Shanghai while seeing her off. If Ken Gieser could get back in the fall of '41, they would be more willing to go on furlough, for otherwise, even with Jim Montgomery acting as administrator, Chal Vinson would have a tough task as the only Western doctor. Nelson wrote: "I know it looks like we are unable to make up our minds and are vacillating, but we are trying to know and do God's will in the matter and that only. How nice it would be to go home and see you precious loved ones and how nice to be out from under the uncertainties of life out here."

The whole region was in turmoil. On this same day, March 7, 1941, Bell wrote to Junkin of Sutsien: "Conditions in the country around here are the worst I have ever known so far as bandits are concerned. The people are crying out in their distress."

In Tsingkiangpu the Japanese, for all their friendliness toward the hospital, had become jealous of the Bells' immense prestige and the love in which they were held, and so remained fundamentally suspicious. Even in a church crowded once again for Communion Sunday, Bell noticed several bad men he knew were spies. On the wider stage, Japanese statesmen had visited Berlin. The Axis would soon become an offensive alliance. In the event of war the Bells would be an immediate liability to their Chinese friends, their work would be snuffed out, and they themselves killed or thrown into concentration camps.

Yet they would not be happy in America if they could still be working in China.

In common with the apostle Paul in another context, the Bells did not know whether to depart or to remain and could echo his words, "What I shall choose I know not."

Their prayer was, "Lord, show me now Thy way....Teach me Thy way, O Lord, and lead me in a plain path....Cause me to know the way wherein I should walk." If God had work for them in America rather than a captivity in China, He must disclose His will beyond a shadow of doubt.

* * * * *

During the second week of March Virginia had a bad recurrence of headache which lasted for two full days and nights. She had omitted her medicine one day, and they thought this the possible cause, but despite careful dosage the headaches did not disappear. She remarked that she felt she could stand a concentration camp if she kept well, but it would be awful if she were sick.

They prayed definitely that if God meant them to stay, the headaches should be removed.

On Monday, March 24, Nelson wrote: "Virginia has been feeling real badly the last week, feeling better today. She had had a bad head cold for six weeks or more and all of her sinuses seem to be congested. She has had some mild kidney trouble too. We are praying for definite leading about going home, and the Lord knows we are perfectly willing to go or to stay and He will surely lead....

"Our indecision regarding coming home may seem hard to understand, especially as both Virginia and I usually are rather quick in making decisions. However, in this case so much hangs on what we do. The station folks are so sweet about putting no obstacle in the way, but at the same time they all realize the need and the opportunity and recognize there are many problems difficult for others to handle, in case evacuation should become necessary. What our final decision will be, I do not know, but I *know* God will make His will plain for He knows we want to do that and nothing else."

By March 30 all doubt had been removed. Virginia was definitely sick with a serious attack of malaria. Nelson decided that he could do no other than take her home. "It is such a hard decision to make," though made easier by the sterling qualities of Chal and Olivert Vinson and Cassie Lee

Talbot, and by the unanimous conviction among the Chinese and throughout the mission that the Bells had made the right decision.

Early in April Nelson wrote: "Now that we have definitely decided to go, the Lord has certainly given His peace in our hearts." But he had to warn Rosa and Ruth that they would be "shocked at how badly your mother looks. Her face is so thin and drawn and I can see such a difference in her strength, so much less pep and ability to keep going."

*   *   *   *   *

They decided to take much more luggage than usual to the States, for neither expected to return to China until after long years of war between America and Japan. Virginia removed favorite pictures from their frames and packed photograph albums, but there would be no space for their wedding presents of silver or glass. She packed little by little, as strength allowed. "I want to finish everything," she wrote on April 20, "and be able to enjoy the yard and birds before we leave. It isn't *easy* to leave; this is *home....*

"MaiMai and DiDi continue to froth at the mouth at the thought of leaving. MaiMai realizes it will be years before she can hope to see home again." Nelson was so sure of war that he forgot to ask for two-way passes. The Japanese official offered them on his own initiative and Nelson accepted with alacrity. The passes would be good until September 1942—by which time Japan had conquered from Manila to Rangoon.

At the end of April the Bells heard a message read over the San Francisco shortwave from Rosa, saying her operation had been successful. As they did not know she had been taken ill again, they were much concerned, and the desire to see Rosa made parting from Tsingkiangpu a little easier. One colleague still believes that except for Rosa's illness they might have changed their minds again at the last minute and stayed.

"The Chinese have been so good to us," Nelson wrote on May 8, "presents, banners, feasts. They have simply showered us with things to show their love and it has been most touching. For instance, the innkeepers and laborers who live on the streets near the hospital got together and sent us a big banner with their names on it and a nice inscription to us." A senior Chinese puppet officer on whom Nelson had operated sent a silver shield and a banner, escorted by a brass band, and some money to Clayton "to buy something to eat when traveling." The gift which was most meaningful to them was the one presented by the hospital staff—twenty-four pieces of beautiful antique china.

Early on the morning of Monday, May 19, 1941, the other missionaries, the entire hospital staff and servants, and a large crowd of citizens, country folk, innkeepers, traders, and Japanese came to the Grand Canal jetty where the Bells had landed nearly a quarter of a century before. Everyone knew at heart how much suffering must pass first, but the cry on all sides was, "Come back soon."

At Hwaian Lillian Wells and a Chinese colleague were waiting to bid them good-by.

Below Hwaian, as if excitements could never cease around Nelson Bell, the launch ran straight through a skirmish.

Part Four
THE NEW FIELD
1941 - 1973

29
Carolina Surgeon

T HE Bells were met by Ruth at Wheaton station at 7:15 a.m. on July 3, 1941. They went to Zace Sanitorium nearby and found Rosa pathetically thin. Her operation three months earlier had revealed tubercular peritonitis. Doctors had ordered complete bed rest for three months, at the end of which she should be able to resume normal life. Her housemother offered to keep her on a sun porch, and Ruth dropped out of school to nurse her. As the third month drew to a close she suddenly had a lung hemorrhage. X-rays revealed both lungs deeply involved with TB. Her situation was very critical.

When she moved to Zace, they performed a phrenicotomy on one side and were giving her pneumothorax treatment twice a week on the other.

Her parents decided to send her to the drier climate of New Mexico, and several months later on the morning she left the other patients gathered around and sang "You Are My Sunshine." Ruth accompanied her to Albuquerque and stayed with her for several weeks.

From Wheaton, Nelson, Virginia, and Clayton went to the Mayo Clinic which quickly relieved them of their various China ills. And then on to Waynesboro where the twenty-two-year-old Billy Graham, who had not been on the Wheaton campus for their brief visit, had been invited to stay. "I had conducted two or three evangelistic meetings in Florida," Graham recalled, "and I drove my secondhand 1940 Plymouth to Waynesboro; I didn't know what to expect. Ruth and I were going together. We were not yet officially engaged, although she had agreed to marry me, and I had not given her a ring. I was scared and nervous about meeting Ruth's parents. I didn't know how they would receive me.

"When I stopped the car in front of the house, Ruth came out. Dr. Bell and Mrs. Bell stood at the door, and after I had grabbed Ruth's hand, he came and gave me the warmest greeting; he said how much they thought of me and that they were so thankful and that they were praying. I just felt at home with them. That night at dinner he asked me many questions about what my views were and what my plans were, and he told a lot of jokes and made me feel quite at home. I was impressed with his humor and his sincerity and his tremendous love of the Lord. I had not expected this." Although already an ordained Southern Baptist minister, Billy Graham at that stage in his life tended to assume that the mainstream denominations held few good and true men.

Ruth's parents and grandmother were most favorably impressed by Billy's sincerity. "It was obvious he knew and loved the Lord. He was very much a gentleman and attractive personally." Old Mother Bell took him to her heart, but her small house had no space for yet another guest. He was lodged at the General Wayne Hotel, and in his inexperience he fretted inwardly because the bill would deplete his slender resources. Next morning he discovered it had already been paid by Dr. Bell.

All the Bells and Billy set off in two cars up the Skyline Drive to Washington, where Dr. Bell had an appointment with the Far Eastern Division of the State Department. That long journey up to Washington and back was every bit as romantic to Billy and Ruth as Nelson's and Virginia's Sunday buggy rides to the mountain mission at Glenkirk long before. But in Washington, as at Waynesboro, nine-year-old Clayton could not understand why Billy and Ruth did not relish his faithful, doglike attendance. "He wanted to go with us everywhere," Ruth recalled, "and Daddy just had to put his foot down and say, 'Now leave Ruth and Billy alone.' Clayton was indignant. He said, 'Well, he came to see me as much as he came to see her!'"

The Bells then rented the Johnson house in Montreat,

North Carolina, a green frame house with warmth and charm. And Billy was with them again later that summer. He remembered that "they always cooked Chinese food and they had garlic, and I didn't like garlic in those days. I didn't like the smell of it, and I could always smell their house. When you walked in, it smelled of garlic. But it was always a happy house, full of fun and laughter and games. You always felt exhilarated when you went in and came out. No matter what the problems were, no one seemed to be aware of any problems. And this greatly impressed me."

Nelson Bell gave one of the main addresses at the World Mission Conference at Montreat, and Billy was "very proud to listen to my future father-in-law speak to such a huge audience. He was so well-known in the church that the auditorium was packed to hear him when there weren't many people going to the conferences....He just started right out on the gospel, and he spoke with such force and such power and such authority that I immediately realized that here was a great man, with great courage and boldness."

Billy was not then aware of the source of Bell's power: "It took me some time to realize that his tremendous strength came from his private devotional life. He was never ostentatious about it. It was a lifetime habit that he took for granted."

* * * * *

Pearl Harbor did not surprise Bell, although the Far Eastern officials of the State Department had not taken him seriously when he tried to convince them that Japan intended war. In Tsingkiangpu Bell's colleagues were able to continue work for a while after his departure because the local commander who had taken office shortly before the Bells' departure was a humane man. Chal Vinson had a hard time, and five months before Pearl Harbor the missionaries were ordered to be held incommunicado for two weeks. A year later (August 1942), the Montgomerys, with Robert, were repatriated in the *Gripsholm* exchange of noncombatants. When they reached New York, they were astonished to see their older children on the dockside. Nelson

Bell had paid their return fares from the South.

Even before Pearl Harbor Bell was so certain of war that he acquired, in October 1941, a surgical practice with an office in Swannanoa and with hospital work in the city of Asheville, fourteen miles from Montreat.

Nelson Bell quickly established a high professional reputation. He was called in when a serious accident caused an unusual injury to a young construction worker. Bell saw at once that the injury was similar to damage he had repaired in China. In saving the Asheville man, Bell made his name. He was soon appointed secretary of the staff of Asheville Memorial Mission Hospital and after five years, assistant chief of staff; only his own illness prevented him being offered eventually the post of chief of staff for the customary one year's tenure.

With a booming practice, for the first time in their lives the Bells could have lived in affluence had they not continued to give systematically, not merely a tithe, but up to twenty-five or thirty percent of net income before tax; Nelson drew enormous satisfaction from having more to give. And there would have been still more had he not followed to an unusual degree the medical profession's practice of treating the needy without payment. For those who were neither needy nor wealthy, Bell charged what they could pay, not what his own services could command. And years of superintending admissions in China made him adept at detecting fraudulent claims, though once or twice he was deceived. Bell also carried his love of other races from China to North Carolina; he refused to follow the southern custom of treating blacks only after whites. Each took his turn.

If the poor and the blacks found in him a friend, so had the student nurses, so that when he offered to start a weekly Bible class, he was surprised how many volunteered. Every Saturday at 11:00 a.m., he allowed time in his heavy schedule to give them a Bible study unless he had an emergency. Nearly thirty years later he still received letters thanking him for those Bible classes.

Many stories are still told of Bell's fifteen years as one of the leading surgeons of North Carolina. "People were drawn to him," said a colleague, "both by his skill and by his reputation as a man of God. The combination is rare."

Nelson bought, for a modest sum, a lot on Assembly Drive at Montreat which included a frame summer house. He had this covered with stone and enlarged, spending much more than the purchase price to create a pleasant residence which quickly became as much a center of hospitality as the superintendent's house at Tsingkiangpu. Virginia made a beautiful garden and in the center stood a stone chimney, all that was left of Montreat's very first building: the Bells turned it into an outdoor grill.

After a twenty-five-year lull, Nelson could now indulge once again his hobby of baseball. He became an enthusiastic follower of the Asheville Tourists, took a season box on McCormick Field, and was invited three times to pitch the opening ball of the season. Sunday games he would neither attend nor watch on television.

*   *   *   *   *

Ever since her illness in high school, Rosa had wished that Jesus were there to heal her. Naturally she had faith in physicians, but they had no thorough cure for tuberculosis. Lying on her bed in the sanitorium, extremely weak, with no appetite she found as the months crawled by "the Lord dealing with me about some things in my life that did not please Him. I had just been putting Him off saying, 'Lord, don't bother me; I'm a sick girl.' One night I came to the end of it all: 'Lord, I'm tired of these things that stand between me and You. I'd rather have a right relationship with You than anything in the whole wide world, so whatever You have been asking of me, I give in to You!'

"I felt as if a big weight had lifted off my shoulders. Then I got tired of being sick, and I thought I would just study the Scriptures and see what the Lord says about healing."

At the end of ten days' study Rosa was convinced that God would heal her if, and only if, she gave Him all the glory. In March Rosa had herself carried to a little church to enable some like-minded friends to pray for her healing and anoint her with oil.

Then she began to eat again and to drink extra milk and build up her body. "And then, as I had the strength, I began to walk around and visit the other patients."

In late May 1942 her father flew out to see her. She was working half a day as a laboratory assistant and half a day running the deep X-ray therapy machine for a specialist downtown, Dr. Van Atta. Van Atta took some X-rays of Rosa during Bell's visit. Nelson recalled: "You couldn't *see* where she had had tuberculosis except for a few fibrous lines outlining where there had been a cavity. Her lungs were completely expanded; she was the picture of health and very active.

"And Dr. Van Atta said to me (and he was a hard-boiled old fellow and an agnostic), 'Dr. Bell, Rosa's feeling that God healed her is the only explanation for what you and I see today on these X-ray films.'"

Since that time Rosa has lived a completely normal life. In 1945 she married Don Montgomery, an electrical engineer with the Atomic Energy Commission at Los Alamos, New Mexico, and now retired.

But the real miracle of Rosa was in the person she became. As Ruth said: "Previously she read her Bible as some people read *Playboy* magazine!—hiding it under her pillow and slipping it out when no one was around and hurriedly hiding it again when she heard someone approaching. But she is now a superb Bible teacher. And from an inarticulate Christian she became a happy witness to her Savior, leading many other persons to faith in Him."

*   *   *   *   *

The very summer of his return from China in 1941 Nelson went to work on his ambition to found an independent Presbyterian journal which would affirm the authority of the Bible, articulate the historic beliefs of the church, offer constructive criticism to the denomination's boards and agencies, and "give a ringing testimony to the evangelical cause." He did this with the help of Dr. Henry Dendy of

Weaverville. This magazine, the *Southern Presbyterian Journal*, had an effective ministry for many years until 1987, when it ceased publication. Nelson Bell wrote several of the editorials or articles for each issue and was the magazine's mainspring.

"He was really the main editor," Dendy said. "I did the legwork—just backing up. While Nelson was doing his heavy surgical practice in various hospitals, he would call me and say, 'Now I'm going to have an operation at such and such a time, but you meet me right outside the door on the third floor of the hospital as I come out of the operating room, and I'll be through at such and such a time.' And almost always it would never be over five minutes variance in the time he'd get through with that operation and be ready to meet me to go to lunch or to tell me something about the paper. He works on the wing!"

Nelson Bell's countless editorials covered a broad range of topics, especially on matters of political or social morality and on any issue which seemed to undermine the Christian foundation of America. An editorial in 1957 received the top award as Editorial of the Year, selected from all American newspapers and journals, secular or religious, by the Freedoms Foundation of Valley Forge. He received a prize of a thousand dollars and an encased replica of George Washington's watch. He also in other years received six lesser awards from the Freedoms Foundation.

Nelson's concern for his church and his commitment to working for renewal within it had a strong influence on Billy Graham's thinking. "Over the years," related Ruth, "Bill saw that to retreat is not a way to fight a battle. When things get difficult, you don't quit your church and join another. This is Daddy's firm policy: you take a stand, you defend the faith, but you don't retreat. Bill has come to admire and respect and to rely on Daddy's judgment."

Billy Graham is in no doubt: "Dr. Bell and Ruth together did more to get my ministry church-oriented than any other single factor and single influence."

Ruth and Billy were married in Gaither Chapel, Montreat, on August 13, 1943, by the Reverend Kerr Taylor and the Reverend John Minder. Uncle Jimmy Graham of

Tsingkiangpu had promised to perform the ceremony but died shortly before. The Grahams went to live in Hinsdale, Illinois, near the town of Western Springs, where Billy had a pastorate. When in 1944 a severe attack of mumps prevented his taking up a commission as army chaplain, Billy became the first traveling evangelist of the new Youth for Christ organization, on a slender stipend; the Grahams moved to Montreat and made their home with the Bells, thus easing a tight budget and giving Ruth a security which made bearable her husband's long absences on the road.

*   *   *   *   *

When the Japanese surrendered in August 1945, Tsingkiangpu fell first to the Communists, then to the Nationalists. The Bells were delighted when the Chinese church particularly asked that "Dr. Lover of the Chinese People" and his family should return with the first party of SPM missionaries.

Then Nelson developed bursitis of the hip. It became so bad that he could not walk, and the SPM had to withdraw him from the first list. His medical colleague at Asheville advised an operation. The night before it was due, the pain ceased: the bursa had spontaneously ruptured, which is the cure for bursitis.

He was "sure the Lord's hand was in it." As he had once written, years before, to Ruth: "We will just take things as they come. After all, God does not want us to expect to see the end of the road from the beginning, but rather to trust in Him for His leading and guidance."

Moreover, though his heart was in China, he felt responsible for his mother who had become totally blind. She now lived with Nelson's sister in Greenville, South Carolina, but because his brother was away in Brazil, Nelson would not leave her to return to China unless the will of God was plain. (She lived on, praying to the last, until 1953 and the age of ninety-one.) While Nelson was still awaiting this clear leading, he heard from two SPM missionaries, Hopkins and Richardson, who had gone to Tsingkiangpu, that the whole region had become a battleground in the civil war. They stressed the tension and unrest, and advised Bell that he would never be able to reestablish a satisfactory medical work and urged him not to come. In a few months they themselves had to leave.

And so Nelson watched from afar the closing, as Ruth commented, "of that phase of God's work." Contact with Tsingkiangpu—except by prayer—was cut off altogether. Lives must not be endangered by letters to Kao or Ts'ao or other dear friends. Yet an experience of Ed Currie, who was able to remain under the Communists at Haichow for a while, shows that when the building is truly founded on the Rock, the gates of hell do not prevail. A young woman dressed like any other Communist soldier disclosed herself as being from a village where many Christians had lived, which Currie had often visited in former times. She had been drafted into the armed forces and had been through many dangerous actions and much indoctrination. After a pleasant conversation in a room crowded with soldiers, she had to leave, and Currie escorted her to the door. "Miss Chin," he murmured, "don't forget what you learned in the little Christian school when you were a little girl."

She looked him full in the face, asking, "Could I forget my Lord?" And she turned and went out.

*   *   *   *   *

Although Nelson Bell was no longer an overseas missionary, he soon resumed service with the Southern Presbyterian Mission, for in 1948 the General Assembly of his church elected him a member of the Board of World Missions.

When his three-year tenure ended, he was reelected a second and third time, until after three terms he retired according to the constitution. But he had been absent only one year when the General Assembly put him back on the board and kept him there each time he came up for reelection. After no less than seventeen years' service, with one more to go before mandatory retirement, he resigned. His resignation was partly on grounds of health. A member rarely served so long, and he was the only ex-missionary with such length of service. In accepting his resignation, the other members wrote in a round-robin: "By whatever yardstick we choose, we find that you stand virtually unequaled among those who have served our church and our Lord as member of the Board of World Missions."

As a board member Nelson made a point of visiting some part of the SPM field for two or three weeks every year at his own expense, and he made several tours as an official representative, especially to Korea. He saw every SPM sphere in the world except Ecuador and Iraq. When traveling officially, he drew expenses in order to regularize his tax position, but he donated to the board the equivalent, glad that financial success as a surgeon enabled him to carry out his duties without depleting the missionary budget.

He was assiduous at attending board meetings, even when once they occurred during the World Series: he brought in a transistor radio and kept the board informed of the score! Nelson still considered himself a missionary, not an ecclesiastical bureaucrat, and he was known for his special concern for the viewpoint of missionaries on the field. His judgment was relied upon in all matters of medical planning, while his desire for truly indigenous churches became even stronger than it had been at Tsingkiangpu; he especially deplored the tendency toward weakening the indigenous works by subsidies from abroad.

In the work of the board Bell grasped points and reached conclusions as quickly as, in surgery, he diagnosed or operated. Bell was never afraid of controversy. "He takes sides; he is a fit protagonist; he is ready to let you know where he stands and to justify and clarify his position," one board member commented. "He takes sides, but he doesn't take over. He knows the fundamental distinction between being passionate and being vehement." And another said: "Nelson Bell's methods were always those of Christian charity. He was always a fair gentleman in anything that he had to say, and time and again he would lighten the atmosphere of the meeting with a little humor. There was a good deal of humor about him—always." When controversy increased toward the end of his membership, with a shifting of emphasis and outlook on the board, a woman member wrote to him: "You are able to differ and yet maintain a sweet spirit and tolerance of the point of view of others." Bell could emerge from a controversy with more friends than when it began.

In 1950, at age 56, Nelson suffered his first heart attack. For several weeks he lay seriously ill. Ruth recalled "visiting him in the hospital room. He was under an oxygen tent, and with him under the tent was his dictating machine." Soon he was back at full tilt, the coronary thrombosis having apparently been completely overcome. At the same time he learned to pace himself (cutting down on his practice by eliminating obstetrics), taking his physical limitations seriously but not allowing them to keep him from doing as much as possible. "His ability to pace himself greatly prolonged his life," Ruth stated later.

30
Neighbor and Writer

BY the early summer of 1954 and the end of the London crusade, Billy Graham had become a world figure.

During his swift rise to national fame in America after the Los Angeles crusade of 1949, Billy had continued to receive unstinting support from his father-in-law. "Many times," recalled Billy, "in the early days when I was severely criticized, he came to my defense publicly and privately." By articles and private letters Nelson expounded and defended Billy's position, aims, and actions. Bell's own stature and prestige helped Graham. This was especially so in the South, while in Philadelphia, as late as 1961, Howard Pew told the presbytery that they ought to endorse the forthcoming Billy Graham crusade because "Nelson Bell is an able and thoughtful individual, and yet he is sincerely convinced that Billy Graham is chosen and inspired by God."

Billy said Dr. Bell "was always encouraging and always thrilled at stories of conversions. I went to him quite a lot for advice. My own father was a dairy farmer, so on many major issues I went to my father-in-law because he was a churchman and a missionary and knew the church situation." But Bell was in no sense the *eminence grise* of the emerging Billy Graham: "I made my own decisions. He rarely came to me and said, 'I want to warn you about this or tell you about this.' He would do it by inference."

Looking back in 1969 Billy felt that Nelson Bell was "one of the great influences in keeping me on the straight course of evangelism....Dr. Bell's strength is that I know that he loves me, but he's never been afraid to tell me what was the truth."

In the summer of 1954 Nelson was able to help his famous son-in-law in quite a different way. When Billy preached in Berlin and Paris after the London crusade, he was wracked with pain from a kidney stone. He sailed back to a hero's welcome in New York and returned to Montreat where the Graham house on Assembly Drive became flooded with telephone calls, mail, and inquisitive tourists. The kidney pains returned. Nelson Bell swept him into Asheville Memorial Mission Hospital where a close friend operated. He ordered Billy to take six weeks of complete rest.

All that autumn while Billy was away again on crusades, Nelson Bell, watching the rising tide of religion in America, dreamed of starting a magazine which could give the whole nation what the *Southern Presbyterian Journal* now provided one denomination: a clear, biblical, scholarly voice to combat the dominant theological liberalism in the seminaries and church leadership. The only nationwide interdenominational paper was the strongly liberal *Christian Century*. It stood unrivaled and, apparently, unbeatable.

At Christmas time 1954 Billy was back at Montreat. He and Nelson were chatting in the Graham home when Billy remarked: "I feel that there is needed in Protestantism today a magazine that is the counterpart to the *Christian Century*. Something that will be evangelical, theologically oriented, and will commend itself to the Protestant ministers of America. I feel it is desperately needed."

The two men discovered their vision was identical. Billy said: "The idea had come to me in the early morning hours about two o'clock, and I got up and laid out the whole thing, including the name *Christianity Today*, the budget, and the various departments that it now has—everything I wrote out. And I feel as I look back that the Spirit of God gave this."

This had happened months before. And now Billy found that his father-in-law's dream magazine not only had the same aim and scope as his own dream, but the very same name, though Billy had never heard of the earlier, defunct *Christianity Today* which had been sent out to Nelson in China. When the dream began to near reality, they acquired the copyright to the name.

That Christmas in Montreat as they talked, Nelson said: "It ought to be done and it can be done." Nelson at once set to work dictating letters, early in the mornings before rushing off to perform operations. He received unanimously enthusiastic replies, though some doubted if it could be done.

To Howard Pew, the Philadelphia layman, Nelson wrote on January 14, 1955, "The greatest single need in Protestantism is a voice which speaks with authority based on God's inspired Word and supported by truly reverent scholarship. This must be done wisely and in love....

"The undertaking is of a magnitude which requires much prayer, spiritual discernment, and Christian common sense. It appeals to me so much personally that I am willing, if God should so lead, to relinquish my successful surgical practice and devote all of my time to the promotion and fulfillment of the objective."

More than a thousand donors contributed to the launching of *Christianity Today*. But if the vision of a strong, sufficient staff, plus a free introductory year's subscription for every Protestant minister in the United States, were to be realized in full, the large-scale support of a man like Howard Pew would be the deciding factor.

On March 10, 1955, Nelson and Billy boarded the overnight train from Black Mountain, the station below Montreat, for the definitive discussion with Pew at Philadelphia. They had a two-berth compartment, and as they neared Philadelphia Billy said, "Let's pray." He got down on the floor, not exactly kneeling but almost as if prostrate before the Lord. "I'll never forget that morning on the train," Nelson told the staff of *Christianity Today* more than ten years later. "I had never seen a man pray like that before exactly. There was an earnestness about his prayers, that the Lord would lead Mr. Pew, if it was the Lord's will, to do something that would insure the beginning of the magazine."

They went to the office on Walnut Street. Pew immediately named a considerable figure which he could give that year and next, the start of a fruitful and happy alliance until Pew's death in 1972.

Nelson had already secured editors, and office space in a modern block in downtown Washington. Billy Graham commented: "When Dr. Bell gets his teeth into something, he never gives up. I get sidetracked. I get interested in other projects. But not Dr. Bell. He just sank his teeth into this, and he wouldn't let me off. He made me stick to it. He made Mr. Pew stick to it." By April 5, 1955, Bell was telling Pew: "I have decided to go into this with everything I have and have completed plans for closing my practice." But no top surgeon whose appointment book is full, with the glow of professional success around him, finds it easy to drop his scalpel for good.

All through the summer and early fall of 1955, which included a visit to Europe where he attended a meeting of the International College of Surgeons, Nelson lived two lives, putting every ounce into both, until, in November, he had a second heart attack.

When he was recovering, the cardiologist, Dr. Samuel Crow, came and sat with him. "Nelson, in four or five months you will be able to resume your practice. But you must remember that at any time you may fall dead across the operating table."

Nelson had no desire to take a patient with him. He realized that this second thrombosis was as clear a divine call as the sudden call to be a medical missionary forty-four years before.

He retired completely from practice as a surgeon and became executive editor of the fortnightly in preparation, *Christianity Today.* The first number of *Christianity Today* appeared in October 1956 and the magazine swiftly became a leading voice in Protestantism.

Nelson Bell's name as a writer became best known internationally for his very personal column in each issue of *Christianity Today,* "A Layman and His Faith," covering every aspect of Christianity. Two collections were published as books: *Convictions to Live By* (Eerdmans, 1966) and *While Men Slept* (Doubleday, 1970).

Nelson was never completely free of his column. Whether driving, eating, watching a ball game, or even when sleeping, ideas would be forming in his mind. He could write anywhere. A colleague commented: "He can work in complete confusion. I have seen him sit at a typewriter turning out a piece of original writing, with all kinds of conversation going on and people moving about."

Perhaps the best comment on Nelson Bell as editor and journalist came from his former China intern, Kirk Mosley, in a private letter from India: "He throws aside the trivia, the inconsequential, the incidental, and concerns himself with the vital issues. His message is on the issues that everyone wants an answer to. This is why in reading an article you can quickly tell whether or not Nelson is the author. He is so full of the message and so imbued with a sense of urgency; he comes quickly to his point and leaves no one in doubt that the real answer to each issue is the way of salvation, which everyone, deep in his heart, is longing for."

* * * * *

T. W. Wilson, an associate of Billy Graham, was in a barbershop in Black Mountain, near Montreat, one day during the later 1960s when he overheard the customers discussing their neighbor, Dr. Nelson Bell. T. W. joined in, declaring his interest, at which a customer said: "That Billy Graham, he's a go-getter; he's a worker, isn't he! But I'll tell you this, Billy Graham and all the others are going to have to get up and go some to do better than his father-in-law Dr. Bell!"

This neatly summed up the admiration and affection felt for Nelson Bell. In October 1965 Nelson and Virginia were honored by a banquet and speeches at the Assembly Inn, when 250 guests, including two senators, church leaders, editors, and heads of great corporations, came from many parts of the nation. Nelson had already been named one of the country's most outstanding churchmen by The Religious Heritage of America.

* * * * *

Whenever he met racial discrimination, Nelson took personal action against it. The blacks of his own community

1971—Dr. Bell and his famous son-in-law, Billy Graham, at Montreat

respected and loved him. At a bus stop in Asheville an old black woman fell into conversation with Chris Jarrett, at that time Dr. Bell's secretary. "You work for Dr. Bell? He treated me once. He's more like Jesus than any man I know." And after Bell's death, a black man who was working for Ruth on a job asked: "Is you Dr. Bell's daughter?" Ruth said yes. "Law," he exclaimed, "he was the awfullest Christian I ever knowed!"

In his controversies, hostility toward Bell could not survive personal acquaintanceship unless the critic was too soured to recognize integrity and love. As a friend once wrote to him: "It has been your love for rich and poor, 'big' and 'small,' sinner and saint, which leaps across ecclesiastical party and theological bias, that has inspired the love and esteem of so many. Yours is an unselfish love which does not compromise your convictions nor obscure your stand."

Nelson had recovered from a third heart attack early in 1965. In March 1966 he had a fourth, and he also had a slight stroke caused by a fall downstairs. His cardiologist advised him to travel less regularly to Washington for *Christianity Today* and to shed any responsibility which engendered tension. Though absent less from Montreat, since much of the work for *Christianity Today* could be done at home, and though slowed somewhat by his cardiac condition, Nelson Bell still lived a full life for a man in his late seventies.

One department grew considerably: his correspondence on behalf of Billy Graham. Many people who wanted Billy's help in a personal crisis wrote to him at Montreat. Yet even when he was briefly at home, his schedule could not include answering about a hundred lengthy letters a week, many of which required deliberation and further correspondence. Nelson found that a reply from Billy's father-in-law would satisfy where a secretary's or associate's would cause resentment. He took endless trouble, yet was so prompt that his own secretary, Winifred Wood, quipped that "he answers them the day before they were written!"

His letters answering those originally addressed to Billy often led to a correspondence. One of the lengthiest was with Mickey Cohen, a well-publicized underworld character, during his long imprisonment.

Cohen had met Billy Graham after Jim Vaus, the gangster's lieutenant, had been converted in the Los Angeles crusade of 1949 and had "quit syndicated crime." The Grahams and the Bells did all they could to help Cohen make a new life. After his arrest and conviction, the Bells visited him in prison; during his parole they had arranged for Cohen and his wife to spend a Christmas with them at Montreat. At the last minute they were told that the plane he had chartered (he did not dare use a commercial flight for fear of other gangsters) had been damaged in takeoff, and he never came.

Cohen wrote long letters from prison over the years: "Dr. Bell," reads one, some months after Cohen had been brutally attacked by another convict, "this letter of yours has done more for me than ten weeks of physiotherapy. And I truly can't find words to express the love that I have in my heart and soul for you and Mrs. Bell, Billy and Ruth."

*   *   *   *   *

Nelson Bell had held a weekly Bible class in Gaither Chapel on Sunday mornings since first settling in Montreat. It was broadcast by a local radio station, reaching seven or eight states.

He was also an elder in the Montreat church. Calvin Thielman, the minister since 1962, recalled how Bell "did more than his share of the work. Rather than see two people quarrel about who did a job to be done, he would do it himself, yet he was the busiest man in the bunch. And he was an irenic spirit in a session meeting; he would be respectful and the people who might have meaner natures would almost be restrained by his presence: it was just a shame to say anything cheap or mean around Dr. Bell.

"And if it was a matter of orthodoxy and faith that came up or a question of morals or conduct he was biblical and he was clear, and he was compassionate and fair. And, he was just about the ideal—in fact, I would say in my thirty-five years of experience as a minister, he was the most ideal elder I ever knew by far."

The Bells were loved in Montreat. They had a knack for knowing wherever there was need, whether material or spiritual. As a neighbor said: "One reason Dr. Bell is a spiritual dynamo in this community is because he finds poor people in the mountains around Montreat and he just goes by and takes them some little bit—maybe it's a chicken, or some sugar and flour, or groceries."

Nelson Bell, though retired as a physician, was constantly consulted informally, and if any neighbor was ill, Nelson dropped around frequently, whether to old China colleagues like the Ed Curries or to a casual acquaintance or a working man. Many old-timers would even call him in the night rather than their own doctors. If a friend was in the hospital, Dr. Bell visited daily, with a smile or a word for all in the ward; and although he would not perform operations since retirement, he attended in the operating room if his presence would comfort a patient.

Calvin Thielman, the Bells' pastor, who knew at firsthand their kindness and generosity, recalled how, "Every morning at five o'clock, summer and winter, Nelson Bell was at his devotions. His knowledge of Scripture would have humbled any preacher. He could always quote the right verse at the right time, and in a way that made one know he believed every syllable of it was true.

"Each Sunday morning I would see this tall, distinguished, white-haired gentleman enter the church at about 9:30 for his morning Bible class. He always seemed to be in a hurry because there was so much he wanted to get done. He followed a schedule that would have exhausted many men. The diversity of his interests and his driving energy were to me a continuing cause of astonishment; but I knew the source of his strength."

31
The Reconciler

I N 1966 Nelson and Virginia celebrated their golden wedding anniversary. By then they were great-grandparents.

In October 1968 Virginia Bell had a slight stroke. She had already suffered much from an arthritic degeneration of the hip joint and in the summer of 1969 underwent major surgery to replace the hip. The operation was unsuccessful; she would never walk again.

A few days after her return from the hospital Calvin Thielman happened to come into Nelson's basement office and noticed a sheaf of letters about to be mailed. "He told me that the letters were resignations from many responsibilities that would have required his absence from home. He said that Mrs. Bell has been everything in the world that a wife could be to him for over fifty years. 'As far as I am concerned, what God wants me to do is to take care of her and I intend to do just that.'"

That fall Virginia had a second and dangerous stroke. Nelson did not panic, or "feel that I had to intercede and plead with the Lord in a special way. He knew what I was trying to do. There was a sense of absolute peace and rest. If you try to live in close contact with the Lord, morning, noon, and night, when an emergency arises you go on and do what that emergency requires and the Lord will take care of you."

Virginia lay seriously ill. She grew somewhat better but her speech remained impaired, a special trial to her active mind, and her hip continued painful and crippling. Nelson was able to continue as executive editor of *Christianity Today*, though going less frequently to the Washington office, and one of his colleagues on the magazine commented on his reaction to Virginia's illness: "Under those circumstances it would be very easy to become impatient; if not with his wife, at least with the circumstances, and thereby you would become perhaps hardened or less concerned or less thoughtful. But in her illness Nelson has again and again said to me that one of the privileges and delights of his life is to be able to care for his wife. He has been to me a shining example of what the ideal husband ought to be in a case like that."

And Billy Graham, certain that he would never be able to live up to his father-in-law's example if the same circumstances should occur exclaimed tongue-in-cheek to Ruth: "Your dad's ruining me! I sure hope when the time comes, I go first!"

The Bells' maid, Zennie, did much but Nelson delighted in preparing supper, as their pastor noticed: "He had all of the instruments for cooking laid out like a surgeon's instruments on the table, and he was very fussy about not being interrupted at this time. He used to say, 'I don't want anybody else in my kitchen.'"

Virginia and Nelson had such empathy that he always knew what she meant to say although her impaired speech was often not clear to others. He would remark that these were the happiest years of their lives. "He looks at Mother adoringly," said Ruth, "as she sits in her wheelchair like a queen on a throne, more beautiful than ever before, her white hair a halo around her face, her eyes, unable to read now or do handwork, still shining with that old fire."

For years Nelson had made a habit of writing poems to Virginia on special occasions—poems which often revealed the joy, quiet humor, and love that had sustained them across the years. An example was the poem he wrote to her for Christmas 1971:

TO MY SWEETHEART

Year by year, my ragged verse
  Just keeps on getting worse and worse;
But none the less, I must do
  One more effort for love of you.

The art of writing, poems or prose
  Depends on inspiration as everyone knows;
So based on that premise—a leading clue,
  My poems should blossom because of you.

Down through the years—sixty next June,
  You have been for me both joy and boon;
You married me for "better or worse,"
  And I'm not talking about my verse.

Our lives have been one, wherever we went,
  And off to China by the Board we were sent;
And where we lived, on land so level,
  To many a person we were just "Foreign Devil."

'Mid joy and sorrow, whatever betide,
  You, precious sweetheart, stayed by my side;
"Helpmate" is often used for a wife,
  And that's what you've been, all of your life.

I saw you in times of danger and stress,
  But you never once faltered, no matter the press;
Midst sickness and sorrow, or wars to dismay,
  You faced every trial, and never turned away.

Yes, in all dangers you stuck by my side,
  Calm and collected, you never did hide;
Day after day you stuck to your work,
  Neither children nor patients, you ever did shirk.

The One Who had called you, to offer your life
  As doctor and nurse and mother and wife,
The life you lived at such wearying pace—

For every duty God gave you the grace.

No praise for you can go too far,
　For what you were, and what you are;
And at this blessed Christmas time
　I sing your praises in ragged rhyme.

To me you're sweetheart and precious wife,
　And to your children a guide in life;
You've made a home, and your husband blessed,
　While blessing your children and many a guest.

Few women indeed have equaled you,
　And what I say I know is true;
For many indeed, both near and far
　Have found in you a guiding star.

And now we come to Christmas day,
　While your husband, children, friends all pray
God's richest blessings on all you do,
　Because we all are loving you.

P. S.—And lest your head should swell and crumble,
　Just count on me to keep you humble.

* * * * *

At this time Nelson began to assist John Pollock, the English author, on the first edition of his biography. "My only prayer," he told the author, "is that God will use the book for His own glory." Although Virginia could not contribute directly to interviews it was she who pointed to the top of the cupboard where his box of letters from China lay, forgotten by Nelson. After the letters were sorted, Nelson would read extracts to her and both the Bells enjoyed reliving the China years. Nelson wanted to call the book *Mending Broken China*, but Ruth knew that this title would relegate it to the ceramics department of a bookstore, and came up with *A Foreign Devil in China*, since foreigners were usually called "foreign devils" in pre-World War II China—and not without reason, in light of the way China was treated and exploited by foreign powers.

God's help, when this time comes next year
be closer together in Him than ever before.
g this year that we may become one in Christ.
particular time, I need love, wisdom, courage
. Please pray for me every day during this
—every day, because I am so fallible and at
able to see all the truth as it should be seen."
mination he'll head for the next year," wrote
d religious correspondent of the Associated
Cassel, "is in grave danger of being torn apart
uarrel between liberals and conservatives. No
s body in America is so perilously close to the
sm as the Southern Presbyterians.
..feels that his mandate is to make peace be-
rring factions of his church.
ation to the church insures that the gray-
ator will give his utmost to this ministry of
. And his immense personal popularity indi-
a chance—probably a better chance than any-
succeeding."

* * * * *

fe hung on a thread; but as Ruth commented:
told the Lord he would have to postpone his
He would say to friends that though he was
ie in harness for the church he loved he had
ord for one more year in order that he might
in a critical hour."
have pleaded ill health and declined to serve,
ready held in high honor. This was symbolized
ty-eighth birthday, July 30, 1972, when the
rary building at Montreat-Anderson College,
en built in his honor, was formally named the
ell Library, with affectionate and laudatory
a bronze plaque. Nelson was handed the key.
red first in her wheelchair, pushed by Nelson,
iced the first volume: a Bible inscribed: The
many books.

taking a relaxed view of the high office of

Billy Graham decided to use it as his gift book for those who wrote in after the telecast of his Dallas crusade. He invited Nelson to the platform of the Cotton Bowl for one of the great meetings in September 1971, a few weeks before publication. Cliff Barrows showed a copy of the book to the Dallas crowd and the future viewers and Billy introduced his father-in-law. Then, as Nelson told the author, "I spoke for a few minutes—first in English, then in Chinese, then back in English. The Chinese I spoke was simply, 'I am not really a foreign devil, but a Christian who loves you very much, and I have one word that I want to say to you.' I then quoted John 3:16, after which I told the audience what I had said. The whole thing probably took no longer than ninety seconds."

Nelson's biography came at a strategic moment, for China was suddenly to the forefront of American interest: In February 1972 President Nixon went to Peking on his official visit. He broke through the Chinese wall which had separated the two nations for thirty-three years, although the land continued virtually closed for nearly another decade.

China had never been forgotten in Nelson's prayers. During the dreadful years of the Cultural Revolution he prayed both generally and for individuals. He did not waver in his belief that Christ's church remained, hidden to Western eyes, persecuted, yet virile; and that God was sovereign, working out His purposes, even through those who denied His existence and tried to root out His Word and liquidate His people. At night Nelson often dreamed of Tsingkiangpu and his friends there—some dead and others presumed to be so. The dreams were vivid, and he found himself talking to doctors and nurses as he joined them in making hospital rounds.

He was asked on television whether he and Virginia ever felt that their years in China were wasted. "Wasted? Never!" he said. "We know that someday in heaven we will meet many who came to know Christ at the hospital. What could be more worthwhile?"

* * * * *

He was now seventy-seven years old, with an invalid wife. He was diabetic, and his heart condition caused frequent attacks of fibrillation which, when uncontrolled, leads to shortness of breath, with distress and poor circulation.

Some friends asked Dr. Bell to run for moderator of the Presbyterian Church in the United States. He replied, with Virginia's brave encouragement: "I will not run. But, if elected, I will serve." If they thought he ought to be moderator, they must do all the campaigning and canvassing.

Most of the commissioners to the Assembly had known him as a powerful conservative speaker; ordinary church members knew they had in their midst a man of conviction who was also a conciliator. As one reader of *Foreign Devil* wrote to *Christianity Today*: "I lived with the Bells until by the end of the book I felt that they were dearly beloved friends of mine. Most of all, of course, I was impressed by Dr. Bell himself, who must be the greatest and sweetest human being I have 'known' in all my life."

The Assembly that year of 1972 met at Montreat. Each candidate (except Nelson) and their supporters lobbied hard. Nelson's friends were worried lest his age be used against him.

When a commissioner demanded, in an almost cynical tone, that each candidate stand up and state his age, Bell, at seventy-seven was the oldest by seventeen years and if elected would become the oldest moderator in Southern Presbyterian history.

The youngest of the four candidates stood to give his age: forty-six; the next was fifty-three; the third was sixty. The inference was obvious. Bell stood up. "Well," he said, "I'm not as old as Moses was when he led the children out of Egypt!" This, recalled Calvin Thielman, "brought down the house with laughter and completely neutralized the age issue."

On the Sunday afternoon when the election was to be held, Calvin went to the Bell home to bring him up early to the auditorium "so that he could go around and glad-hand." He found Nelson washing up the dishes from Sunday lunch.

"What are you doing, Dr. Bell! You should be up there

showing them you ar[...]

Nelson laughed, a[...] and then he would g[...] that he must be the fi[...] of the church who w[...] hour before he was el[...]

On the second ball[...] out of 434 total—alm[...] nearest opponent.

His predecessor in[...] moderator's badge of [...] monial gavel. Bell told[...]

Dr. Bell with the gavel of offi[...] in the United States.

applause: "B[...] we're going [...] I intend duri[...]

"For this [...] and patience[...] coming year [...] times I am un[...]

"The den[...] the celebrat[...] Press, Louis [...] by a bitter [...] major religio[...] brink of sch[...]

"Dr. Bell.[...] tween the w[...]

"His ded[...] haired mode[...] reconciliatio[...] cates he has[...] one else—of[...]

Nelson's [...] "Daddy just [...] departure." [...] wishing to [...] "asked his [...] minister to [...]

He could [...] for he was [...] on his seve[...] new large [...] which had [...] L. Nelson [...] speeches an[...] Virginia ent[...] who then p[...] *Book amon[...]

Far fro[...]

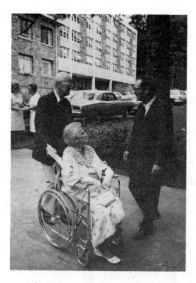

Nelson and Virginia Bell with Dean Donald Mitchell at dedication of the L. Nelson Bell Library, Montreat-Anderson College, July 30, 1972

moderator, Nelson embarked on a strenuous program although declining many lesser engagements to speak. "Such a continued pressure of things to do," he wrote to his children. He never knew when his heart might play up. As he left one meeting, "I started fibrillating badly and it lasted into the night. For the first time I took a stethoscope and listened to my heart and it sounded pretty bad—weak, very irregular in beat, and with varying intensity. Wednesday morning and since have been OK."

His resilience amazed those who knew his uncertain health. Then he bought a pair of cheap shoes made of a new plastic which he realized—too late—didn't allow his foot to breathe as leather would. (And he had been so proud of his "bargain.") An ulcer formed on the little toe of his left foot and refused to heal because of his diabetes. He took to using a wheelchair at airports but the ulcer was sometimes agonizing. "I really had a bad night," he wrote after a heavy day's work in the church's offices at Atlanta. "Cramps in left foot and leg kept me awake until a quarter of five—then got one-and-a-half hours sleep. The circulation in my left leg is very bad. Sooner or later I will have to do something about it but I have some engagements I feel I must meet first."

He would not drop his work as moderator. His great aim was to bring the denomination back to the primacy of its spiritual message, and to evangelism. In his talks to churches and lay groups he stressed "our need to trust in the presence and power of the Holy Spirit as we are not doing. We are trusting in organizations and programs and forgetting that He must devise and implement them.... There is such emphasis on *organization*; and while that is important the church is *primarily an organism*, a spiritual one at that, and I often feel that is being forgotten.

"We are living in a sinning and deeply disturbed world, and the church of Jesus Christ alone has the message of redemption and hope. But only too often, the world is not hearing that message, because the church cannot agree on its content or its urgency. It is high time for all of us to put first things first."

Yet he never wavered in his belief in the providence of God. Therefore, Nelson Bell remained an optimist. "Dad was always up, I never found him down," recalled Clayton Bell. "It came from that great sense of joy, and knowing that God is in control."

* * * * *

In Nelson's constant traveling Virginia sometimes could come too (they took her wheelchair). On those occasions they brought along their old China companions, the Ed Curries, or sometimes Winifred Wood, Nelson's secretary, to keep her company when Nelson was in board or presbytery meetings, but if he was addressing a church dinner Virginia would be at his side. "Three-hundred-forty-six at the dinner," he wrote after a visit to Johnson City in Tennessee, "and a number of our friends and we enjoyed it all so much."

Their travels could be adventurous. Once they nearly got stuck in snowdrifts at Christmas time. On another speaking tour they stayed the night with the McCue cousins at the old plantation home, Belvidere. Next morning the brakes on Virginia's chair gave way as they were helping her down the ramps which Margaret McCue and her sister had thoughtfully laid from their front door. "The chair started fast—backward," he told the children in his weekly letter, "and I could not keep up and my heel caught and I was catapulted down to the yard, the chair landing on top of me. Then your mother and the chair rolled over on her side. Margaret, bless her heart, tried desperately to hold the chair back and was dragged down the concrete steps badly skinning one shin. "There the three of us lay on the ground and Margaret said, "My, it looks like we have been bombed!" She and I got up, collected glasses, pens, etc. which had scattered from our pockets, then turned your mother's chair over on its back and then lifted her up. The chair had protected her, otherwise she could have been seriously injured. We were all so thankful it was no worse."

If Virginia could not be with him, Nelson would call her three times a day. If he was to be gone for several days, Ruth would have her up to her house to stay; if for a shorter time she would bring down supper and Zennie, the maid, would move in for the night that Nelson was away.

"Mother would wait impatiently for his return," recalled Ruth. "She knew the approximate time the plane would land and how long it would take him to drive from the airport. He always honked twice as he approached the house. She would be the first to hear the wheels on the gravel in the driveway, the first to hear the car door slam, and his quick step on the back porch.

"If he was not fast enough to suit her, in her impatience she would give an imperious little cry that sounded more like 'Nelsoo' than 'Nelson.' Or an impatient little hoot. In either case, his step would quicken. Her dim eyes would be looking anxiously toward the dining room through which he must enter. Then he would be beside her, bending down to kiss her long and tenderly, coming up for air, and going down for seconds."

Ruth loved to watch her parents' devotion to each other after fifty-seven years of marriage. "One morning when I dropped by to see how they were, I found Daddy on his knees in front of Mother, helping her put on her stockings.

"Daddy had reached the point where he got up and down with difficulty. He, who had been an athlete in his younger days, and had always kept himself in top physical shape, now found himself with a painfully ulcerated toe that refused to heal due to the fact that he was a borderline diabetic and had lost circulation in his left leg.

"He glanced up at me over his glasses, giving me his usual broad smile of welcome. 'You know,' he said, returning to Mother's stocking, 'these are the happiest days of our lives. Caring for your mother is the greatest privilege of my life.'"

32
Up Before Dawn

ON the morning of April 1, 1973, Nelson was in Gaither Chapel at Montreat addressing his Sunday school and wide radio audience. He had a new strong light which had been set on the podium because a fast-growing cataract had made his left eye useless for reading, a fact of which even his children were unaware. He never complained. After fifteen minutes he sensed that he was about to faint. He closed hurriedly with a short prayer and sat down. Ruth and others hurried to him. He agreed to go home and lie down.

On Monday he talked by telephone to his friend, Dr. Carl Morlock at the Mayo Clinic who urged him to come to Rochester, where they gave him thorough tests, changed his medication to control the fibrillation better, and let him go home; as he remarked, "Right now I cannot have my leg operated on—will wait until after the General Assembly— God willing." While he was away the Grahams installed an electrically controlled bed like the one already used by Virginia, and a two-way radio telephone in his car.

He resumed his duties and travels as moderator and chairman of the General Executive Board but arranged for others to take the weekly Sunday school until the Assembly. Yet he was never short of time or energy to help strangers who called in spiritual need, or friends in distress. When he heard that a Montreat neighbor's husband had died in a car crash in Virginia, he not only rushed up to comfort and help the widow but made a dozen long-distance calls to alert relatives.

Nelson was now nearing the end of his year of office. On May 18 he flew to Omaha, Nebraska, and addressed the General Assembly of the Northern Presbyterians. He was back at Montreat that night after two changes of plane.

A few weeks later, in mid-June 1973, the Bells went to Fort Worth, Texas, in a private jet loaned by a Texan friend of Billy Graham, for the General Executive Board followed by the 113th General Assembly. Nelson had completed his year of office: he had been able to give a fresh emphasis to the spiritual priorities of the church; and although the plan of union with the United Presbyterians had not been abandoned, only postponed, and the consequent movement to secession had gathered pace, Nelson's leadership had ensured that the break would come with much less bitterness.

For his retiring moderator's sermon at the opening session on Sunday, June 10, Nelson preached a masterly address which pointed the church to the path it must take, and enshrined the convictions by which he had lived. It also brought China—still a closed land, for Chairman Mao did not die until three years later—right back into his hearers' consciousness. His theme was "Humanism—Counterfeit Christianity."

"The church," he began, "is in the gravest danger of changing her message, which is the saving and keeping power of Jesus Christ, and the Living Water, for the dry and hopeless mirage of a 'changed world,' through humanistic endeavor.

"Humanism says, 'change man's environment and living conditions.' Christianity says, 'You must be born again'— that in and through Christ we become a 'new creation.'

"Our world is a prodigal world, estranged from God by disobedience. The world is populated by prodigals. Humanism would make the prodigal comfortable, happy and prosperous in the 'far country' and leave him there. Christianity seeks man's immediate welfare, but above and beyond all else, it brings the prodigal back to his Father through the Lord Jesus Christ."

He emphasized the difference between humanism and humanitarianism, "which is the duty of every Christian"; and he rejected the charge that his emphasis meant he was "blind to the misery of hunger, oppression, disease and poverty." Nelson Bell made the telling point that relief alone cannot meet man's final need.

"For twenty-five years," he said, "I worked in a 380-bed hospital in China, and during that time we treated hundreds of thousands of patients. We gave them the best we could from a professional standpoint. Where are they today? I would guess that 90 percent of those patients are now dead. And death is the ultimate end of all human existence—a fact that the so-called social gospel seems to ignore.

"We saw the great majority of those patients leave the hospital physically cured or improved. But while they were in the hospital we earnestly sought to give them the message of Christ's death and resurrection—the Door to eternal life which He offers."

He added a touch of humor: "During those twenty-five years I spent more time in jail than all of you probably put together! Almost every Sunday morning I went with a nurse to the city jail and the penitentiary, treating the sick and telling of Jesus' love. I saw men (and women) living in unspeakable filth and enduring various forms of torture. And I saw many of these people come to be gloriously saved through faith in Jesus Christ. Treatment of their diseases was a humanitarian effort, but it would have been mere humanism had I not told them of the One who died for their sins."

When Nelson had delivered his moderator's report on the state of the church the entire Assembly and guests gave him a standing ovation. When his successor, Dr. Charles Kraemer, in his first speech as moderator, made a warm reference to Dr. Bell the Assembly burst into applause and again gave him a standing ovation which lasted on and on.

*   *   *   *   *

The next seven weeks for the ex-moderator were a time of much personal happiness and physical pain.

He continued traveling and speaking, and attending board meetings, but in the last week of July, while in Maryland, he had several days and nights of "increasing pain in my little left toe, pain like an exposed nerve in a tooth." He slept only two hours one night but next day "the Lord gave me the strength needed" for two sermons.

Back at Montreat the pain became so bad that he discussed amputation. The doctors doubted he could stand surgery and gave him treatment which controlled the pain in the toe. On Tuesday, July 1, he was delighted when the Family Life Conference met in the Montreat Auditorium and a prominent minister, after praising Nelson's work as moderator, said that Virginia deserved special recognition for her patience and help to him. The entire audience of three thousand stood and applauded her. "Bless her heart, she deserved it," Nelson said.

Two weeks later the toe became so painful that Nelson called the Mayo Clinic and was told to come back at once. As he checked into the Kahler hotel at Rochester he felt a tap on his shoulder and turned to see Ken and Kay Gieser, his China colleagues and devoted friends: they had been having tests. Next morning when he arrived at the clinic building where scores of patients "were checking in at various windows (like a bank) the gray-haired woman who was writing my name, etc. said without looking up, 'You are the "Foreign Devil" in China, aren't you, and Ruth is your daughter?' When I came to my room at the hospital an elderly nurse came in and said, 'I know all about you. I have read *Foreign Devil*.'"

China seemed all around him.

The doctors warned Nelson that owing to blocked blood vessels they might need to amputate not merely the toe but the leg to above the knee. He did not feel he could undergo surgery yet—he was too busy. He was much amused that at one point "There were eight doctors in my room at once and I have had as many as thirteen in a day and some of them come back several times. They are so nice to me."

Dr. Morlock was surprised and deeply touched when, the day he left, Nelson walked all the way from the Kahler by way of the underground passageways, and made his way to the nineteenth floor of the clinic building to thank him personally for his kindness. "Knowing the terrible pain he was in," Dr. Morlock told Ruth, "I just could not believe he did this."

On the Thursday he was discharged a man from the Billy Graham Association office drove him from Rochester to Minneapolis, where Billy was holding the Twin Cities crusade at the Fairgrounds. Nelson sat with his son-in-law before the service. Billy said to Ruth afterwards that he "never considered him old—not even when his strength began to fail. His spirit was young and strong as ever. Stronger, in fact, as his body wore out." Nelson sat on the platform for the first hour rejoicing at the huge crowd hearing the gospel, but had to leave early for the airport.

On Sunday afternoon, July 29, a telephone call came from Dallas: Clayton (after being unanimously recommended by the nominating committee) had been unanimously appointed senior pastor of the Highland Park Presbyterian Church in Dallas, which had the largest membership of any congregation in the denomination. The news gave spice to Nelson's seventy-ninth birthday celebrations on Monday.

On Wednesday, August 1, 1973, Nelson was as usual up at dawn for his devotions, then at seven o'clock he woke Virginia with her cup of coffee and they listened as always to the radio news. That day was a normal, busy day with letters to dictate or type and talks to prepare, and with much laughter as always, and visits with friends dropping by. At night there was time for a game of Scrabble with Virginia.

The World Mission Conference of the Southern Presbyterians would open that night in the auditorium at Montreat. Past and present missionaries and their children were gathering. Many old China friends looked in to say hello and share encouraging stories which had filtered out. Nelson invited them and their families to join him on the next Saturday for a hot dog get-together: some seventy-five were expected.

That night, as ex-moderator and their most eminent missionary, Nelson had been asked to open the Mission Conference with prayer.

All ages packed the auditorium, from retired veterans to teenagers. After the hymn he mounted the podium and without notes, but "with considerable vigor and enthusiasm," he gave a "brief but moving and eloquent invitation."

"Before I pray," he began, "I have a few words to say. After hearing that singing, no one can deny that our Presbyterian church is waking up!

"Now in this place there are two groups of people. There are those who know they are saved and love the Lord Jesus Christ, and there are those here who as yet may not know Christ."

And then he said, "My hope is that before you leave this place you will come to know Him as your personal Lord and Savior. The Lord said, 'Behold I stand at the door and knock; if any man hear my voice, and open the door, I will come in to him, and will sup with him and he with me.'"

*   *   *   *   *

Virginia woke on the morning of Thursday, August 2, and was surprised to see Nelson still in bed—he who was always up at dawn. She called to him. No reply. Then she knew something was wrong. She managed to get out of bed by herself and across to the telephone. She tried to dial Ruth's number but her dim sight made her dial at random. She might have gotten any stranger in the Black Mountain area but the telephone rang in the home of a dear missionary friend on furlough from Korea, R. K. Robinson, who had been at the meeting the night before and recognized her voice and that something was wrong. He hurried across to T. W. Wilson's, knocked at the door and told them.

T. W. went down immediately, while his wife Mary Helen called the doctor, the Grahams, and Calvin Thielman. When Ruth arrived, still in her bathrobe, she had but one thought in mind—she did not see anyone there—she only wanted to get to her mother and let her know she was there and loved her. She went directly to her mother and kissed her gently, then after a bit she turned to her father's bed. "It was as if he was asleep," she wrote, "on his left side, his face against his curved left arm, his right arm comfortably resting back across his neck. But when I kissed him, he was cold."

Dr. Knoefel said Nelson's heart had stopped at about dawn. "As Bill said, 'It was about the time he usually got up,' and," Ruth exclaimed, "he did!"

Virginia's courage that day so impressed Ned, the Grahams' youngest son, then aged thirteen, that he remarked to his parents "She's a little Peter, a little rock. It is on people like her that God builds His church." And Ruth noted in her diary: "There has been a lot of laughter today. How can we remember Daddy and not laugh? Humor was as much a part of him as his walk and the tone of his voice. And tears sprang unbidden, too."

They held a private funeral for family and close friends on Friday. Virginia and John Somerville were on furlough from Korea; Billy Graham had put off his departure to the Middle East; Clayton and Peggy had driven fast back from their vacation to New England; Rosa and Don Montgomery had flown in from Los Alamos.

They buried him on a gently sloping plot facing east in the cemetery at Swannanoa, where he had practiced, for Montreat had no burial ground; and as they lowered the casket into the ground there was a rumble and crash of thunder. Rosa said it was a twenty-one-gun salute.

The telephone lines in Montreat were jammed with callers wanting to express sympathy or tell of his kindness: church leaders, statesmen, editors; blacks, Chinese, young people. A nurse told how the student nurses at Asheville, usually terrified of surgeons, used to line up to operate with Dr. Bell because he was always so kind and gentle if they made a mistake. A social worker told how she had telephoned to him her concern that black children in the Piedmont were not receiving medical treatment: "Dr. Bell's reply was positive and immediate. He took his surgical nurse and held clinics, removing tonsils and giving the black children the medical attention they needed." Mickey Cohen, the former mobster called. Ruth answered the phone. "Give your mother my damndest condolences," he said, not knowing how else to express it. Ruth understood.

Saturday, Ruth had the Chinese missionaries to their home for the annual hot dog roast knowing that was how Nelson would have wanted it. Virginia held court from her

The graves of Nelson and Virginia Bell in Swannanoa, North Carolina. At top of each gravestone is their name in Chinese; at bottom are the Chinese characters for the Gospel terms "righteousness" and "come".

wheelchair, surrounded by old friends, including Kerr Taylor and Ed Currie. On Sunday, August 5, a great memorial service took place at Montreat. The auditorium, holding three thousand was full to overflowing. "Without any fear of contradiction," said Calvin Thielman at the beginning of his address, "I state that Dr. L. Nelson Bell was far and away the best-known and, I believe, the best-loved Presbyterian layman in the whole world."

* * * * *

In the year and three months that Virginia was left

without Nelson, her children felt that keeping her happy was more important than just keeping her well. Years before, Ruth had designed a downstairs room in their home on the mountain with her parents in mind. Ruth let her know she would be warmly welcomed when she wanted to move up the mountain, but to take her time. After a few weeks she moved up. Ruth loved having her. After a couple of months, she wondered if Ruth would mind her going back home. "Whatever will make you the happiest," Ruth said. The Grahams needed privacy; Virginia needed people. They secured a housekeeper and a companion and neighbors and friends and students were in and out, as she loved to have it.

The following September, 1974, Virginia sent for her daughter in Korea to fly home and spend five weeks with her. It was a happy time. Virginia (MaiMai) Somerville drove her all around, once to Charlotte and back. They read, they played games. They entertained friends.

Then Virginia Somerville had to return to Korea—to her husband and her children.

Two weeks later Virginia Bell had a stroke.

In October 1974, when Billy had left for his crusade in Brazil, Ruth had a serious fall when preparing a swing for her daughter Gigi's children in Milwaukee. She was recovering from her injuries when word came that her mother was in the hospital. Still on crutches she flew home with Gigi.

"Rosa came, too, and Clayton from Dallas. We found Mother helpless and furious. Tubes were extending from everywhere. Her rings had been forcibly removed, and when the nurse tried to remove her partials as well, Mother, with her old spunk, snapped at her. Although she was unable to speak, I could read the anger and frustration in her eyes.

"This might be a postponement of death for her, but it was certainly not a prolongation of life. So I asked the doctor who had cared for her and Daddy for so long, if we could take her home. She might not live as long, but she would die happy.

"'If all you children agree,' he replied, 'you have my permission.' Rosa rode in the ambulance with her. She said Mother looked worried till they passed through the arched stone Montreat gate. Then her face lit up. In her slightly confused state, she may have thought we were taking her to a nursing home (a thing she dreaded).

"It was a joy to see her settled comfortably in her own bed, in her loved and familiar surroundings. Rosa was able to give her the necessary shots to keep her comfortable.

"Mother, who all her life had loved music, who used to play the piano and sing like a bird, now asked only for 'The King Is Coming.'"

Ruth gathered a great pile of Christian records and selected every hymn that would speak to the dying. The local Christian radio station put them on cassettes. "Mother had a simple cassette recorder she was able to work, and she listened to those grand old hymns by the hour," recalled Ruth.

"Then, quietly, on November 8, 1974, she joined Daddy."

Five and a half years later their four children were back in China and driving towards Tsingkiangpu.

The Bell children today. Left to right: Clayton Bell and wife Peggy; Rosa and husband Donald Montgomery; Ruth and husband Billy Graham; Virginia and husband John Somerville

Epilogue
RETURN TO CHINA

ON May 13, 1980, Rosa, Ruth, Virginia and Clayton drove north from Nanking towards Tsingkiangpu.

They went in two cars with Mr. Yao Jin Rong, their government companion, and escorts from the Chinese Friendship Association.

The whole journey took four and a half hours, instead of the three days on the Grand Canal as they remembered when growing up. The road was now a two-lane highway, paved, and shaded by many more trees than they recalled. Their father had written in a letter dated 1938 that General Chiang Kai-shek had built this new road to Tsingkiangpu for which they were most deeply grateful. But the rice paddies and the wheat fields, the water buffalo, and the little mud farmhouses with their thatched roofs evoked memories, and when hogs ran across the road, and when a curious but friendly crowd surrounded them at one stop, the Bells felt they were coming home.

Their father would have been amazed and delighted that his children were nearing "TKP" within six years of his death. Chairman Mao had died in 1976. The Gang of Four had been overthrown and Deng Xiaoping was rebuilding China after the excesses of the Cultural Revolution. The people had more freedom. In 1979, worship in church became legal again, though restricted; and Ruth had heard "from many reliable sources" that "there are more Christians—and stronger than when the missionaries left."

In 1980 China was slowly re-opening to the West. Tourists were not yet encouraged, but high-level American-Chinese contacts had led to an invitation to the Bells' children to visit China and to go to the city where three of them had been born and all had spent their childhood and youth.

As they entered the city soon after midday, "nothing looked familiar," noted Ruth. "We saw smokestacks in what was formerly a low-profiled city; two-laned streets whose sidewalks were wider than the old streets we had known. The ancient city wall had been torn down but for us the driver stopped where the city gate used to be—the gate over which Daddy had seen hanging the head which he had patched up two days before."

The hosts in Tsingkiangpu had frantically called the Friendship Association in Beijing saying they could find no one in the entire area who knew how to cook American food and were greatly relieved to be told, "They want only Chinese food."

They were eager to get to their old compound but lunch made the waiting worthwhile, reviving as it did happy memories of the local dishes. Soon they piled back into the cars and suddenly things looked familiar. They were at the Grand Canal, about a hundred yards wide at this point, which had flowed for nearly 2,400 years, since the third century B.C., and had seen dynasties, civil wars, and revolutions come and go. They drove over the ancient lock and asked the drivers to stop so they could have a few minutes to soak it all in, spotting the *old* houses, so different, so much more picturesque than the newer ones, to remember the many times they had arrived at or departed from this very spot. In the old days from here they could have seen the red tin roofs of the hospital compound. Now taller buildings usurped the view.

Back in the cars, it was only a short time till a brick wall appeared on their right. The cars turned into a wide gate and there before them stood a familiar-looking foreign house. It was their old home. It looked pitifully battered and run down "like an old lady no longer loved or cared for," but across the front steps hung a red banner with yellow lettering: *American friends, your coming is warmly welcomed by the people in your birthplace.* And a group of Chinese on the front porch did just that!

The Bell children return to their old home in Tsingkiangpu, welcomed by the townspeople and their hosts

"It was all unbelievably small and pushed together," Ruth noted. "Like people, places and buildings seem to shrink with age. The men's hospital, the boys' school and Dr. James Woods's home were gone. All of the rest of the buildings, some partially destroyed and repaired almost beyond recognition, are still being used as a technical school. A few small unfamiliar buildings have been added."

The Bell children went over the house, enjoying their memories, and then across to other former missionary houses. Friendly, enthusiastically clapping crowds lined the streets, for Dr. Bell's children had come home! Contact with individuals was impossible, though they were sure that many of the older ones remembered *Chong Ai Hua*, "The Bell Who Is Lover of the Chinese People." Ruth thought to herself, "How nice of the Chinese government to arrange such a warm welcome for us!" Later when Shorty Yeaworth[1], who was filming their pilgrimage, went back to China to show the Friendship Association the hour-long film they

---

[1]Irvin S. Yeaworth, Valley Forge Films, Inc.

had made from what was to have been strictly home movies, and to ask their permission to use it on TV, the Friendship Association was amazed at the crowds of friendly people. They recognized it as a spontaneous outpouring of love and appreciation that had spanned thirty years of separation from their missionary friends.

The Bell children asked to go shopping. Instead, the next day they were presented with toothbrushes and small lion figurines. When Virginia spotted bricks from the old porch balustrade lying behind the house, they asked if they could possibly have two bricks each. When they got to their rooms that night, they found eight bricks cleaned and neatly wrapped awaiting them. Ruth had hers made into bookends.

That night, after a formal dinner of delicious Kiangsu dishes, they had a surprise visit from Miriam Chen, whose eldest sister had been Rosa's best friend. Miriam was now widowed and had come all the way from Shanghai. When she was born, delivered by Dr. Bell, her Christian parents had been disappointed at another girl. "Never mind," Nelson had said. "Next year you will have a son, and call him 'Moses.'" And here was Moses, smiling beside her and a younger sister with them. Their eldest sister, Mary, had died. "Your father led me to Christ," Miriam said, adding almost defiantly, "and I am still a Christian!"

As they talked of old times Miriam remarked, "The seed your father sowed is bearing fruit. Most of the older Christians have died, but the younger ones are carrying on."

Next day, a day of rain, the Bells watched four surgeries (including a stomach resection done under acupuncture) at the new Peoples' Hospital, then returned to the old mission compound. The Giesers' house was standing but empty. Then they went to the home of Uncle Jimmy and Aunt Sophie Graham. It was now a wholesale grocery outlet, the former living room dominated by a picture of Chairman Mao.

*   *   *   *   *

Nelson Bell's influence is still being felt in China, in more ways than one.

In 1987 Uncle Jimmy Graham's granddaughter, Mary

Abbot Reid, wife of a missionary in Japan, and her daughter had been among the many tourists now welcomed in China. From Nanjing (Nanking) they had taken a taxi to Tsingkiangpu, now part of Huaiyin. Mary Abbot wrote Ruth that as she looked at the Bells' home, "I thought of your mother sitting at the upstairs bedroom window in the afternoon—crocheting or knitting. I remember her giving me pink and white marshmallows out of a can...." Mrs. Reid visited a Christian family "and they told me there are now *two hundred thousand* Christians in the Huaiyin area."

Back in Shanghai at the conclusion of their 1987 tour, Mrs. Reid and the tourists were taken to the Bund, the wide commercial street beside the Huangpoo river. It was crowded with friendly Chinese who soon surrounded the tourists to practice their English. "The young man who accosted me said: 'How do you like China?' When I told him I was born there he told me that when he was studying in the United States someone gave him *A Foreign Devil in China.* He had read it and *memorized* it. He knew everyone mentioned in the book." He was not a Christian and Mrs. Reid "took the opportunity to witness to him. It was remarkable to me that out of that throng of people, the Lord would bring this young man to talk to *me*!...He was impressed with your father's life."

* * * * *

On April 19, 1988, Ruth came again to her birthplace. This time she came with her husband and their eldest son, Franklin. Billy Graham had preached to overflow crowds in two churches in Beijing (Peking) and had been received by the new premier, Li Peng, for an unprecedented fifty-minute discussion—the first time a foreign religious leader had ever been received by a premier of the People's Republic.

The Grahams, Franklin, and their party had flown from Beijing in a small plane to the port city of Lianyungang in the northern corner of Kiangsu Province. Ruth's memory went back to the day in 1937 when Shanghai fell to the Japanese. They had been advised to go north on the Grand Canal because Japanese warplanes might have attacked a

The fulfillment of a dream: Billy and Ruth Graham come together to China. In Beijing the Grahams were warmly welcomed by Premier Li Peng at his official residence. At left is Irvin (Shorty) Yeaworth, who accompanied the Bell children on their 1980 visit and helped arrange the 1988 trip.

A historic first: Billy Graham's message in China at Beijing's packed Chongwenmen Church, the first time the globe-trotting evangelist had preached on Chinese soil

At the service in Shanghai's Mu-en Church crowds not only filled the church but spilled over into adjoining rooms and buildings to hear Billy Graham.

Billy Graham's busy speaking and preaching schedule in China included several leading universities and academic institutes. Here he answers a question at Nanjing University.

convoy of cars. The party transferred to the railway and was held up by air raids; they went to the port of Lianyungang where they took a launch out to the American destroyer, USS *Pope* in a choppy sea. All, wondering how the bedridden Aunt Sophie on her stretcher could be transported safely from the little launch to a higher destroyer, held their breath and prayed. Suddenly the sea went calm for a few moments and she was carried across the gang-plank safely. ("The rest of us," Ruth remembered, "had to make it across the best we could.") Fifty-one years before...Ruth had left home from Lianyungang. Now it was through Lianyungang she was returning.

From Lianyungang the Billy Graham party of 1988 drove almost due south. "I was heading home," wrote Ruth in her journal. "We passed through miles of 'old China'—little villages, mud farmhouses with thatched roofs, each with their own little pond of *green* water, a few ducks, chickens, sometimes a water buffalo, an occasional dog. It was growing dark as we finally entered Huaiyin. Nothing remotely familiar. Huaiyin is a new city made up of the old Tsingkiangpu, Hwaian and the old Huaiyin.

The Grahams were overwhelmed by the way their hosts at Huaiyin had knocked themselves out to make them comfortable and feel welcomed. At the welcome banquet that night Ruth did not find *one* of the old Kiangsu dishes with which she was familiar. All was new. The charming and attractive young mayor (who "made it quite clear that she is an atheist") presented Ruth "with an exquisite framed relief picture of the old compound in mother-of-pearl."

"The stone," she said, "reflects the strength of the relationship between you and the Huaiyin people. The pine represents the everlasting nature of our friendship. The maple tree (feng tree) symbolizes the warmth of the feelings of the Huaiyin people for you when the leaves turn red in autumn."

*   *   *   *   *

Next day, when they drove to the old compound, thousands lined the streets—curious rather than warmly enthusiastic as in 1980. In the eight years that had passed many of the older folks had died. It was forty-seven years since Nelson Bell had left China: the crowds were probably curious about the invasion of foreigners, some having never seen one before (Huaiyin not being an "open city").

At the old compound, the Bell house had been emptied and swept clean. As they went around together, Ruth poured out her memories to Billy and Franklin, who had heard so much of this place but had never seen it.

Chinese friends had also located the Chinese house where Ruth was born, had it emptied and swept clean. In one of the two small upstairs rooms they had benches around the walls and flowers on a table. Ruth told them how in later life someone had asked her father how many of his old patients were still living. He thought a moment, then replied, "I would guess 90 percent are now dead." Adding, "Which only shows that what we did for them spiritually is the most important." A face in the crowd listening lit up with a big understanding smile and Ruth recognized there

A large crowd turned out to greet the Grahams as they visited the city of Huaiyin (formerly called Tsingkiangpu), the city of Ruth's birth and the location of Dr. Bell's quarter century of work among the Chinese.

Madame Xu Yen, the mayor of Huaiyin, presented the Grahams with a beautiful picture done in mother-of-pearl.

was one who remembered and believed what the missionaries had taught.

They went to other buildings in the compound. "We met an old lady—a Christian who had known the missionaries. 'I am a Christian' she said in Chinese, her strong old face calm, unsmiling for the pictures. She gave me an old faded picture of the hospital staff. They took pictures of us together and when I said in Chinese, 'God bless you,' she replied with a smile, 'Thank you and God bless *you.*'"

As they neared the Giesers' old house, now an office, "suddenly there was Miriam Chen, all the way from Shanghai, and Moses Chen, and their younger sister. With them was Yang Jin Fang, daughter of our former cook and Virginia's special friend. This was the closest link with home. What a warm, loving welcome they gave us. And we them. It was like a real homecoming."

A few minutes later, in the office, the civic leaders proudly showed the Grahams a large stone slab which had been

Ruth and Billy Graham outside the Bells' home

Ruth delighted in showing her husband the attic room which had been her favorite playroom as a child.

Ruth watching the children doing exercises outside the school

A joyous reunion with friends who came from Shanghai and Zhenjiang. Ruth recalled in her diary, "Daddy delivered Miriam Chen, (center), who at age sixteen became a nurse in our hospital, and a year later delivered her younger brother Moses Chen (right), now organist in the church. To my right is Yang Jin Fang, the daughter of our former cook, and at my far right the younger sister of the Chens." In the inset: Miriam's younger sister and Yang Jin Fang during Dr. Bell's days

Friends meet again in Huaiyin

unearthed during the excavation for the new hospital. It was the stone which had been above the main gate of the hospital compound, with the characters for "Love and Mercy Hospital" carved on it in old Chinese letters.

Then they presented Ruth with a handsome brocade box. Opening it she found the old, rusty swing hooks from their front porch! Rosa had spotted them back in 1980. Nothing could have touched Ruth more.

From the hospital they drove to the school building where Rosa, Ruth, Sandy Yates (Gartrell), Hampton and Bill Talbot had been tutored by Miss Lucy Fletcher. At the entrance to the school was a double row of children, brightly rouged cheeks and bows in their hair, chanting at the tops of voices, "Welcome! Welcome!" And as they left, the children shouted "Come back! Come back!" (or "So long! So long!") Ruth shook hands with every old granny in the narrow street who watched them walk by in case there might be one who would remember the missionaries. And then, with Billy, they walked the few steps to the house next door. They were standing in front of the former home of Uncle Jimmy and Aunt Sophie Graham, which in 1980 had been a wholesale

A brief boat ride on the Grand Canal near one of the old canal locks, with hundreds watching

grocery outlet.

Suddenly her mind went back to 1937, shortly before the Japanese war. "The Grahams' bedroom was upstairs to the right as you faced the old square, gray brick house. Aunt Sophie had suffered a stroke and was bedridden. I was visiting there with her one afternoon. Uncle Jimmy sat across the room watching her with loving concern.

"I was asking about the old days—when they first arrived, those difficult times when the Chinese neither liked nor trusted (and not without reason) the 'foreign devils' with their light hair, strange eyes, and big noses.

"I listened as Uncle Jimmy told of visiting village after village telling people throughout the area of a God who loved them enough to send His Son as a Savior to die for their sins and to share their lives, their sorrows, to bring them joy. Inscrutable eyes watched him. A scornful comment by one. An angry second. And the people would become a mob. Stones fell. People spat, contemptuously.

"'Once,' Uncle Jimmy added a little sorrowfully, 'something soft hit the side of my head. I looked down. On the ground lay a newborn puppy—dying.'

At the conclusion of the trip to Huaiyin the Grahams visited the former home of missionaries James and Sophie Graham.

1988—Billy and Ruth Graham met with the pastor of a thriving church which now meets in the old James Graham home. In 1980 the building was used as a wholesale grocery outlet (see inset).

"Aunt Sophie, who had been following him closely, spoke up. 'He'd come home,' she said, 'and there'd not be a place on his body where I could put my hand (holding up her hand palm forward to demonstrate) that was not black and blue with bruises. And his clothes would be running with spit where people had spit on him.'

"Three years and only one convert."

"'Were you ever discouraged?' someone asked.

"'No,' said Uncle Jimmy in his gentle southern voice, shaking his head at the thought of it. 'No. The battle was the Lord's and He would deliver it into our hands.'"

Only one convert. And now, in 1988, ninety-nine years after Uncle Jimmy and Aunt Sophie had arrived, and seventy-two after Ruth's parents had joined them, Ruth, Billy, and Franklin mounted the thirteen steps to the porch of the square and ugly house—no longer a missionary's home—and no longer a wholesale grocery outlet: it was the local church.

Beside them walked the elderly pastor, Pastor Fei. He told the Grahams that there were now "130,000 Christian believers among the nine million people of the greater Huaiyin area." (Mary Abbott Reid had been told 200,000—"Only God knows how many: who and where," thought Ruth.)

They entered the house. "The walls to the living room and dining room have been removed, and a partition built at the foot of what used to be the divided staircase. Here the pulpit stands. The old living room fireplace mantle is still in place but Chairman Mao's picture has been removed."

*   *   *   *   *

"A sower went forth to sow…"

Robert Morrison
J. Hudson Taylor
Jonathan Goforth
John and Betty Stam
Absalom and Carrie Sydenstricker
The Woods family

Order extra copies of *A Foreign Devil in China* to share with family and friends! They'll be inspired by the thrilling story of Dr. Bell's mission work in China, which helped lay the foundation for the great spiritual awakening in China today.

Suggested retail price $8.95   Your price $6.95

. . . and here are some more key resources on Christian missions in China:

Miracle Lives of China, by Jonathan and Rosalind Goforth $3.25

Hudson Taylor's Spiritual Secret, by Dr. and Mrs. Howard Taylor $2.95

Hudson Taylor (Autobiography), by J. Hudson Taylor $2.95

cut along dotted line and mail to:
Grason, Box 1240, Minneapolis, Minnesota 55440

- -

❏ Please bill me for the following order (I understand a postage and handling charge will be added).

❏ Enclosed is my check (or money order) of $_____ for the following order (I understand there is no postage or handling charge when my check accompanies my order). Minnesota residents add 6% sales tax.

Please send me the following:

___ additional copies of *A Foreign Devil in China*

___ copies of *Miracle Lives of China* (41454)

___ copies of *Hudson Taylor's Spiritual Secret* (41403)

___ copies of *Hudson Taylor (Autobiography)* (41402)

Name

Address

City   State   ZIP

XR